MODERN

THE MODERN MOVEMENT IN BRITAIN

First published 2005 by Merrell Publishers Limited

Head office
81 Southwark Street
London SE1 0HX

New York office
49 West 24th Street, 8th floor
New York, NY 10010

www.merrellpublishers.com

Publisher Hugh Merrell
Editorial Director Julian Honer
US Director Joan Brookbank
Sales and Marketing Manager Kim Cope
Managing Editor Anthea Snow
Editor Sam Wythe
Junior Editor Helen Miles
Art Director Nicola Bailey
Junior Designer Paul Shinn
Production Manager Michelle Draycott
Production Controller Sadie Butler

British Library Cataloguing-in-Publication Data:
Powers, Alan, 1955–
Modern : the Modern Movement in Britain
1. Modern movement (Architecture) – Great Britain
2. Architecture – Great Britain – 20th century
I. Title II. Von Sternberg, Morley
720.9'41'0904

ISBN 1 85894 255 1

Designed by Karen Wilks
Edited by Matthew Taylor
Proofread by Sarah Yates
Indexed by Hilary Bird
Printed and bound in Slovenia

Jacket front: Patrick Gwynne, The Homewood, Surrey, 1937–38 (see pp. 132–33)
pp. 6–7: Berthold Lubetkin, Holly Frindle ('Bungalow B'), Whipsnade Park,
Bedfordshire, 1933–36 (see p. 175)
pp. 42–43: Sir Ove Arup, Labworth Café, Canvey Island, Essex (see pp. 46–47)

DEDICATION
To the owners of the buildings pictured within, who
care for their treasures and share them with us.

ACKNOWLEDGEMENTS

There are many people to thank for helping to bring
this book into being. Hugh Merrell and Julian Honer
had the vision to commission it, and to bring the
author and photographer together for what became a
most enjoyable two-year project. I am deeply grateful
to Morley von Sternberg for his dedication to the
task and his commitment to travel to far-flung places
at my bidding. His work involved the co-operation of
the numerous private and institutional owners of the
buildings included within these pages, who have been
exceptionally generous. Our knowledge of whom to
contact has been gathered from many sources over
many years, chiefly from the collective memory of the
Twentieth Century Society, as a result of its casework
and visits, and from the architects who have worked
on restoring many of the buildings, especially John
Allan and John Winter.

The research could not have been done without
the background provided by a survey undertaken
in 1992–93 for DOCOMOMO UK as part of the
international DOCOMOMO register project. I was
funded by the Architects' Registration Council of
the UK to visit and report on the present condition
of Modern Movement buildings in Britain. This work
was not formally published at the time, and the
present book, although driven by somewhat different
criteria, is the closest to publication that it will
probably ever get.

In my research, I have used the resources of the
RIBA Library and Photograph Collection, and
additional archive photos have generously been lent
by Dr Lynne Walker.

Karen Wilks has brought the material together
with a design worthy to stand alongside the best of
the architecture depicted, and Sam Wythe has been
the most conscientious text editor one could wish for.

Alan Powers

Photography by
Morley von Sternberg

MODERN

THE MODERN MOVEMENT IN BRITAIN

MERRELL

LONDON · NEW YORK

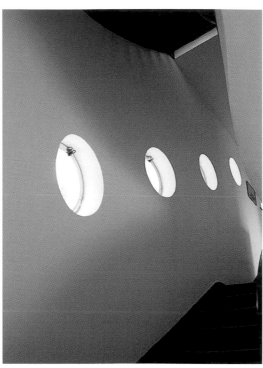

Preface

This book brings together the largest collection of pictures of Modern Movement buildings in Britain from the 1930s ever presented between two covers. The core of this body of work is not difficult to define, and some of it is now extremely well known, but despite this, some buildings are published here for the first time, and many others are shown for the first time in colour.

Some explanation of the selection principles is needed. The purpose of the book from the outset was that it should be illustrated with new photographs in colour. Many of these buildings are known only through black-and-white images, and even if the buildings themselves are mainly white, a colour picture can help in interpreting the design and making it appear a part of our world rather than of the world of seventy years ago. Obviously, buildings that have been demolished or radically altered could not be photographed afresh, and while many private and corporate owners of buildings have been extremely generous in allowing photography, others declined or could not be contacted, thus introducing a further element of self-selection. In some cases a whole building has been represented with old photographs, because we considered it and its architect important enough to warrant this treatment, often to correct what might otherwise have been an imbalance in the coverage of different building types or in the representation of women architects.

To set against losses by demolition, extension and alteration there are many buildings that ten years ago were considered virtually lost, owing to their poor condition. A gratifyingly large number of these have now come back to life, looking as good as new, thanks to the skills of architects specializing in their repair and to owners dedicated to caring for their properties. While more will undoubtedly benefit from this treatment in the future, this book is partly a celebration of the reclamation and reconstruction of Charles Rennie Mackintosh's interiors at 78 Derngate, Northampton, and the long hoped-for repair and refurbishment of the Lawn Road flats in Hampstead, London, by Wells Coates, among other examples.

The principle was that each building should, so far as possible, be shown with more than one picture, and in some cases many more, so that depth was preferred to breadth. Again the buildings themselves provide unequal pictorial rewards, and the number of pictures allocated to each is not automatically a reflection of merit. They could have been organized chronologically or by building type, but a decision was made early on to go by an alphabetical sequence of architects. Although there are merits in the other systems, this was considered most practical for reference purposes, and in some cases a conspectus of work by one architect or practice offers a microcosm of the main historical changes.

Who was in and who was out? The cohort of modern architects in the 1930s was relatively small, and we have been able to include nearly all the well-known names. The fringes are in some ways more fascinating and fall into several categories, including Art Deco and stripped classical. Fairly tight control has been kept around these edges, at the risk of omitting work that is good of its kind but only ambiguously modern. The received wisdom concerning what Modernism is has therefore tended to prevail in the choice of examples, even if the text questions it at times. The growth of diversity in Modernism in the second half of the decade, which has generally received less attention than the 'high' period at the beginning, is treated with special attention here, both as a significant development in its own time and as an indication of the direction of post-war architecture in Britain.

Three other kinds of marginality are significant. First, geographic margins: the main concentration of Modernist buildings was in the

south-east of England. As far as possible this has been offset by including buildings from the north of England, Scotland and Wales (excluding Ireland, the result of logistics rather than ideology), but, even so, I am conscious that justice has not really been done to Scotland in particular. Linked at times to geography is the notion of stylistic margins, for architects based outside London tended to make their own rules about what they wanted 'modern' to be. Thus, for example, the fine group of Co-Op department stores in northern cities designed by W.A. Johnson and his assistants would appear slightly conservative for their date compared with, say, the Peter Jones building in London but are nonetheless architecturally and socially interesting.

The second marginality is gender. The 1930s was the first decade in the history of British architecture in which women made a major contribution, beginning with the unsurpassed feat of Elisabeth Scott in winning the competition for the Royal Shakespeare Theatre, Stratford-upon-Avon, in 1929. Other women architects produced important buildings, among which are designs as avant-garde as any by men of the same period, such as Norah Aiton and Betty Scott's Aiton Factory

Offices in Derby. Every effort has been made to represent them here, although both these particular buildings have suffered from alterations that mean that old photographs present them more satisfactorily than new ones.

Finally, there are building types and works by individual designers that have failed to survive, and whose full representation would have diluted the original concept of taking new photographs. In many cases these buildings were created for industries, and when they became obsolete a combination of economic and political factors, added to the fact that their architects were usually largely unknown, meant that efforts to save them were unsuccessful. Thus the amazing glass curtain wall of Dunston B power station on the River Tyne by Merz and McLellan went in the mid-1980s, followed by nearly all the buildings from the coalmining industry. The latter included the pithead baths by architects of the Miners' Welfare Fund, which were important social documents as well as examples of moderate Modernism.

The book is divided into five unequal sections. The first discusses the origins of Modernism among earlier architects in Britain, and carries the story up to the end of the 1920s. The second part discusses what happened in the 1930s and why, and reflects on the commentaries and interpretations that have influenced our view of it. Following the main body of the book, which catalogues the contributions of individual architects and partnerships, a further, brief text looks beyond the cut-off date of 1939 to summarize the significance of the Modern Movement in Britain and to question the way it is seen now. The final section then offers a brief review of issues affecting the conservation of Modernist buildings.

Introduction

When one of the twentieth century's greatest masters of Modernism, Ludwig Mies van der Rohe, accepted the Royal Gold Medal for Architecture in London in 1959, he listed C.F.A. Voysey, Charles Rennie Mackintosh, Edwin Lutyens and M.H. Baillie-Scott as the architects whose work he had come to Britain to study fifty years earlier.[1] Apart from being a compliment to the country making the award, Mies's roll-call shows that Modernism as whole owes much to British architecture from the period around 1900, and that the understanding of Modernism in Britain in the 1930s should properly start there.

It may be helpful to define Modernism in architecture first, but it is not as easy as it used to be. For some authors the story goes back to the beginnings of self-conscious rationalism in the mid-eighteenth century. More commonly it starts in the 1880s, following the development around that time of a technocratic, urbanized society. So momentous were the changes that between 1900 and 1930 more hope was invested in architecture's ability to bring the emerging condition of the world under control and to rescue it from disaster than at any previous point in time. From the outset this gave Modernism its distinctive and over-reaching craziness, for there was no proof that any architecture could achieve such a redemption. On the other hand, as with any form of art, when the user, spectator or recipient meets the creator half-way in a sympathetic suspension of disbelief, the illusion may become real. In architecture, furthermore, there are practical as well as emotional problems to solve, and the Modern Movement set out to do this better than any other kind of architecture.

In modern architecture submission to the existing order of things was mixed with a desire to oppose and change it. In Germany, where most of the initial thinking behind a modern architecture was done, the tension between these two components was always manifest, so that in the 1920s architects including Mies and Walter Gropius, who initially adopted a spiritualized and idealistic Expressionism, switched within a year or two to *Neue Sachlichkeit* or 'New Reality' architecture, which was the epitome of cool, rational, technological progress, inside which the flame of poetry and passion was, nonetheless, still burning.

There was nothing inflammatory about British architecture at the end of the First World War, in which Germany had been defeated. From 1900 the development of modern architecture went by one route through mainland Europe, carrying a selective baggage based on abstract architectural form and the idea of living closer to nature in a reformed industrial society. British architecture followed a different track, retaining the idea of nature and the garden city, but discarding abstraction in favour of Tudor and Georgian styles, for domestic architecture, with Neo-classicism for civic and public buildings. Edwin Lutyens, although an architect increasingly designing with formal abstraction as his goal, felt no need to abstract his style to the point where all historical reference disappeared – unlike his contemporary in Germany Peter Behrens, whose office around 1910 contained Mies, Gropius and Le Corbusier, three of the most important names in European Modernism. Goddards, a typical Surrey house of 1900, is a good representative of the period, dating from nearer the beginning of Lutyens's career than the end, when he came closest to the Modernist idea. Charles Rennie Mackintosh suffered for his commitment to abstraction in an Edwardian society that responded artistically to modernity chiefly by play-acting. While he could have been an onshore link between 1900 and the Modernism of 1930, the only substantial work he was able to complete after 1905 was the interiors of Derngate, and when these were published in the *Ideal Home* magazine, his name was not even mentioned. The developments on the Continent that we now recognize as the essential groundwork of Modernism were similarly almost totally ignored by British publications until the 1920s.

Defined as a purely aesthetic concept of abstraction, the potential for a modern architecture was seen in Britain as nothing more troublesome than a resumption of late Georgian or Regency simplicity. Equivalents to this elegant escape from Victorian eclecticism can be found in most other European countries that experienced a revival of simple, regionally based classicism around 1910. Many architects who later became famous Modernists started this way, including Mies, Le Corbusier and Gunnar Asplund, while others, such as Bruno Taut, expressed admiration for this period of work in Britain, where those such as Albert Richardson, who began their careers believing that such classicism was modern, saw no reason to change their minds later on. Regency classicism is the ghostly presence in nearly all British Modernism, even in the 'pioneer' work of Mackintosh's Glasgow contemporary George Walton, and can be seen

grinning through the vertical proportions of the Peter Jones store in Sloane Square, the Gilbey offices in north London by Serge Chermayeff or the elegance of some of the villas. It was such a familiar presence that it was taken for granted and scarcely noticed, even though very different modernisms could have arisen if freed of its gently regulating control. Curiously, the same quality is seen in the Roche offices at Welwyn Garden City, by the Swiss architect Otto Salvisberg, who had no cultural roots in Britain.

The aesthetic issues of Modernism did not stand in isolation, and in this it tried to follow the morality of the Arts and Crafts movement in avoiding a split between outward appearance and inner structural truth. The Gothic Revival in Britain and France laid important ground rules for restoring the integrity of materials and the way they were treated, but it remained within the architectural language of the past. The Arts and Crafts, if never actually non-historical, treated the past as a more eclectic and mutable source of images. Good materials and workmanship were a substitute for trying to address the nineteenth century's awkward question "What is the style of our time?", and many architects in England in the first quarter of the twentieth century avoided the question too. In this they gained theoretical support from Geoffrey Scott, who had absorbed

BELOW: Charles Holden (1875–1960), Zimbabwe House (originally British Medical Association), 429 Strand, London WC2, 1907–08. This building shows that when Edwardian architects wanted to experiment the classical language was often their laboratory. The two lower floors are faced in granite, against which the mutilated remains of Epstein's Portland stone sculptures stand out.

RIGHT: H.P. Berlage (1856–1934), Holland House, Bury Street, London EC3, 1910–14. Henry-Russell Hitchcock considered this building "comparable in quality if not in size or significance" to Berlage's most famous commission, the Amsterdam Stock Exchange.

the latest German theories about art and empathy, and who wrote in *The Architecture of Humanism* in 1914 that the ideal architecture would combine abstract formal qualities with the familiar language of classicism.

Scott referred to the belief that materials and building techniques shape architectural style as "the mechanical fallacy", but two technical developments at the end of the century finally provoked the crisis out of which Modernism was born. The availability of cheap steel and the discovery of reinforced concrete meant that buildings could be lighter, thinner and taller than ever before. Capitalist development had uses for such buildings, including steel-framed skyscrapers in Chicago, where Louis Sullivan gave them forms that were classical in spirit if not in detail, and the accidentally sublime concrete grain elevators in Buffalo. In London passers-by in the 1920s could see steel frames go up one month and be covered in Portland stone a few months later, almost as if they had never been there, classical in detail but not in spirit. Geoffrey Scott could not convince them all that the disconnection was irrelevant to fine architecture. Well before the moment of Modernist breakthrough in 1930, thoughtful architects were worried by this and looked for solutions.

Sir John Burnet's Kodak House in Kingsway, London (1909), for example, had larger windows than normal and a clear classical organization of its stone cladding, with minimal ornament. The new building for Heal's in Tottenham Court Road, by the Arts and Crafts architects Smith & Brewer, completed in 1916, clothed its steel frame without hiding its lines. Charles Holden, whose early career indicated that he might have been an English equivalent of Mackintosh, brilliantly took up the fashion of Michelangelesque Mannerism in the design of the British Medical Association (now Zimbabwe House) in the Strand, which incorporated controversial sculptures by Jacob Epstein.

Almost unnoticed in 1914, London acquired a major building by an international modern architect: Holland House in Bury Street, by the Dutch architect H.P. Berlage, commissioned by the Kröller-Müller shipping company. In his refusal to treat the regular grid of a steel frame as a classical composition of horizontal layers Berlage introduced an effect that became common in London between the wars. His glazed faience may have looked old-fashioned at the time and has a dark tonality that is the antithesis of later Modernism's love of light.

S.E. Urwin, Sawston Village College, Cambridgeshire, 1930. Neo-Georgian was the normal style for public service architecture throughout the 1930s, although Urwin, the Cambridgeshire County Architect, and his patron, Henry Morris, abandoned this style for the later village colleges.

While in Germany defeat in the First World War had the effect of accelerating architectural change, it was the opposite for the British, whose victory ushered in a period of architecture in which few buildings in any style shone with lustre. Why didn't more of the originators of the Arts and Crafts movement provide an alternative to the prevailing classical revival of the period 1905 to 1930 and develop a continuity between their work and Modernism, as Frank Lloyd Wright, who was no younger than Lutyens, did in the United States? Historical accident meant that several of the most prominent among them retired from practice, and those remaining longer, such as Voysey and Baillie-Scott, either repeated their earlier work or became more historical. There was apparently little demand for proto-Modernism of the kind promoted by Edgar Wood's flat-roofed houses, before or after the War, or by C.H.B. Quennell in the houses he designed for Crittall's workers in Braintree, Essex, in 1919, so anything unconventional was either confined to industrial work or remained on paper.[2] Only Charles Holden ended up with a foot strongly placed in both the Arts and Crafts and Modernist camps, but even he went through a period of producing dull work in between, indicating that there were no opportunities in the years 1910–25 to do much else.

If Modernism was the winning game, then the dominance of classicism at this time is historically anomalous, but it did catch the imagination of most of the profession, and some of them made it the vehicle for real architecture. The Regency revival of around 1910, associated with C.H. Reilly and the Liverpool School of Architecture, was a different kind of classicism from that of Lutyens and can be followed through to the Peter Jones building in 1935, which Reilly undertook with his former student William Crabtree, who shared his concern for seemly and reticent street architecture.

It has been usual to talk about social purpose as the third leg of the Modernist tripod, after the aesthetic and the technical. The social dimension could simply be the outcome of putting the other two together and making buildings that were both cheaper and more beautiful than the alternatives, but if maintenance and other life-cycle costs had been factored in, the relative gains would often have been cancelled out. Social purpose usually went further, however, to include a concern with working out the 'programme' for the building, something more demanding than a

mere brief, and then taking advantage of the freedom from ready-made forms and solutions to develop the optimum design.

Modernists believed that their way of building alone would achieve the best results, but a non-partisan comparison between, say, the neo-Georgian Sawston Village College near Cambridge of 1930 and Walter Gropius's Impington of ten years later showed that the programme had not changed in essence, and that while the spacious, informal layout of Impington produced tangible benefits in such skilled hands, Sawston, practically speaking, was nearly as good.[3]

If, on the other hand, as German theorists were more apt to insist than English ones, Modernism was fundamentally a question of creating qualities of enclosed space that gave expression to 'the will of the age', then this was much more difficult to achieve within the conventional languages of architecture.[4] Space was a form of aesthetic expression and also seen, in Germany at least, to be essential to the social programme of architecture. This idea has now become a commonplace in the discussion of modern architecture, but it is arguable that British Modernists in the 1930s were relatively unadventurous in their use of space. In houses the conventions of lifestyle meant that open planning was limited, and in general, as Nikolaus Pevsner noted in 1939, "it can safely be said that spatial movement is not what British architects wish to express in their buildings".[5]

The architectural historian John Summerson was more emphatic that space alone was the defining feature of modern architecture, even if it was not actually a new experience, when he made a comparison between a conventional neo-Georgian house by Oswald Milne at Dartington (where Milne was also originally engaged to design the headmaster's house before William Lescaze took the job) and Shrub's Wood, by Erich Mendelsohn and Serge Chermayeff (pp. 188–89). Milne's house answered all the functional requirements, but, as Summerson wrote:

The sweep of the Chalfont plan, its generous terrace and dramatic asymmetry, all have a tremendous psychological appeal. Here is a 'space consciousness' very like what the Elizabethans must have felt when they added long windowed galleries to their old halls, opening out their houses to the light and the newly-discovered pleasures of English landscape and Italian garden.[6]

OPPOSITE: J.M. Easton (1889–1972) and Sir Howard Robertson (1888–1963), The Royal Horticultural Society New Halls, Vincent Square, London SW1, 1926. "Serene buoyancy, vivid freshness, luminous gaiety … this is architecture without yawns", wrote P. Morton Shand in 1929.

LEFT: Peter Behrens (1868–1940), New Ways, 508 Wellingborough Road, Northampton, 1925–26. The *Architectural Review* commented: "Mature judgement will realize that the somewhat bizarre exterior of the new is conditioned not so much by the demands of internal efficiency as by the fact that its owner desired an exercise in modernity."

BELOW: Serge Chermayeff (1900–1996), Cambridge Theatre, Seven Dials, London WC2, 1930. Chermayeff's interiors were commended for their freedom from eccentricity. The relief sculpture is by Anthony Gibbons-Grinling.

Apart from a growing general dissatisfaction with the way things were, where did Modernism in Britain come from? The architecture schools were a likely entry point, not because they taught modern architecture, but because students thought for themselves and looked around, particularly after the First World War had made it necessary to challenge existing beliefs. R.A. Duncan, a teacher at the Architectural Association, recalled that the ex-service students after 1918 questioned things as never before. "The atmosphere was extremely stimulating but unsettling", he wrote. "I defy anyone but a hidebound dogmatist to have passed through this ferment without finding his ideas reduced to a state of flux."[7]

Howard Robertson, the Principal of the Architectural Association between 1920 and 1935, was trained in Paris at the Ecole des Beaux-Arts but viewed the emerging Modernist scene with benevolent curiosity. With John Murray Easton, Robertson was the designer of the British Pavilion at the Exposition des Arts Décoratifs et Industriels Modernes in Paris in 1925, a deliberately frivolous and decorative effort, in contrast to Le Corbusier's Pavillon de l'Esprit Nouveau, which the exhibition's organizers tried to hide among the trees at the back of the Grand Palais. The following year, however, Easton and Robertson built the Royal Horticultural Society New Halls in London, where behind a rather conservative brick front there was a dramatic hall with tiered clerestories of windows, supported on concrete arches. The basic idea was copied from a timber exhibition building in Gothenburg in 1923. In addition, Robertson was responsible for the most significant publications of new buildings from Europe in the later 1920s, including many by Le Corbusier.

Le Corbusier's own books circulated sporadically, first in French and then, after 1927, in translation. His name was often in the press, since his extreme ideas provided good copy. Many students refused to take his work seriously. More immediate impact came from the decorative style of the 1925 exhibition, now known as Art Deco but usually called 'Jazz Modern' or 'Modernistic' in the 1930s. Its gestation went back to the end of Art Nouveau, but it incorporated colours and forms from early abstract and Expressionist art, and could be applied as an overlay on essentially classical structures, as seen in the Hoover Factory by Wallis, Gilbert & Partners in Western Avenue, Greenford, Middlesex. The symmetry of the main elevations, combined with bright colours and abstracted decoration,

make New Ways, the house at Northampton that Mackintosh's patron Wenham Bassett-Lowke built in 1925–26 to move to from Derngate, look essentially Art Deco, although it was the work of one of the more serious German Modernists, Peter Behrens. New Ways was a strong influence on Modernism in Britain for several years to come, particularly through the work of Thomas Tait at Silver End, Essex, and elsewhere.

Interiors were often more modern in style than the buildings that contained them. Art Deco was popular for places of entertainment, such as bars and restaurants; some of the best examples survive in London hotels, such as Claridge's and the Savoy, where a French or American atmosphere was considered appropriate, and in a more assertive form at the Strand Palace (where despite the loss of the main foyer, the lower parts remain) and the Regent Palace, these last two the work of the architect–decorator Oliver Bernard. Art Deco can also be found in theatres and cinemas, including the Savoy (by Basil Ionides, 1929), the Apollo Victoria (by E. Wamsley Lewis, 1929) and the Cambridge Theatre (1930), where interiors by Serge Chermayeff were the culmination of his

first job in association with the furnishing company Waring & Gillow. Art Deco was an entrance into Modernism for some, a permanent stopping point for others; a few years later it was seen as a blockage in the path of Modernism that must be cleared away. As J.M. Richards wrote in 1940:

If people understand the point of genuine modern architecture and appreciate what it is trying to do, they will see quickly enough that the ungenuine – which is often called 'modernistic' – has no basis in itself. It consists only of a few flashy tricks and the use (often the wrong use) of a number of fashionable materials.[8]

In more recent times the terminological difference between Art Deco and Modernism has become less clear, with the recognition of a middle spectrum where they overlap. Other criteria, contrasting puritanism and pleasure, and masculine and feminine principles, are perhaps as valid for diagnostic purposes as a traditional stylistic analysis. It is at least an entertaining speculation that British intellectuals accepted Modernism not because they liked it but because it was sufficiently uncomfortable and self-righteous for them to feel at home with it, whereas Art Deco was evidently not a style for serious thinkers.

The interiors at Finella in Cambridge, a house converted for an English don, Mansfield Forbes, by a young Australian architect, Raymond McGrath, between 1928 and 1929, look Art Deco but were more than a superficial imitation. Forbes had an infinitely playful imagination and led a revolt against all kinds of conformity. The house followed a symbolic programme based on a Scottish legend of a Pictish queen, Finella, who is said to have invented glass and died by plunging down a waterfall. It used as many as possible of the new materials from glass, metal and plywood manufacturers for decorative purposes, and it served as the venue for almost continuous parties. At the same time Forbes had a serious purpose: to encourage McGrath and a group of other designers and patrons who gathered there, along with unconventional thinkers of all kinds. The short-lived Twentieth Century Group began there and represented Forbes's vision for a Modernism of spiritual regeneration, although he found that the architect members were too quarrelsome to organize themselves.[9] Thus Finella was one of the unlikely launch-pads for Modernism.

In the United States, where Art Deco was a more mainstream style than in Britain, there was a shift towards the style known as 'Streamlined Moderne', which relied less on surface pattern and ornament but still fails to qualify under the stricter definitions of Modernism proposed by Gropius or Le Corbusier because of its desire to manipulate the forms and materials of the building to achieve a decorative effect. Streamlined Moderne was widely found in Britain, and its boundaries with 'true' Modernism are often unclear. The streamlined style was popular for cinemas, both inside and out, and for blocks of flats. Where these buildings have survived, they are now much valued as period pieces; the condemnation they received from J.M. Richards and others seems hard to understand, although it undoubtedly holds a key to unlocking some of the less obvious meanings of Modernism.

The Royal Shakespeare Theatre at Stratford-upon-Avon is harder to classify. The architect, Elisabeth Scott, is notable as the first woman architect in the world to have won a major competition for a public building and to have carried out the scheme. Her scheme was as 'advanced' as could have been found at the time of the competition in 1929 and did not flinch from having the look of an industrial structure. It is usually described in terms of German Expressionism, a movement associated with jagged geometric decoration and a sense of northern solidity and mass, although there is also a quality of restraint about Scott's design. The geometrical chromed steel ornament is clearly related

Wells Coates (1895–1956), shop for Cresta, Brompton Road, London W1, 1929 (demolished). This was the first in a series of similar shops that shook off their Art Deco touches and became a well-known demonstration of 'real' modern design.

to Art Deco, but the mood is somehow different. The term 'Medieval Modernism', coined by the American historian Michael T. Saler in relation to the ideology of Frank Pick, the design chief of the London Underground, perhaps describes it best.[10] This putative style was in many ways a continuation of the Arts and Crafts movement and its values, although crucially different in its acceptance of the products of machinery and industry. It was strong in its belief that modern design should act to achieve social cohesion, offering the public symbols of continuity and effort. For this purpose classicism was too Mediterranean and too much associated with Imperial power, while Art Deco was too frivolous, although a certain amount of brightly coloured, quasi-heraldic ornament was not prohibited.

The ethos of Medieval Modernism can be recognized in many other examples of British modern architecture, probably owing to the deep-rooted effects of the Arts and Crafts movement, and it had counterparts in the Modernism of other countries. The worthy intentions of communal living behind Thomas Tait's houses at Silver End mark these out as Medieval Modernism, alongside buildings by more conservative architects that make up this paternalistic village for workers in the Crittall steel window factory. The windows themselves were intended not only for modern buildings, and the company's catalogues took care to show them in neo-Tudor and neo-Georgian settings. The horizontal emphasis of the casements links them to the traditional proportions and forms of Essex farmhouse and cottage windows.

Like Wenham Bassett-Lowke, Frank Pick, Ambrose Heal and other patrons of proto-Modernist buildings in Britain, the Crittall family were active members of the Design and Industries Association (DIA), founded in 1915 to improve the design of industrial goods, with the slogan "fitness for purpose". During the later 1920s DIA lectures and tours were among the best ways in which architects could find out, for example, about the new housing in Frankfurt under the direction of Ernst May, where all the components of living were researched and refined for mass production – including the earliest fitted kitchens – or about the Deutsche Werkbund's housing exhibition at Stuttgart, the Weissenhofsiedlung, on which Bassett-Lowke reported in 1927, and which brought together actual houses by a dozen or so leading modern architects in Europe.

In 1932 the painter Paul Nash wrote that "Whether it is possible to 'Go Modern' and still 'Be British' is a question vexing quite a few people today."[11] By then the breakthrough had taken place, but it is not difficult to see why it had taken so long. The Weissenhofsiedlung was a long way from the Arts and Crafts movement, and when British Modernism finally gathered pace around 1930, the influence from 1900 was traceable not only in the half-way stage of Medieval Modernism, but in those designers and their works that are taken to represent 'the real thing'. The earliest designs by Wells Coates, in 1929–30, for example, were for shops and offices for Cresta Silks, a company that hand-printed artist-designed dress fabrics. Serge Chermayeff acknowledged the wisdom of an elderly designer who, from his account, sounds like C.F.A. Voysey.[12] In a typically British way a movement that thought it was going forwards was also going back.

Notes

1. "I was in this country 50 years ago, on my first and last trip here, to study the great architects of that time. I studied Behrens, Olbrich and van der Velde. I wanted to study Lutyens, Baillie Scott, Voysey and Mackintosh." *RIBA Journal*, vol. 66, 1959, p. 308.

2. The best summary of would-be Modernism before 1914 remains Nikolaus Pevsner's 'Nine Swallows, No Summer', *Architectural Review*, vol. 91, August 1942, pp. 109–12.

3. The architect of Sawston was S.E. Urwin, Cambridgeshire County Architect. After 1930 he built village colleges at Bottisham and Linton that were Modernist.

4. "Architecture is the will of the age conceived in spatial terms", Mies van der Rohe, 1923; translation by Michael Bullock in Ulrich Conrads (ed.), *Programmes and Manifestoes on 20th-Century Architecture*, London (Lund Humphries) 1964, p. 74.

5. Nikolaus Pevsner, 'The Modern Movement', unpublished text prepared for the *Architectural Review*, 1939, Box 18, Pevsner Papers, Getty Center for the History of Art and the Humanities, Los Angeles.

6. John Summerson, 'Romance and Realities', *Country Life*, vol. 81, 13 February 1937, supplement, pp. ii–iii.

7. R.A. Duncan, *Architecture of a New Era, Revolution in the World of Appearance*, London (Denis Archer) 1933, p. vi.

8. J.M. Richards, *An Introduction to Modern Architecture*, Harmondsworth (Penguin Books) 1940, p. 11.

9. An account of the Twentieth Century Group is given in Alan Powers, *Serge Chermayeff: Designer, Architect, Teacher*, London (RIBA Publications) 2001, pp. 39–41.

10. See Michael T. Saler, *The Inter-War Avant-Garde in England, Mediaeval Modernism and the London Underground*, New York and Oxford (Oxford University Press) 1999.

11. Paul Nash, "'Going Modern' and 'Being British'", *Week-end Review*, 12 March 1932, p. 322.

12. Interview with Chermayeff in *The Cabinet Maker and Complete House Furnisher*, 25 January 1930, p. 159.

R.A. Duncan (1889–1960), The House of the Future, Ideal Home Exhibition, Olympia, London W8, 1927; perspective drawing by Walpole Champneys, garden designed by Geoffrey Jellicoe.

Burnet, Tait & Lorne, Evelyn Court, Amhurst Road, London N10, 1934. Francis Lorne was a member of the Council for Research on Housing Construction, and planned this scheme of 1125 flats in Hackney for the Four Percent Industrial Dwellings Company, a housing organization founded in 1887.

A Decade of Modernism: 1930–1940

Apart from its convenience as a round number, the year 1930 has special significance in the history of the Modern Movement in Britain, as external economic and political factors influenced and accelerated the emergence of a new idea of architecture at this time. It was the beginning of three or four years of instability, when unemployment rose at home, the pound fell against other currencies when Britain left the gold standard, and there was much talk of the need for a completely new start in Britain, after the promises of reconstruction in 1918 had turned sour. The rise of extreme political movements in Europe, right and left, tested the moderation of the British parliamentary system. This was a climate in which gestures of allegiance, particularly among the young, assumed a magnified importance.

In architecture schools 1930 was the year in which the change to a distinctly different modern architecture became visible, when several future founder members of the Tecton partnership, plus Elisabeth Benjamin, Denys Lasdun, H.T. Cadbury-Brown and Mary Crowley, were students at the Architectural Association. Few of the tutors were yet convinced about the change, although in some cases the students helped to teach them, as Richard Wilson did Geoffrey Jellicoe in the design of the Caveman Restaurant in Cheddar Gorge, Somerset.

There was a public, although not necessarily a large one, for a new style. In some cases the patrons were feeling the same desire for change as the architects themselves. It is interesting that at least two of the earliest Modern Movement buildings in Britain were associated with advertising: Crawford's in High Holborn, London, and the Royal Corinthian Yacht Club at Burnham on Crouch, Essex, commissioned by Philip Benson, head of another of London's leading advertising agencies. Lord Beaverbrook understood the publicity value of modern design with the *Daily Express* building in Fleet Street, London, upstaging its heavy Art Deco–Classical neighbour the *Daily Telegraph*. The *Daily Mail* Ideal Home Exhibition was inconsistent in its representation of Modernism, but its House of the Future in 1927, by R.A. Duncan, was an early attempt to imagine a completely new architecture, and in 1934 the first models of Wells Coates's 'Sunspan' design were shown there.

For a style associated with left-wing politics it is also surprising that several of the early Modernist commissions came from the aristocracy, such as Lord Weymouth, for the Caveman Restaurant, and Lord De La

Warr, who had a guiding hand in the selection of Mendelsohn and Chermayeff's scheme for the Pavilion at Bexhill, East Sussex. *Country Life* magazine, associated with hunting and shooting, gave the movement an unexpected degree of support at the beginning of the 1930s, although later on this declined. Lifestyle magazines such as *Ideal Home* mixed modern and more traditional new houses in their pages, while *The Studio* published a wider range of modern design from Europe than most of the architectural papers.

The years 1930–32 were perilous ones in the politics and economics of Britain, owing to the world slump, which exposed long-standing structural weaknesses in the economy, together with the inadequacies of training in many areas. Modern architecture was encouraged by many members of the establishment, especially men close to the Labour Cabinet of Ramsay MacDonald, the Prime Minister at the beginning of the decade, as a necessary part of the modernization of Britain. These included Earl De La Warr and Sir Ralph Glyn, who persuaded the LMS Railway to employ Oliver Hill for the design of its new hotel at Morecambe,

Lancashire, in 1932 as a way of boosting wealthier middle-class seaside holidays in Britain rather than abroad. Set against this was a persistent conservatism, but Modernism took on forms that succeeded in satisfying progressives and many conservatives alike.

As the reality of economic depression impinged on even the middle classes, the solution of the 'slum problem', essentially unchanged in form since it had first been noticed nearly a hundred years earlier, became a matter of wide concern once more. It has been said that the development of cheap houses in the suburbs by the private building industry, which appalled left-wing politicians and aesthetes of all political colours alike, did more to solve it than any deliberate move by government or philanthropy. Modernism had only a limited impact on the local authorities, who were given funding to address the issue. They found that they could build brick flats, usually with timber sash-windows in a restrained Georgian style, in the inner cities and semi-detached houses of similar character in the new suburbs without having recourse to any of the new techniques and aesthetics that modern architects so strongly believed would offer the best solution. The outcome in Britain in the 1930s was that few Modernist housing projects were built to rival those of Berlin or Frankfurt, and most of those that were built emanated from outside the charmed circle of the MARS Group (or the Modern Architectural Research Group, to cite its little-used full name), many of whose members wanted more than anything else to work in this field. In London, Burnet, Tait & Lorne built Evelyn Court in Hackney using a repetitive steel-frame design in 1934. The almost forgotten architect Edward Armstrong built Loughborough Park in Brixton for the Guinness Trust in 1938 with a rather Dutch-looking yellow brick. The most visually impressive and socially and technically progressive development, Quarry Hill at Leeds (1934–39), was the work of a local authority architect, R.A.H. Livett.

Admittedly, these schemes lacked the architectural polish that was brought to the design of the Kensal House flats by Maxwell Fry or to Highpoint in Highgate by Berthold Lubetkin and the Tecton partnership, but the intentions were similar. The friendship and architectural collaboration between Jack and Molly Pritchard and the architect Wells Coates, who designed the Lawn Road flats for them, remains emblematic of the almost unavoidable confusions of the period. Jack Pritchard, apart

A PELICAN SPECIAL

ANTHONY BERTRAM

DESIGN

TOP: Edward Armstrong, Loughbourough Park, Brixton, London SW9, 1938.

ABOVE: Neil & Hurd, flats at Ravelston Garden, Edinburgh, 1938. A rare private development in a modern style in Scotland, with an interesting X-shaped footprint.

LEFT: R.A.H. Livett (1898–1959), Quarry Hill flats, Leeds, 1934–39, shown in model form on the cover of Anthony Bertram's *Design* of 1938.

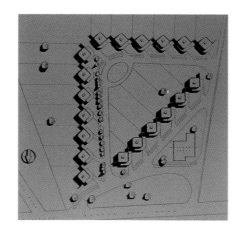

from his day job as a plywood salesman, was a founder member of a freelance think-tank, PEP (Political and Economic Planning), closely associated with the magazine *The Week-end Review*, edited by Gerald Barry from 1930 to 1933. Molly was a psychiatrist, active in the discipline that many believed to offer man's best insight into his own sorry predicament. At Lawn Road they first of all, in 1930, sacked a neo-Georgian architect whom they had commissioned to build them a private house and then employed Coates initially to design a single house, then two, and then a block of flats intended as a demonstration model for future minimal dwellings, although it was occupied by artists and intellectuals rather than workers. It was a brave effort, but only an exemplar rather than a practical contribution to the main social problem.

Housing in flats was widely seen by many architects and design thinkers as the right solution, for all social classes, to the spread of the suburbs that had left many British people in a state of shock by 1930. Roadside advertising and uncontrolled ribbon development of semi-detached houses and bungalows along the roads into towns and cities were eating the countryside away. The Modern Movement saw itself as part of a broad coalition in favour of a better-quality environment, furthering the work of the Council for the Protection of Rural England (founded in 1926), and the Design and Industries Association (DIA), which in 1930 published *The Face of the Land*, edited by Noel Carrington, as a manifesto for greater planning control in town and country. The moderns, however, set themselves apart by seeing 'period' styles as part of the problem. It was not difficult to show Modernism in a better light than the speculative builder's standard product. The architect Hugh Hughes, discussing an early flat-roofed house in Cambridge by George Checkley, felt that, "at the worst, a flat roof does not mar the countryside as does a pyramid of shrimp-pink asbestos".[1] Philip Morton Shand went further, including the 'polite' neo-Georgian of post offices and telephone exchanges as "a symptom that our cultural decay is as pronounced as our commercial decline", seen through the eyes of more culturally advanced foreigners.[2]

There were attempts to beat the speculative builders at their own game, by offering standard Modernist house designs capable of being cheaply built. The most successful of these was the 'Sunspan' house by

Wells Coates, in conjunction with the builders E.L. Berg, launched at the Ideal Home Exhibition in 1934, a year after Serge Chermayeff's 'Kernal' house, which was derived from German prefabrication. The contractors Haymills developed the Hanger Hill estate at Ealing with houses, hotel and Underground station (Park Royal) in a moderate modern style by Welch & Lander in the mid-1930s. Other builders, such as John Laing, went cautiously modern, while it is not uncommon to find streamlined styling and curved windows applied to what were otherwise essentially standard houses.[3]

Despite such attempts to stand apart from the architecture of the previous generation, Modernism in Britain shared most of the underlying principles of the Garden City movement, which, although expressed in cosy vernacular revival design, was an important source for the principles of modern city planning in Europe.[4] The result was a widespread lack of belief in the traditional city, with its dense urban blocks or streets of terraced houses, and a concern that now seems excessive for provision of green open space. One must remember that smoke output from domestic coal fires and industry in cities continued unabated and that antibiotics were still in the future, while TB was a real danger at all levels of society. Even the effort to keep things clean in a house without detergents could be achieved only with paid domestic help, and escape into an unpolluted countryside seemed to offer the quickest route to a decent life. Many of the 1930s Modernists, such as Frederick Gibberd and Geoffrey Jellicoe, were involved in planning the post-war New Towns that perpetuated most of the features of earlier garden cities, but there was a countervailing admiration among nearly all the Modernists for the orderly design of Georgian cities in Britain, which began to influence their designs after 1935.

In the suburbs Modernism after 1930 began to contribute to the new patterns of life, putting its mark on building types such as Underground stations, schools and lidos that, when built in the previous decade, had normally been Georgian in style. The new stations on the Piccadilly line by the Underground's favourite architect, Charles Holden, began in 1930 with Sudbury Town, which set a standard pattern of forms and materials that was developed by Holden and other architects. In 1930 Holden, whose pre-1914 work, such as Zimbabwe House, was often radical for its time, travelled with his patron, Frank Pick, to The Netherlands, Germany and

Gunnar Asplund (1885–1940)
and Nils Einar Eriksson, Paradise
Restaurant at the Stockholm
Exhibition, 1930. The restaurant
was named after a hanging
sculpture of Adam and Eve, with
an elephant and a 15 ft (4.5 m)
stripy snake, suspended in the
projecting glass bay. The wall was
dark blue and merged with the
sky at night.

Sir Albert Richardson (1880–1964) and C. Lovett Gill, St Margaret's House, Wells Street, London W1, 1932. A classicist's response to the fashion for austerity.

Sweden to look at new architecture. They rejected the more extreme examples and synthesized the rest, with results that have always been admired. In 1942 Nikolaus Pevsner ended his *Outline of European Architecture* with an illustration and description of one of the most elegant stations, Arnos Grove.

Near these Underground stations, the schools designed by W.T. Curtis, the Middlesex County Architect, were built in a similar style, representing an emerging idea of modern architecture as a public service, aimed at seemliness and efficiency. The mainstream of architectural debate tended to view such buildings as relatively uninteresting, but they set a pattern for the great expansion after the War in the architectural status of county councils and other local authorities, especially in the design of schools.

Included in Holden and Pick's itinerary in the summer of 1930 was the Stockholm Exhibition, visited by many other leading British thinkers on architecture and design. During the 1920s the preceding classical style in Sweden had been highly influential in Britain, and several of its exponents, such as Gunnar Asplund and Sigurd Lewerentz, suddenly changed horses for the 1930 exhibition, which helped to dispel the idea that Modernism was culturally alien to Britain. It was possible to believe that, for all their differences, the Swedes represented a model of what the British might become, both socially and culturally, if Modernism were accepted and the consequences of the first industrial revolution reversed. Prudence Maufe, the wife of the architect Edward Maufe, told radio listeners that the air in Sweden was so unpolluted that "a cotton frock will last clean for a week in Stockholm, and you know what it would look like in London after a day or two".[5]

More than anything, the Swedes had succeeded in making the change to Modernism seem less alarming than the French had done, and more fun than the Germans. Philip Morton Shand wrote in the *Architectural Review*: "We should be wise to back the Swedes, if only because it will save us a lot of time and trouble – things we invariably grudge. And this is not only because their instinct is sure, their technical and intellectual equipment more than adequate, but because their sense of beauty and fitness of things is more akin to our own than other people's."[6]

Modernism is often associated principally with the use of new building materials, and the early histories and polemics of modern architecture celebrated the prowess of the engineer, as opposed to the timidity of academic architects. Reinforced concrete and structural steel were late nineteenth-century materials, the adoption of which saved time and money because as frame structures they removed the need for load-bearing walls. Building design since the demise of timber framing had depended on massive construction, but the vision of a lighter future offered by the steel skeletons that more frequently emerged from behind the hoardings of new buildings after a change in building codes in 1909 was lost when they were covered up with a coating of Portland stone or brick.

The right response to these developments was an issue that worried architects all through the 1920s, and the absence of alternatives consonant with the ideals of structural honesty that most of them had learned from the Arts and Crafts movement made the Modern Movement, in some form or other, an almost unavoidable choice. For Albert Richardson there was an acceptable way of using steel within the classical tradition, and before 1914 he was at the forefront of exploring a thinner and more rational application of the style. In 1932 his St Margaret's House in Wells Street, London, stripped off more of the ornament than ever before, without losing the classical organization. In Battersea Power Station, London (1933), Giles Gilbert Scott chose instead to emphasize through three-dimensional geometric composition the solidity of the brick skin, even though it was actually a thin wall for a building of this scale. Because of its plainness and functional purpose this was seen by many as a modern building and became a popular landmark.

By 1930, for any architect without a strong commitment to using the dress of a historical style, the issue for office buildings had resolved essentially into a question of whether to stress verticality or horizontality. Casing the steel stanchions in accordance with London building regulations with the amount of masonry required for a load-bearing structure led to loss of daylight in commercial buildings, so instead the solid panels between the windows became the main expressive element of the design, as seen at High Holborn, London, by Etchells and Welch. The stainless-steel casing of the stanchions helps to draw the eye and balance the composition. At Hay's Wharf, London, H.S. Goodhart-Rendel tried to provide a balance, using faceted Portland stone cladding combined with other forms of decoration. The further alternative, less frequently adopted, was that of the *Daily Express* building by Owen Williams, where the load-bearing frame was concealed entirely behind a continuous skin of glass, varied between black and transparent – the effect known as a 'curtain wall', although this, technically speaking, is not built as one.

Steel not only saved money on solid walling but also shortened construction time. Oliver Hill's Midland Hotel, Morecambe, was completed in twelve months between 1932 and 1933, and the speed produced a substantial cost saving. At the De La Warr Pavilion further time and money were saved by welding the frame rather than riveting it with red-hot rivets tossed from the ground up in the air to the riveters aloft, the terrifying but normal method of the time. Owing to the fire safety provisions in the building regulations, actual steel always had to be concealed on the exterior and in the inhabited parts. Lighter welded-steel frames, such as were used in the French Mopin system at Quarry Hill, Leeds, in 1935, offered more advantages of cheapness and speed, although they were not widely adopted.

Concrete had the advantage of being fireproof and could act either as a frame or as a form of panel or walling. Before 1914 it was almost exclusively used in civil engineering, achieving architectural respectability of a kind in 1924 in the Empire Exhibition at Wembley, including the famous Wembley Stadium, where Owen Williams collaborated as engineer with the classical architects Simpson & Ayrton. Soon afterwards Williams began to design complete buildings himself, with striking results. His Boots D10 building of 1930–32 seemed to realize the elusive ideal that 'form follows function' to produce a lucid plan and section with a fully visible concrete post-and-slab structure behind its floor-to-ceiling perimeter glazing. Williams, who was knighted in 1924, was one of the few engineers in Britain in the 1930s whose name was well known by the public.

The role of the consulting engineer, sympathetic to architects' design intentions and offering friendly collaborative advice, began to emerge during the 1930s. The Danish engineer Ove Arup was educated partly in Britain and worked for the Anglo-Danish practice Christiani & Nielsen at the beginning of the 1930s, mainly in dock and sea defence structures. At Canvey Island, Essex, he took the opportunity in 1932 to build a cylindrical café on top of the sea wall, and this offered useful experience for the Gorilla House at London Zoo, which was Arup's first of many collaborations with Berthold Lubetkin as a consultant engineer.

Arup, Felix Samuely and Oscar Faber emerged as modern architects' favourite engineers, but many architects, including Amyas Connell, made their own engineering calculations, while others may have considered the engineer's role insufficiently important to record at the time. Even though the ideology of the Modern Movement promoted the engineer to a high status, the two cultures generally remained distinct. Arup later recalled:

The puzzling part was that these architects professed enthusiasm for engineering, for the functional use of materials, for the ideals of the Bauhaus, and all that; but … this didn't mean quite what you might suppose. They were in love with an architectural style, with the aesthetic feel of the kind of building they admired; and so they were prepared and indeed determined to design their buildings in reinforced concrete – a material they knew next to nothing about – even if it meant using the concrete to do things that could be done better and more cheaply in another material.[7]

Flat roofs were important as a signal of Modernism, and yet they were also one of the main causes of scepticism and opposition. Modernists could argue that they had a long tradition in Britain, going back to medieval castles, Elizabethan prodigy houses and, so far as external appearance goes, Georgian urban terraces. Their practical use as roof terraces and gardens was stressed, although not all house designs provided access. The architect Manning Robertson wrote in 1935: "As regards the use of the flat roof as a garden or sun loggia, this is of value under crowded conditions, but is quite useless where there is a garden which can give the same benefits, and shelter from the wind at the same time, without running into the cost of stairways, parapets, etc."[8] Even so, many flat roofs were optimistically equipped as play spaces for children, as at High and Over, Amersham, Buckinghamshire, and 31 Madingley Road, Cambridge, and may also have been used for sunbathing. Not much gardening was attempted on them, perhaps owing to a lack of knowledge of appropriate plants.

Initially, the 'white box' look that the flat roof permitted was virtually synonymous with modern architecture and could in fact be achieved either with concrete or steel as the main structural material. Henry-Russell Hitchcock and Philip Johnson's *Modern Architecture: International Exhibition* at the Museum of Modern Art, New York, in 1932 gave the impression that modern architecture was exclusively based on box-like forms, in what Hitchcock later called "a convergence of long imminent ideas", but it was supposed to be only a snapshot of a moving subject. Hitchcock and Johnson preferred the 'International Style', as they called it, to be viewed as "the frame for potential growth, rather than as a fixed and crushing mould".[9] The leaders of the movement were more flexible, and Mies van der Rohe used exposed brick walls for the majority of his villas, while Le Corbusier, with whom the white style was so strongly associated, never in fact built another white box after the Villa Savoye in 1930.

In Britain, however, many young architects considered not just that concrete was the only possible material but also, at least until experience made them wiser, that it should as far as possible be 'monolithic' – that is to say, cast in one continuous piece, comprising walls and roofs, all 4 inches (10 cm) thick. Interruptions such as columns and downstand beams in the ceilings were avoided where possible, or concealed. When the shuttering was taken away and the walls painted white, the effect could be beautiful. The inside and the outside corresponded exactly, like the soap bubble that Le Corbusier invoked as a model for architecture. There were no obscuring cavities, usually only an internal lining of cork for insulation, cast as 'permanent shuttering'. The steel windows, with their razor-thin bar sections, were placed in the openings.

The problems began when the houses had to be inhabited, for the insulation was never adequate, and the whole structure lacked 'thermal breaks' of any kind to buffer the transmission of heat or cold. Sometimes the flat roofs leaked, and they certainly acquired a dubious reputation. In honour of pure aesthetics copings at the head of the walls were eliminated as a fussy and historical-looking detail, but the result was that rain streaked down the surfaces that were intended to look as pure as a Ben Nicholson white relief. Some of these problems were exacerbated by the damp English climate, which can freeze and unfreeze daily during the winter. The changes that came over most architects' choice of materials and styles after 1935 (discussed below) were to a large extent guided by

the realization that the purity they once held so dear came at a heavy cost in maintenance and utility bills.

One convincing argument for using a flat roof was less frequently articulated: that it allowed the designer more freedom to build with a deep plan, because skylights could light stairs and, in some cases, bathrooms without other external light. Paradoxically, the typical Modernist house plan of the 1930s would be long and thin, a perfect shape for a conventional roof. Rudolf Frankel's house of 1938 (see pp. 108–09) and Dora Cosens's of 1937 (pp. 94–95) are rare examples of houses that do make good use of a compact square mass on plan, while at 2 Willow Road, Hampstead, the living-rooms get the best available daylight from the windows, and bathrooms and staircase have skylighting, adding to an effect of mystery.

Whatever the practical pros and cons of a flat roof, there is a symbolic quality about it that eluded expression in the 1930s and is still seldom discussed today. To understand it, one needs to approach the subject through a thinker such as the French philosopher Gaston Bachelard, who interpreted houses as images of the individual psyche, with the implication that a flat roof allows a swifter passage upwards to a kind of transcendental state, which may also be interpreted as a sexual arousal. No other explanation seems quite to account for the fervour with which this particular aspect of building was contested by supporters and opponents alike.[10]

Some of the problems of total concrete construction could be avoided if the house was actually built out of brick or blockwork, and then plastered inside and out. In fact, Le Corbusier did not mind publishing photographs showing that his own villas were built this way, but in Britain this was seen by some as a shameful compromise. At Frinton Park, Essex, in 1934 several work-hungry architects even turned down the offers made by Oliver Hill on behalf of the developers for building small houses because they were not allowed to use pure concrete. Then the fanaticism began to wear off. In 1936 F.R.S. Yorke's partner Randall Evans made him promise that he would never build a concrete house again, which for the author of *The Modern House*, a book published in 1934 promoting concrete houses, was some undertaking. The reason was the difficulty Evans had experienced cutting openings at

Raymond McGrath
(1903–1977), Carrygate, Galby,
Leicestershire, 1939. A notable
example of a modern house in
timber and brick (salvaged from
an Elizabethan house) at the end
of the 1930s, influenced by work
in Japan by Frank Lloyd Wright's
pupil Antonin Raymond.

Torilla, Hatfield, to connect to an extension that he was in charge of building.[11]

The fact that local councils often forced architects to build in brick rather than concrete in order to fit in, as happened to Maxwell Fry at Little Winch, meant that concrete was the 'heroic' choice for many, but fewer of them tried to contest the struggle as the decade went on. In his row of cottages at Stratford upon Avon in 1938 Yorke was one of several architects to try using a monopitch or single-slope roof, probably inspired by houses designed by Sigurd Lewerentz at the Stockholm Exhibition of 1930. Mary Crowley roofed her group of three houses at Tewin, Hertfordshire, with monopitches in 1935, and Max Lock followed with a house at Stanmore, Middlesex, in 1938.[12]

Having built one monolithic concrete apartment block, Highpoint I, Highgate, London, in 1935, Berthold Lubetkin completed its neighbour and successor, Highpoint II, with a frame-and-panel construction three years later. In line with the doctrine of structural honesty he made this difference legible on the exterior with tile panels inset in the frame. Similarly, after the pure concrete of Lawn Road flats, Wells Coates chose a surface finish of artificial stone, ingeniously cast as 'permanent shuttering', in conjunction with pouring the structural concrete, for 10 Palace Gate, Kensington, London.

Brick and timber made a comeback after 1935 and by the end of the decade had given a new face to modern architecture. To commentators then and subsequently there has been an implication of compromise about this, as if the 'heroism' of modern architecture depended on the pursuit of impracticality for aesthetic ends at all costs. It is notable, however, that this shift was not just the cop-out of the half-hearted but often the preferred route for architects with impeccable credentials of purity.

Ernö Goldfinger, a pupil of Auguste Perret, who had virtually reinvented architecture in terms of concrete, was enthusiastic for the material but equally opposed to 'Casbah' architecture, as he described the white boxes. Nikolaus Pevsner, who found that "there is in this reversion to a traditional material ... something typically British", believed that "brick must have something extremely appealing and convincing for the English atmosphere, if it could even attract these foreign architects working in London".[13] The English understood brick, and it suited the climate, so Goldfinger used it

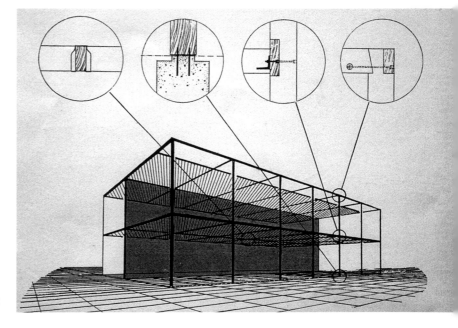

Serge Chermayeff, Bentley Wood, Halland, East Sussex, 1938. A diagram showing the non-traditional jointing of the timber frame.

for both his domestic projects before the War, even though the structure at 1–3 Willow Road is concrete underneath. Ernst Freud and Rudolf Frankel came from Berlin, where brick had never been excluded from the Modernist vocabulary, and like Goldfinger they used it to get a sober flatness of texture, unlike the variety associated with brickwork in England and seen in Holden's station buildings. Walter Gropius chose brick for the Impington Village College, although he wanted to import the bricks from The Netherlands to achieve a smooth effect, until the cost implications showed this could not be done.

By the end of the decade timber was a popular material for modern houses. It was easily available, good for insulation and cladding as well as structure, and quick to erect. In Germany it had always formed one strand of the Modern Movement, as seen in Konrad Wachsman's book of 1930, *Das Holzbauhaus*. Once again Gropius set an example, with The Wood House, Shipbourne, Kent, designed in 1936. Shortage of concrete in the years before the War, when supplies were commandeered for building airfields, was the main reason why Shawms, Cambridge, was built in timber. However, it was a material more widely favoured among the student generation to which Justin Blanco White belonged, and there was a vigorous commercial promotion of the material in books and magazines.[14] At Bentley Wood in Sussex, a house much admired by students of a younger generation, Serge Chermayeff developed special ways of fixing the timber frame, probably based on German experience, and in many people's view elevated timber to the highest level of modern architectural use. Frank Lloyd Wright, a pioneer Modernist with a special fondness for timber, visited Bentley Wood in 1939, by which time there was already an emerging school of Modernist timber building in the San Francisco Bay Area.

Stone was less frequently used, owing to its cost and associations of luxury, but Le Corbusier had given a lead, as in so many other matters, when in 1930 he included a long curved wall of rough rubble in the entrance building of the Pavillon Suisse in Paris, before going on to develop several other designs in which the roughness of masonry was an important aesthetic component. He may have been partially influenced by the emblematic significance accorded to stone by Surrealist artists such as Max Ernst. The ancient and chthonic quality of stone contrasted with the transitory modern age. Marcel Breuer used Cotswold stone, a material associated with most traditional English attitudes, in his temporary pavilion at Bristol in 1936, and probably drew on the technical expertise of his partner Yorke, who also gave his Stratford terrace a stone end wall. Although no other architects used stone so prominently in this Modernist way, Breuer's design, in particular, was the beginning of 'feature fireplaces' in stone, in his own work and in that of countless imitators in the United States and Britain.

This survey of materials shows some of the aspects of the 1930s that divide architecturally into at least two parts. The first few years of the decade were spent assimilating ten years of existing experience in Europe, but when that was done, and when conditions in Britain returned to something more normal, it was possible to take stock in a less fevered manner. Sixty years later there remains a conflicting body of written and built evidence for those trying to establish whether there was an essential form of Modernism in Britain.

To answer this question, it is essential to try to enter the minds of a group of perhaps a hundred key architects and to deduce, usually from

Le Corbusier, Pavillon Suisse, Cité Universitaire, Paris, 1930. The mixture of materials made this a particularly influential building for English modern architects after 1935.

inadequate evidence, their ideas and intentions during a period of ten or more years. In addition to individual architects, there are patrons to consider as possible influences, and implicated in each project is a set of ideas and expectations connected with each type of building. Although it is tempting to pick certain main lines of the story, the conclusion that the Modern Movement in Britain was both complex and contradictory is unavoidable, as even a surface inspection of the built evidence reveals. Had this not been the case, it might have been the arid, over-theorized movement that was all its detractors could see it as, rather than something of much greater cultural depth.

The critical debate around Modernism was not merely a question of opposite sides, as it appeared when Sir Reginald Blomfield confronted Amyas Connell on the radio in 1934, or when Evelyn Waugh wrote contemptuously in *Country Life* in 1938 of "villas like sewage farms, mansions like half-submerged Channel steamers, offices like vast beehives".[15] Even the issue of whether Modernism was a 'foreign' style was influenced by its origins in Britain within close memory, the fact that British architecture was a story of successive waves of European influence, and the skills brought by émigré architects that were lacking among professionals at home.

A deep sense of national cultural inferiority was present not only in architecture but also in music and the other arts, with the possible exception of literature. Even the more traditional architects of 1900, with their shifting affections for the United States, France and Sweden, had experienced it. Foreign influences came, furthermore, in many forms that allowed a wide range of choice. France, represented above all by Le Corbusier, appeared to take precedence, closely followed by Germany and The Netherlands, but Sweden, Czechoslovakia and Italy all had different modulations of Modernism to offer. After Alvar Aalto showed his furniture in London in 1934, an event rather surprisingly held at Fortnum & Mason's high-class department store in Piccadilly, his influence began a long hold on the British imagination that has never ended.[16]

When architects themselves came from Europe to settle and work in Britain, it is less clear whether they influenced their host country, or whether the influence travelled the opposite way. They certainly experienced the great difference in ideas and manners between Britain and the rest of the Continent, finding it well disposed in general but hostile to aesthetic challenges. Charlotte Benton lists some sixty individuals who arrived in Britain during the 1930s, the majority of them as a result of political pressure to leave Germany or Austria, although a few, such as Berthold Lubetkin and Ernö Goldfinger, had already settled in the relative security of Paris. Both of these brought considerable experience not only professionally but also in terms of their experience of life in the artistic and intellectual swim of Paris.[17] Both tended to appear arrogant and impatient of the muddled English way of doing things, but Lubetkin was undoubtedly the most brilliant individual working before the War in his field, while Goldfinger had a remarkable late flowering as a housing architect in the 1960s.

Erich Mendelsohn formed a partnership at the end of 1933 with Serge Chermayeff, who, although born in Chechnya, had been educated in Britain and was naturalized in 1928. Within a few months they won the competition for the De La Warr Pavilion, although Mendelsohn spent the majority of his time living and working in Palestine until 1939, when he moved to the US. Henry-Russell Hitchcock commented favourably on the change in Mendelsohn's style that he believed had taken place since his arrival in Britain.[18]

Walter Gropius, the founder of the Bauhaus school, arrived in October 1934 and formed a partnership with Maxwell Fry. He was very short of money but too proud to lower his standards of work. Although he felt a lack of opportunities, his final project, Impington Village College, begun on site only after he left to become chairman of the Department of Architecture at Harvard in 1937, shows how strongly he had absorbed the influence of English informality and given Modernism a new and unexpected direction. Gropius's ideal of the suppression of ego in design connected back to the Arts and Crafts movement and struck a chord in the English heart, casting a retrospective glow of precocious modernity on the Georgian building tradition, with its semi-industrialized components and its compositions of repeated units.

Marcel Breuer, one of Gropius's star pupils at the Bauhaus, arrived in Britain in 1935 and worked in partnership with F.R.S. Yorke until 1937. Thanks to the patronage of Jack Pritchard, he was able to develop plywood and laminated furniture, with designs that have been

The range of the *Architectural Review*: two sample spreads from 1930. The top spread shows decorative treatments by Fernand Léger and Marcel Breuer (left), and a design for a cinema floor by Raymond McGrath (right). The lower spread is taken from an article by Philip Morton Shand and illustrates work by Gabriel Guévrékian, Robert Mallet-Stevens and Jean Lurçat.

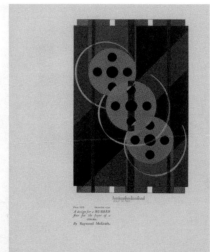

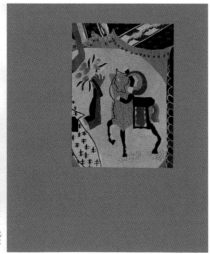

reproduced almost continuously ever since, and, although he lacked many opportunities for new buildings, he designed some elegant interiors. Less well known were architects such as Ernst Freud and Rudolf Frankel, but their work is instructive since in their cities of origin (Vienna and Berlin respectively) they were not the most avant-garde of their generation, and when their moderation was transplanted to Britain, it demonstrated how modern architecture could become a matter of pleasant common-sense planning and careful rational use of materials. The careers of other émigrés took them into many fields, including teaching. Some, such as Peter Moro, were only just old enough to get a building finished before the War, while others, such as Walter Segal from Germany and Eugene Rosenberg (later in partnership with Yorke and Cyril Mardall) from Czechoslovakia, made their mark entirely after it.

It has often been remarked how many of the active figures in British Modernism before the main wave of immigration came from what was still described as 'the Empire'. Amyas Connell, Basil Ward and George Checkley were all from New Zealand, Raymond McGrath came from Australia, and Wells Coates was a Canadian citizen, although he had been born and raised in Japan. It is possible that their familiarity with the need to make the most of available materials without a fuss helped the New Zealanders in their handling of concrete. All of them seem to have felt less inhibited than some of the native Britons in challenging architectural conventions.

It is an interesting speculation whether the émigrés, with their experience and sophistication, had the unintended effect of nipping in the bud some more nationally distinctive variety of British Modernism that might have been emerging before 1934. Nikolaus Pevsner believed that Owen Williams was "one of the outstanding independent British leaders of the Modern Movement in the international sense" and a truly original creator, but otherwise identified a desire for compositional balance and poise as the essential qualities of British Modernism.[19] Comparing Connell and Ward's White House, Haslemere, Surrey, completed in 1932, with the work of their partnership with Colin Lucas two or three years later, one can see that with submission to the almost irresistible lure of Le Corbusier came a loss of the oddity and eccentricity that make the earlier work so appealing. An anonymous reviewer of Hitchcock's 1937

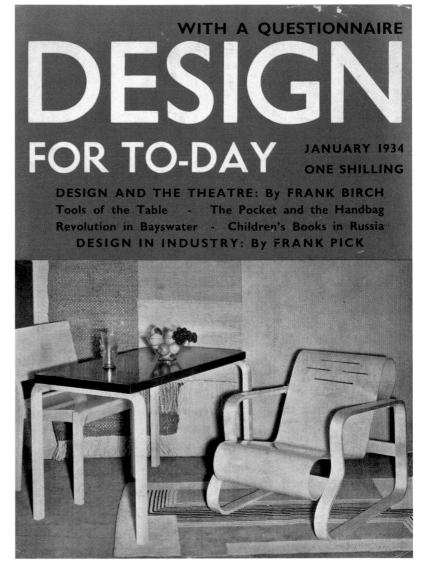

book *Modern Architecture in England* believed that "national temperament and conditions", including the suspended animation of the slump years, contributed to shaping this dominant influence.[20] Yet nationalism, particularly for a culture such as Britain's, assembled from different elements, is inherently paradoxical, often recognizing itself only through the mirror of another culture. One could contend that it was through this mirror of intense admiration for something different that Britain was able to rediscover a more secure sense of identity, at least in the medium term. The Czech architect Karel Honzig was sure that the roots of Modernism were already there and wrote in 1937 that:

In such a country it was not necessary to wage such a bitter struggle against historism or formalism as had frequently to be waged by countries of a different psychological nature. In time we realize something more, and that is, that it is not necessary in the case of the English consumer or producer to inculcate a sense for type and standard, for it is precisely this sense that is the fundamental element of English tradition and conservatism.[21]

Chermayeff was one semi-outsider who, early in his career, believed that English Modernism must adapt to the manners and customs of the country. With Coates and McGrath he was especially favoured by the *Architectural Review* in the years after 1930, when the journal's proprietor–editor, Hubert de Cronin Hastings, called them "The Three Musketeers". After 'H de C', as his colleagues knew him, became editor of the *Review* in 1929 at the age of twenty-six, it began to play an important role in the culture of British Modernism, never as a simple-minded advocate but always with the aim of helping architecture break out of its narrow culture. The elusive figure of Philip Morton Shand was an important mentor to Hastings and to the poet John Betjeman, who was on the staff from 1930 to 1933, and literary friends of his such as Cyril Connolly and Robert Byron wrote about a wide range of subjects. Shand wrote frequently for the *Review* in the early 1930s and, as a traveller and linguist, made contacts with architects abroad whose ideas and work were not yet well known, such as Adolf Loos and Alvar Aalto. Significantly, perhaps, neither Shand nor Hastings came from a background of architectural

The Empire Exhibition at Glasgow in 1938 displayed a consistent range of modern buildings by a team of Scottish architects working under the direction of Thomas Tait, who was the designer of the Coal Pavilion (bottom) – a building that would not have been out of place in 1930s Italy. The Industry Pavilion (right) was designed by Jack Coia, an architect who specialized in churches. After the War his practice became widely known as Gillespie, Kidd & Coia. The cover of the special issue of the *Architectural Review* for August 1938 (far right) recreates the sensation, hitherto unknown in Britain, of a complete Modernist environment.

training or practice.[22] Their ability to see architecture from the outside assisted the creation of a critical culture in the 1930s, and the *Review* campaigned to improve the quality of design not only in buildings but across the whole spectrum from consumer goods to landscape, and to recover a genuine sense of national style as opposed to the sentimental imitation of old design that had been prevalent since the nineteenth century. The topographical painters Paul Nash and John Piper helped to show how all periods of architecture in Britain were, at their best, a response to a spirit of place, balancing the internationalism of the new movement with a regional inflection that was, in fact, a feature of modern movements in all countries.

The *Review* was only one of many journals, among which the three weekly professional papers *The Builder*, the *Architect and Building News* and the *Architects' Journal* had begun during the nineteenth century. The latter came from the same publishers as the *Architectural Review* and reflected a similar outlook, with a useful annual round-up of new work written by C.H. Reilly.[23] The *Architect and Building News* was even more inclusive, and from the 1920s published F.R. Yerbury's photographs of Continental modern buildings with Howard Robertson's commentaries. In 1934 a young architect named John Summerson, later famous as a historian of English architecture after deciding that writing rather than practice suited him best, became a staff member; he contributed many perceptive articles on Modernism, not always signed, that show the influence of Shand's impassioned scepticism on him as well.

When writing his *Introduction to Modern Architecture* for Penguin Books at the end of the 1930s, J.M. Richards, who became the nominal editor of the *Review* in 1935 (with H. de C. still driving from the back seat), put forward his theory of Englishness:

As modern architecture matures, a new differentiation according to national characteristics is inevitable – not on the basis of the racial exclusiveness of Naziism, and not so clear and distinct as would have been the case many years ago … but Englishness is a definable quality found in things English, as Frenchness is found in things French, and these qualities are not incompatible with modern architecture as we have described it.[24]

Richards's unthinking equation of England with the rest of the British Isles may jar on present-day ears. Modernism in Scotland was hampered by a worse economic depression than in the south, but architects such as Basil Spence and William Kininmonth were interested in creating distinctive forms in ways that were fruitful after the War. The greatest demonstration of Scottish Modernism was the Empire Exhibition at Glasgow in 1938, for which the chief designer was Thomas Tait, who had a firmly established reputation in London as well as Edinburgh and Glasgow. In Wales a national identity for modern architecture was less easily established, although studies in vernacular building by scholars such as Iorweth Peate, based in the pioneering open-air museum at St Fagan's, near Cardiff, prepared the way for a well-grounded understanding of national traditions.

Richards's mention of Nazism raises the question of the political positioning of modern architecture in Britain. This complex issue really needs exploring on a case-by-case basis, since there was no simple equivalence between Modernism and left-wing politics, although this is commonly assumed and has a good basis in fact. Indeed Marshall Sisson, whose work is represented in this book, was briefly a member of Sir Oswald Mosley's British Union of Fascists (BUF), while by contrast Clough Williams-Ellis, remembered primarily for his candy-coloured Italianate hotel village of Portmeirion more than for his campaigns for the preservation of landscape and old buildings, was a socialist who believed in "more fun for more people". Interest in Modernism did not automatically ensure political correctness. Morton Shand was anti-Semitic, while John Gloag, a popular advocate of modern design, published some embarrassing articles in praise of Hitler's Germany. The clearest distinction was made when members of the BUF criticized the selection of the 'foreign' architects Mendelsohn and Chermayeff for the design of the De La Warr Pavilion at Bexhill, perhaps owing to the fact that two of the organization's members, Marshall Sisson and James Burford, had been unsuccessful in the competition, but their protest was never clearly against Modernism as such. Even so, the Nazis' opposition to modern art and architecture and the association they made between it and Jewish practitioners – the reasons for Mendelsohn's presence in London together with that of many other artists and intellectuals – made its alignment with the left virtually a foregone conclusion.

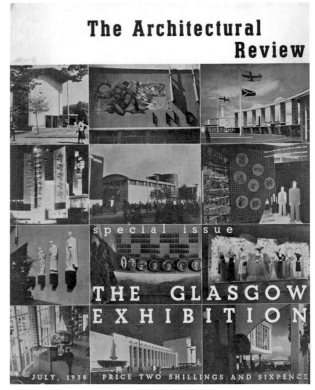

stood for 'Modern Architecture Research', and it was based on the Marxist view that scientific information was the proper basis for decision-making. Exhibitions on housing, probably its most important contribution, made a direct link between the misery of slum-dwellers, the rapacity of landlords and the apathy of the authorities, which could, if they chose, solve the problem faster and more effectively.[25] But most MARS Group members were too busy trying to make a bare living to put their time into research, and the group was riven with petty quarrels between large egos. It took until 1938 for the MARS Group to stage an exhibition to persuade a wider public – a stylish but essentially aesthetic presentation of completed projects lacking a strong philosophy.

It was among the 'lower' ranks of assistants in offices and students in schools of architecture that the more effective ideological battles took place. The ATO (Architects' and Technicians' Organization) was founded in 1935 by Lubetkin and members of Tecton, partly in response to the lack of political effectiveness in the MARS Group. It was concerned chiefly with housing, although it turned its attention later to air-raid protection.[26] What at the beginning of the decade might have been a politics of gesture from a country where the professional classes were still relatively secure had turned into a matter of survival for everyone.

There was undoubtedly a need for research of various kinds. Technical testing and experiment were, however, adequately covered by the Building Research Station, which grew to become a major resource in transforming the manner of building after the War. Offices increasingly carried out their own research, such as the standardization of detailing promoted by Burnet, Tait & Lorne and similar studies by Tecton, and they gave a lot of time to refining and improving the ergonomics and performance of building components and their assembly; they often also published their findings as part of the description of new buildings.

The political mood changed during the years of the Spanish Civil War (1936–39), when idealism and disillusion were competing responses. At the Architectural Association the members of a newly politicized generation of students interpreted their rather dilettante training as a symptom of the wider malaise of smug apathy that was so clearly leading to disaster. Even their pantomime in 1937, *Jack and Jill*, based on W.H. Auden and Christopher Isherwood's *The Dog Beneath the Skin*,

In Italy, Mussolini's opposition to Modernism came later and took a less extreme form, while the rise of Stalin in Russia created the anomaly of a Communist country banning its own modern architecture in favour of a return to classicism. It was rare, therefore, to hear classical architecture denounced as inherently Fascist, something reserved for later decades. Indeed, despite admiration on the left for Roosevelt's New Deal policies, American official architecture tended to be conservative and 'stripped classical'. It was in the social democracies of Sweden and other Nordic states, if anywhere, that the ideal correlation of politics and style was found.

Marxism was fashionable in the early 1930s among artists and intellectuals of all kinds and was for a time a genuine stimulus to rethinking the past and planning the future. Rumours still circulate about which architects were members of the Communist Party and which were only sympathizers. Modern architects' own organization, the MARS Group, was founded at the end of 1933 in order that Britain could have representation through a national group at the international conferences of the Congrès Internationaux d'Architecture Moderne (CIAM). The organization's initials

Gordon Cullen, opening screen for the MARS Group Exhibition, London, 1938. Godfrey Samuel proposed the adoption of the well-known quotation from Sir Henry Wootton's paraphrase of Vitruvius in *The Elements of Architecture*, 1624. The exhibition texts were written by John Summerson and the exhibition design was by Misha Black.

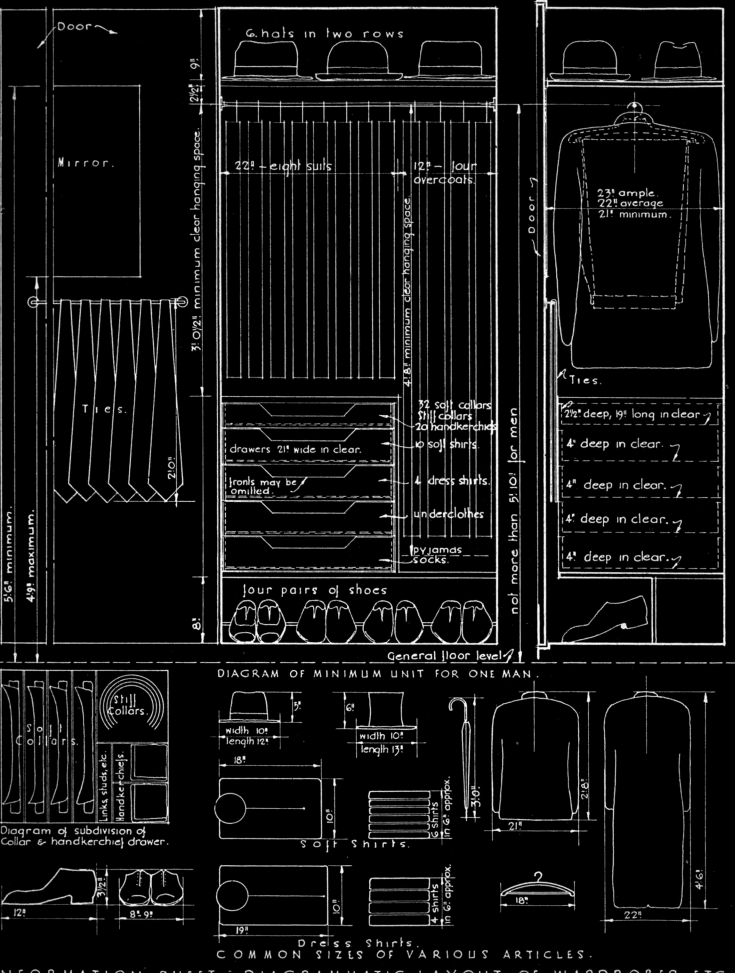

Door

Mirror.

Ties.

5'6" minimum.

4'9" maximum.

2'0"

6. hats in two rows

9"

2½"

3' 0½" minimum clear hanging space.

22" – eight suits

12" – four overcoats.

4'8" minimum clear hanging space.

not more than 5'10" for men

drawers 21" wide in clear.

fronts may be omitted.

32 soft collars
Stiff collars
20 handkerchiefs
10 soft shirts.

4 dress shirts.

underclothes

pyjamas
socks.

four pairs of shoes

8"

General floor level.

DIAGRAM OF MINIMUM UNIT FOR ONE MAN.

Door

Ties.

23" ample.
22" average.
21" minimum.

2½" deep, 19" long in clear.

4" deep in clear.

4" deep in clear.

4" deep in clear.

4" deep in clear.

Soft Collars.

Stiff Collars.

Links studs, etc.

handkerchiefs.

Diagram of subdivision of Collar & handkerchief drawer.

5"

width 10"
length 12"

6"

width 10"
length 13"

18"

10"

6 shirts in 6" approx.

Soft Shirts.

3'0"

21"

2'8"

3½"

12"

8"-9"

19"

10"

4 shirts in 6" approx.

Dress Shirts.

18"

22"

4'6"

COMMON SIZES OF VARIOUS ARTICLES.

INFORMATION SHEET : DIAGRAMMATIC LAYOUT OF WARDROBES, ETC.

SIR JOHN BURNET TAIT AND LORNE ARCHITECTS ONE MONTAGUE PLACE BEDFORD SQUARE LONDON W.C.I.

was a call to action, with words and music that matched the wit of
Auden and Benjamin Britten. These students went further, however, with
encouragement from the young Principal of the school, E.A.A. Rowse, who
took over from Howard Robertson in 1935. Rowse had a strong interest
in the social function of architecture and planning, and reorganized the
curriculum, but the more conservative members of staff felt that objective
standards would be lost by too much engagement with the real world
early on. Anthony Cox was one of the student leaders, engaged in a battle
of polemics with H.S. Goodhart-Rendel (in the thankless post of Director
of Education), and with symbolic appropriateness their showdown
coincided with the Munich crisis in 1938. Rowse moved across to direct
the Architectural Association's Planning School, and Geoffrey Jellicoe was
appointed as the new Principal.

The cluster of beliefs held by the rebellious students, and by several
of the staff who backed them, represented an attempt to get back to
the purity of the Modern Movement, which they believed had been
compromised, and even matched the more extreme ideas of the Arts
and Crafts period in the 1890s. Emphasizing social and technical research
as the most valuable aspect of their training, they believed in hands-on
experience, and one group conducted its own building project, while
another three students were given access to the building site of the
Finsbury Health Centre, London, to investigate how the actual process of
construction was carried out and to find ways of improving its efficiency.[27]
Groups of students were also involved in real-life planning exercises for a
new town at Faringdon in Berkshire, and a re-planning of Wantage.

Another group, tutored by Max Lock, studied a slum-clearance area
of Stepney called Ocean Street. As a result of interviewing the residents,
they learned that 55% preferred to be rehoused in two-storey terraces
like those due to be demolished, only better built and equipped.[28] This was
a challenge to the untested assumption that flats were superior to houses,
but it was in line with the ideas of the housing consultant Elizabeth Denby,
who, despite working with Maxwell Fry on the design of Kensal House
in 1936, believed that this was not the best solution. In her book *Europe
Re-housed* (1938), based on research in The Netherlands, Sweden and
Austria, Denby cast doubt on the paternalistic Victorian idea that social
housing required a distinctive architecture that created an enclosed island

of territory in the urban fabric; she suggested instead that it should be virtually invisible from the outside view and integrated with privately owned houses.

Anthony Cox wrote disparagingly about the direction taken in Lubetkin's work, especially the way that Highpoint II differed from Highpoint I. 'Formalism' was the word used to describe the result of what Cox called "the retreat from function". "Behind this", he wrote, "may be a more general frustration, eating away like a slow poison, and perhaps unrealized – the uneasy feeling of the insecurity of life, a war fatalism that makes a travesty of long-term thinking, and a dread that civilization everywhere may revert to the barbarism and bullying of a hysterically defensive Fascism."[29] He accurately identified the slightly febrile quality that can be found, not only in Lubetkin but also in Lasdun's 32 Newton Road, London, in aspects of Goldfinger's 1–3 Willow Road, London, and in Peter Moro and Richard Llewelyn-Davies's Harbour Meadow, Birdham, West Sussex. Le Corbusier had given the lead for this attitude of "curly sophistication, as brittle as the laughter of the Dadaists … the flippancy of people with the jitters", as Cox called it.[30] Other architects, however, seemed able to humanize their style while still keeping a serious demeanour – Chermayeff, for one, not only at Bentley Wood but also in the urbane but unpretentious urban architecture of the Gilbey Offices in Camden Town, London, which Hugh Casson described as "sound vernacular design".[31]

Walter Gropius admired Cox and his fellow editors of *Focus* magazine from the other side of the Atlantic.[32] They in turn admired Impington Village College, which was brought into being after Gropius's departure by Maxwell Fry's assistant Jack Howe, who had to apply the greatest ingenuity to cutting down the original design in order to keep within a tight budget. The common-sense materials and plan form of Impington are the opposite of 'masterpiece' architecture, and yet the design has an unforced grace that fulfilled the ideals of Henry Morris, the visionary Education Officer of Cambridge County Council, who inspired it.[33]

Leslie Martin was a figure who commanded the respect of the serious, politically motivated students, since he was closely involved with abstract artists such as Ben Nicholson and Naum Gabo, with whom in 1937 he edited the book *Circle*, subtitled 'International Survey of Constructive Art'. The book, with an accompanying exhibition, remade links between architecture and the fine arts in the strictest forms of abstraction, as a deliberate antidote to the Surrealist exhibition held in London in the previous year. Martin himself published designs for prefabricated unit houses for the sea coast, using the Bauhaus-inspired idea that remained with him for many years after, of a building form that could be infinitely repeated.

Martin was head of the Hull School of Architecture. His connections with the Nicholson family and abstract art brought him the patronage of the textile manufacturer and painter Alistair Morton for the construction of Brackenfell, Brampton, and a house extension for the collector Helen Sutherland at Dockray, also in Cumberland. His nursery school at Hartford, near Northwich, Cheshire, although a tiny building, indicates in its extendible unit plan and simple use of materials many of the principles that Martin applied after the War as an influential Chief Architect of the London County Council.

Schools were a particular concern in the final years of the 1930s, symbolizing the fragile hope that architecture could make life better for a younger generation. From its earliest origins the Modern Movement had been strongly child-centred. Reforming ideas in health and child welfare alike indicated the desirability of making schools light, open and attractive. The *News Chronicle*, a daily paper with a strong commitment to design, ran a serious competition in 1937 for three different types of school design. One of the categories was won by Denis Clarke Hall, and this led directly to his employment to design a girls' high school at Richmond, Yorkshire. Goldfinger made theoretical designs for nursery schools, and designed for Paul and Marjorie Abbatt, suppliers of educational toys and equipment such as slides and climbing frames for outdoor use at home. Oliver Hill designed several schools, although only one, at Whitwood Mere, near Castleford in Yorkshire, was actually built.

Most local authorities during the 1930s employed their own architects to design schools and other buildings. Their designs were disparaged by Goodhart-Rendel as being "like chocolate from a machine, repetitive and rather stale", but this was intended as a stimulus to improvement. Among the younger Modernists at the end of the 1930s the idea developed that an architecture of social service would in future best be conducted through the work of publicly employed architects rather than private practitioners. During and after the War many of them made good their claims, above all through the London County Council Architects' Department and Hertfordshire County Council.[34]

Thus, despite set-backs and frustrations, it could be claimed that when the development of modern architecture was effectively curtailed by the outbreak of war in September 1939, it was in a flourishing condition and had learned many of the lessons of the earlier years in terms of real rather than symbolic practicality and the need to appeal to its users rather than alienate them. It had come to terms with issues of national identity, and, as Henry-Russell Hitchcock wrote in 1937, there was hope that "the modern school or schools of the British Isles may, within a decade or more, be one of the most firmly established in the world".[35]

By 1939 the trend in all the arts in Britain was towards romanticism, or Neo-romanticism, as the movement soon became known. In architecture this embraced the soft but elegant pragmatism of Tayler & Green's Studio in Highgate, London, as well as the brittle self-consciousness of Lubetkin's Highpoint II penthouse, half a mile distant. The *Architectural Review* played an important role in fostering this all-round sensitivity to places and people, making connections with the Picturesque movement of the late eighteenth century, which in its own time had loosened the rigidity of Palladian classicism. The English were pleased to be told that this earlier movement of theirs had not only changed radically the style of gardening across Europe but had even helped to form the political thought of Goethe and Rousseau. Interest in landscape design as a distinct discipline

from architecture (albeit related to it) developed from the founding of the Institute of Landscape Architects in 1929, and when one of its members, Christopher Tunnard, tried to formulate a distinctly Modernist attitude to landscape, the result was pluralistic and often historically based.[36] Two practitioners who were less conspicuous in the 1930s, Brenda Colvin and Sylvia Crowe, became major post-war exponents of landscape architecture as a creative art with social and scientific dimensions.

Although the path of romanticism might appear to lead directly to nostalgia, it offered the promise of popularity, as an approach to design that was sensitive to places, people and the context of nature, while academic and traditional architecture was seen as having failed in these respects. As an anonymous member of the MARS Group wrote in 1938: "It is not with the green forms of Nature that the new architecture will be out of harmony, but with the work of man in the landscape during the period now happily passing, which has been marked by individual instead of collective control."[37]

In a long perspective the Modern Movement can be seen as an investigation into the nature of reality, in response to a crisis in which nothing seemed real any more. It can be doubted whether any question of such depth can have a conclusive answer, and Modernism took some strange pathways in searching for it. The Platonist strand of Modernism, which underlay its tendency to seek certainties of a classical kind, could become distorted into a false picture of the world when it denied the changeability of things. In Britain, Leslie Martin encouraged several generations to believe that architecture must eschew fashion if it is to

Connell, Ward & Lucas, Greenside, Wentworth, Surrey, 1938. A classic serenity tempers the structural gymnastics of one of the practice's finest smaller houses. Although protected by listing, it was demolished in 2003 (see p. 233).

find the truth, yet this unyielding sense of high purpose inevitably appealed more to the authors of the buildings than to their users. Those who shared his view believed that science was on their side, but science has subsequently come to be seen as in many ways less objective than was formerly thought. In fact C.H. Waddington, a scientist married to the architect Justin Blanco White, welcomed the romantic tendency in the arts and wrote in 1941:

> I do not think that an increase in the importance of a romantic view of life would make it any more difficult to achieve a scientific society. The substitution of a romantic ideal for our recent pallid and inhibited one would, I think, simply release enormous potentialities for action which have been suppressed. It would be incompatible with the myriad of vested interests, large or small, which sit on our heads like tin-pot or cast-iron lids. They would go flying.[38]

In the freeze-frame of 1939 it is possible to see the potential for pluralism as an essential aspect of Modernism, offering a better interpretation of the world and a better way of dealing with it in practical terms. When architects in following decades contested this view, they could find evidence in the 1930s for both sides of the argument, but the subtlety of different positions was ignored, and there is still much work involved in constructing a truer picture of this extraordinarily complex period.

Notes

1. H.C. Hughes, 'Recent Building in Cambridge', *The Listener*, vol. 6, 23 March 1932, p. 407.

2. P. Morton Shand, 'The Post-War Post Office', *Architectural Review*, vol. 68, 1930, p. 153.

3. See Simon Pepper, 'John Laing's Sunnyfields Estate, Mill Hill', in *The Cambridge Guide to the Arts in Britain*, vol. 8: *The Edwardian Age and the Inter-war Years*, ed. Boris Ford, Cambridge (Cambridge University Press) 1989.

4. See Robert Fishman, *Urban Utopias in the Twentieth Century: Ebenezer Howard, Frank Lloyd Wright and Le Corbusier*, Cambridge MA (MIT Press) 1982.

5. Prudence Maufe, 'A Visit to the Stockholm Exhibition', *The Listener*, vol. 4, 20 August 1930, p. 287 (text of a talk broadcast on 4 August 1930).

6. P. Morton Shand, 'Stockholm 1930', *Architectural Review*, vol. 68, August 1930, p. 71.

7. Ove Arup, 'The World of the Structural Engineer', Maitland Lecture, p. 5.

8. Manning Robertson, 'The Trend of Modernism', *The Builder*, 30 August 1935, p. 357.

9. Henry-Russell Hitchcock, 'The International Style Twenty Years After', *Architectural Record*, vol. 110, August 1951, p. 91; and Henry-Russell Hitchcock and Philip Johnson, *The International Style*, 2nd edn, New York (W.W. Norton & Co.) 1966; p. 20.

10. See Alan Powers, 'A Zebra at Villa Savoye', in *Twentieth Century Architecture*, vol. 2: *The Modern House Revisited*, London (Twentieth Century Society) 1996, for a further exploration of this theme.

11. Information from conversation between the author and Randall Evans in 1992.

12. The Cedar House, Common Road, Stanmore, Middlesex. The house still stands, although it has been enlarged.

13. Nikolaus Pevsner, 'The Modern Movement', p. 38, Special Collections, Getty Center for the History of Art and the Humanities, Los Angeles (unpublished typescript for special British number of the *Architectural Review*, 1939).

14. The Timber Development Association ran a competition for modern house designs in 1935, won by Reginald Kirby. His design is illustrated in the *Architectural Review* special number on timber of February 1936 and in S.P.B. Mais and Robert Furneaux Jordan, *The Charm of the Timber House*, London (Ivor Nicholson and Watson Ltd) 1936.

15. See Reginald Blomfield and Amyas Connell, 'For and Against Modern Architecture', *The Listener*, vol. 12, 28 November 1934, pp. 885–88.

16. The exhibition was organized by P. Morton Shand. See Kevin Davies, 'Finmar and the Furniture of the Future: The Sale of Alvar Aalto's Plywood Furniture in the UK, 1934–1939', *Journal of Design History*, vol. 11, no. 2, 1998, pp. 145–56.

17. See Charlotte Benton, *A Different World: Émigré Architects in Britain, 1928–1958*, London (RIBA Heinz Gallery) 1995.

18. "The English work of Mendelsohn in partnership with Chermayeff … is distinctly superior aesthetically to most of his German work." Henry-Russell Hitchcock, 'An American Critic in England', *Architect and Building News*, vol. 149, 15 January 1937, p. 69.

19. Pevsner, 'The Modern Movement', p. 35.

20. Review of *Modern Architecture in England*, in *RIBA Journal*, 22 May 1937, p. 746. Internal evidence suggests that Summerson may have been the author.

21. Karel Honzig, 'England's Part in the Modern Architecture', *Stavba* [Prague], vol. 14, no. 4, April 1937, pp. 57–58.

22. Hastings was briefly a student at the Bartlett School of Architecture under Albert Richardson; Shand was a writer and translator. A selection of Shand's writings, with a bibliography and commentary, was published in the *Architectural Association Journal*, vol. 75, January 1959.

23. F.R.S. Yorke was the technical editor of the *Architects' Journal* and editor of *Specification*, an annual reference book containing product information, also published by the parent company, the Architectural Press.

24. J.M. Richards, *An Introduction to Modern Architecture*, Harmondsworth (Penguin Books) 1940, p. 80.

25. In September 1934 the MARS Group took up the offer from the Housing Centre to contribute to the exhibition 'New Homes for Old' at the Building Trades Exhibition, Olympia, London. See the account in John Gold, *The Experience of Modernism: Modern Architecture and the Future City, 1928–1953*, London (Spon) 1997, pp. 120–24.

26. See Gold, *The Experience of Modernism*, pp. 113–15. The ATO was amalgamated in 1938 with the Association of Architects, Surveyors and Technical Assistants (AASTA).

27. The students were David Medd and Bruce Martin, who after the War made an important contribution to the school building programme, together with John Madge. The reconstruction of a cottage is described in the *Architectural Association Journal*, vol. 55, September 1939, pp. 75, 81–82.

28. Information on this project is scanty. The main evidence is in the *Architectural Association Journal*, vol. 55, August 1939, pp. 60, 68.

29. Anthony Cox, 'The Retreat from Function', *Architect and Building News*, vol. 153, 13 January 1938, pp. 43–44. Cox was one of the editors of the magazine *Focus*, which emanated from the Architectural Association and appeared in four issues between 1937 and 1939.

30. ibid. Le Corbusier's quasi-Surrealist penthouse for Charles de Bestegui in Paris of 1930 included incongruous 'collaged' elements, and his whole palette of materials and forms developed during the course of the decade.

31. Hugh Casson, 'Good Building and Bad Theatre', *Night and Day*, 9 September 1937, p. 118.

32. "I enjoyed it so much that I spontaneously wrote them a letter, giving their ideas my strong support. I think it is a most promising sign when a young group goes ahead with clear ideas in their minds and the activity among them which we missed in former years." Walter Gropius to Maxwell Fry, 27 October 1938, Gropius Archive, Harvard University, Cambridge MA.

33. In an unpublished recollection of Gropius written in 1985 Howe quoted Morris's words: "When an original idea becomes incarnated into fact, God has an orgasm."

34. See Andrew Saint, *Towards a Social Architecture: The Role of School Building in Post-War England*, London and New Haven CT (Yale University Press) 1987.

35. Henry-Russell Hitchcock, 'An American Critic in England', *Architect and Building News*, vol. 149, 15 January 1937, p. 70.

36. See Christopher Tunnard, *Gardens in the Modern Landscape*, London (Architectural Press) 1938. In the second edition after the War, Tunnard, by then in the US, rejected the possibility of finding a landscape equivalent to modern architecture.

37. 'Modern Architectural Research and Planning', *Landscape and Garden*, Summer 1938, p. 101 (article by a member of the MARS Group).

38. C.H. Waddington, *The Scientific Attitude*, Harmondsworth (Penguin Books) 1941, p. 123.

restaurant
entrance

CANVEY

THE LABWORTH

ISLAND

FAR LEFT: The thin profiles and pure geometry of the entrance canopy shows the influence of De Stijl buildings in The Netherlands. The reflections in the glass turned the semicircular supports into full circles. Aiton & Co. manufactured steel tubing, so its display was particularly appropriate.

LEFT: The offices' internal linoleum floors were red, and the walls and steelwork grey-green. The staircase is reduced to its constructional minimum, and the glass partition extends the sense of space into the ground-floor drawing office.

Norah Aiton and Elizabeth (Betty) Scott 1904–1989; 1903–1983

Norah Aiton met Betty Scott at the Architectural Association School in London, where they overlapped in the years 1926–28. Aiton then travelled with her parents while Scott worked in an office in New York.

John Aiton, Norah's father, the director of an engineering business in Derby, commissioned Norah and Betty to design one of the most radical modern British buildings of the period. This was probably mainly due to Norah, who had travelled to The Netherlands and had seen some of the most advanced architecture of the time. The extreme clarity of Dutch Modernism is apparent in the Aiton Factory offices more than in any other English Modernist building. Aiton and Scott never had the opportunity to repeat this feat, and, although the building survives, it needs careful restoration to re-create the original effect.

Betty Scott married the architect Stephen Rowland Pierce, who was a tutor at the Architectural Association. Pierce designed several town halls, including Norwich City Hall, in a Swedish classical style, although he had been the anonymous designer of grain silos at Northfleet in Kent in 1915 (which were later recognized as potential 'pioneer' works of Modernism), and had collaborated with R.A. Duncan on the House of the Future at Olympia, London, in 1927 (see p. 18).

OPPOSITE TOP: By means of their overlap and colour contrast the two volumes of the building appear to interlock, although the flatness of the façade reduces this to an illusion.

OPPOSITE BOTTOM: The director's office contains two Marcel Breuer chairs and a desk lamp from the 'Bestlite' range by Best & Lloyd of Smethwick, introduced in 1930 and popular in Britain up to the present day.

AITON & CO. FACTORY OFFICES
Derby, 1930–31

The building is a steel-framed structure with a plinth level of blue brick. The smooth-rendered upper level was originally painted partly in grey and partly in white, to enhance the contrast of the two planes of the building. The vertical lettering in red and the horizontal in jade green added colour accents.

The interior was spacious but starkly simple, with an open metal staircase balustrade and a broad landing, and internal glazed partitions into the drawing office. The boardroom was equipped with Marcel Breuer chairs, ordered from Thonet, and a table specially designed by the architects and made by Arundell Clarke, with a hammered aluminium base.

REFERENCES
Architect and Building News, vol. 125, 2 January 1931, pp. 18–20; vol. 126, 16 July 1931, pp. 117–19
Architectural Association Journal, vol. 48, 1932, pp. 71–73
Lynne Walker, 'The Forgotten Architecture of Vision: Aiton & Scott's Factory Office for Aiton & Co., Derby, 1930–1', *Twentieth Century Architecture*, no. 1, *Industrial Architecture*, London (Twentieth Century Society) 1994, pp. 23–30

REFERENCES

Architects' Journal, vol. 156,
8 November 1972, p. 1051
(illustrated with an early
photograph)
Ove Arup, 'The Built
Environment', *Arup Journal*,
vol. 20, no. 1, Spring 1985,
p. 41
John Allan, *Berthold Lubetkin:
Architecture and the Tradition
of Progress*, London (RIBA
Publications) 1992

LABWORTH CAFÉ

Western Parade, Canvey Island, Essex, 1931–32

Two concentric monolithic reinforced-concrete drums are mounted on top of the sea wall of this low-lying island on the Essex side of the Thames estuary.

The café, an added extra to Christiani & Nielsen's sea defences, was over-modestly described by Arup as "architecture on the cheap by an amateur architect employed by a contractor, and a client with no money to spend". Arup later recalled that he was allowed by his employer to visit the site only once. He also proposed a spiral tower at the end of Clacton Pier (Ove Arup, 'The World of the Structural Engineer', 1968, reprinted in *Arup Journal*, vol. 20, no. 1, Spring 1985, p. 5).

Sir Ove Arup 1895–1988

Ove Arup was the most important figure to bridge the worlds of architecture and engineering in Britain before and after the Second World War. Although he was born in Newcastle upon Tyne, his family was Danish, and he was educated first in Denmark and then in Germany, where he studied philosophy and mathematics.

Arup worked in London after 1923 with the Danish company Christiani & Nielsen, and from 1934 to 1938 with J.L. Kier & Co., collaborating with Berthold Lubetkin on the design of concrete structures. In 1938 Arup set up his own company, and in 1949 he established Ove Arup & Partners, which attracted brilliant collaborators and encouraged an atmosphere of shared effort and enterprise that was sympathetic to the creative ambitions of architects. Arup's post-war collaborations included the Brynmawr Rubber Factory (with Architects Co-Partnership), Coventry Cathedral (with Basil Spence) and the Sydney Opera House (with Jørn Utzon).

Arup hoped to integrate every aspect of building design and procurement in a single organization, and established Arup Associates as an architectural practice in 1963. He designed relatively few structures independently, his other main design as a soloist being the Kingsgate footbridge at Durham, completed in 1963.

ABOVE LEFT: The interior of the café shows the ring beam and columns that form the main load-bearing structure. Large windows overlook the Thames estuary, and the glazing originally had a continuous transom with top-hung casements in the upper part.

ABOVE: The two wings of the building form outdoor terraces accessible from the main room of the café. These originally had a timber framework on top that unintentionally resembled certain paintings by Paul Nash. Another timber framework rose from the centre of the roof.

OPPOSITE: The café was built in conjunction with the sea wall. The side wings had open seating areas with slender columns, and the central section was not glazed at ground-floor level.

Geoffrey Bazeley 1906–1989

Bazeley's family were shipowners and commodity traders in Cornwall, and Bazeley himself was born in Penzance. He studied architecture at Cambridge University in 1926–29 and at the Architectural Association in 1929–32, before going to work first as assistant to G. Grey Wornum on the Royal Institute of British Architects building in Portland Place, London. In 1933 he began working for Serge Chermayeff, with whom he was the principal assistant for Shrub's Wood, Chalfont St Giles, Buckinghamshire, having been the means of introduction to the client, R.L. Nimmo.

With the commission for Tregannick, Bazeley returned to Cornwall to set up in independent practice, initially in Penzance but ultimately with offices in three different Cornish towns. Tregannick has never been published before, but it has survived in excellent condition, with some careful repairs by recent owners.

Bazeley's later work included the modernization of the Seaton Barracks at Plymouth, new offices for the E.C.L. group of companies at St Austell and the new See House for the Bishop of Truro. He won an award for a housing scheme in the Isles of Scilly.

ABOVE: The cutaway corner adds an element of volumetric excitement to the otherwise calm garden aspect of the house and provides a sleeping balcony for the main bedroom. Sleeping balconies were included in many houses of the early 1930s, although probably not so often used.

TREGANNICK

Sancreed, Penzance, Cornwall, 1935–36

One of the best Modern Movement houses in the west of England, Tregannick was commissioned by W.L. Oats, a local dairy farmer whose Primrose Dairy business formed a substantial part of United Dairies.

The plan is compact, in the form of a long rectangle. The house has a relatively plain entrance front and opens out on the south-east garden front to face the view, with a balcony providing shade for the three broad drawing-room windows. A single-storey service wing, with a courtyard, adds length to the elevation and helps to ground it on the hilltop.

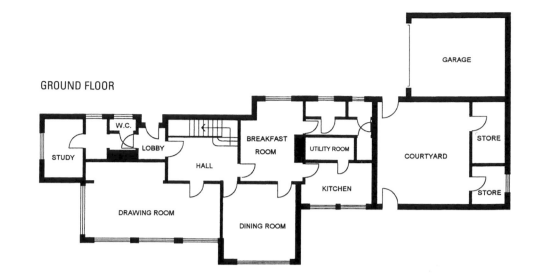

GROUND FLOOR

STUDY

W.C.

LOBBY

HALL

BREAKFAST ROOM

UTILITY ROOM

KITCHEN

GARAGE

COURTYARD

STORE

STORE

DRAWING ROOM

DINING ROOM

ABOVE: Tregannick's interiors are beautifully crafted in timber, as are the interiors of Chermayeff's houses, which reflect his early career as an interior designer. The glass balustrade of the staircase helps to achieve a sense of transparency.

LEFT: The fine original light fittings are rare survivals.

Elisabeth Benjamin 1908–1999

Born in London into a liberal Jewish family, Benjamin was educated at St Paul's School for Girls, London, and became interested in modern architecture while staying in France and Germany. She went to the Architectural Association in 1927 and was a member of one of the first student cohorts to produce a substantial number of modern architects. She later recalled: "We did a lot of talking. We were all very influenced and excited by Le Corbusier and Gropius."

Benjamin then worked for a time in the office of Sir Edwin Lutyens, on Liverpool Cathedral. With her student friend and contemporary Godfrey Samuel, she was involved in building a school for German refugee children. She collaborated with the émigré architect Eugen Kaufmann on a small modern house in Wimbledon, south-west London, before starting her major work, East Wall, in 1935. This house was a collaboration with Samuel, but entirely to her own design.

After her marriage in 1937, motherhood and the War took Benjamin away from architecture, although she did small jobs for family members and for the St Austell Brewery, while living for a time in Cornwall.

ABOVE: This early photograph shows the intricate and mannered composition of East Wall, with its contrasts of form and material. The extension of the wall on the right serves no practical purpose but completes the geometry of the rectangular volume. By cutting a tall slit through it, Elisabeth Benjamin emphasized its symbolic function and allowed a masked view of the driveway from the bedroom terrace.

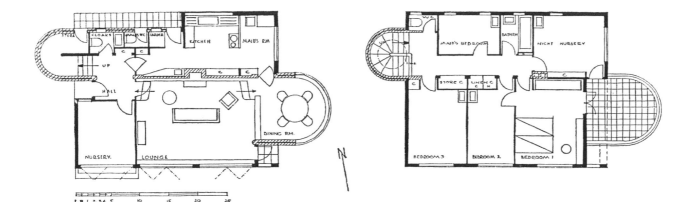

REFERENCES
F.R.S. Yorke, *The Modern House in England*, London (Architectural Press) 1937, pp. 131–32
Elisabeth Benjamin, interview with Lynne Walker, *Twentieth Century Architecture*, no. 2: *The Modern House Revisited*, London (Twentieth Century Society) 1996, pp. 74–84

ABOVE: The kitchen is laboratory-like in its neatness, although the stove seems out of place.

ABOVE RIGHT: The lounge shows how the dark brick wall was carried through the interior of the house, and the semicircular elements of the plan are echoed in the outline of white concrete around the fireplace.

EAST WALL
Hedgerley Lane, Gerrards Cross, Buckinghamshire, 1935–36 (with Godfrey Samuel)

East Wall was built, principally from reinforced concrete, for Arnold Osorio, a director of Ripolin paints. The spine wall, in blue sewer bricks, extends into a semicircular stair turret and a dining-room bay at either end of the house; the opposition between the concrete and the bricks led the designers to call it the 'George and the Dragon' house.

Several works by Tecton partners (of whom Samuel was one until 1936), such as Six Pillars, Dulwich, and houses at Haywards Heath, East Sussex, have a similar, slightly ironic contrast of brick and concrete, but at East Wall this becomes a dominant and poetic architectural theme.

Margaret Justin Blanco White 1911–2001

Justin Blanco White, as she was known, was the daughter of the social thinker Amber Reeves (H.G. Wells's 'Ann Veronica') and the lawyer Rivers Blanco White. A childhood friend of Myfanwy Evans (later the wife of John Piper), she was educated at St Paul's School for Girls, London, where she sang under Gustav Holst, and then in 1929–33 at the Architectural Association, where she won awards for her student work, especially in construction. In 1936 she married the biologist Conrad Hal Waddington (1905–1975), who became a Fellow of Christ's College, Cambridge, where he was able to persuade the Fellows to commission a design for a new building from Walter Gropius in 1936, although this was never built. Shawms was commissioned during the same period by Dr W.A.W. Rushton, also a Fellow of Christ's. Blanco White had an additional planning qualification from the Architectural Association and worked on the Middlesbrough Plan survey with Max Lock.

Waddington was appointed to a chair at the University of Edinburgh in 1947, and Justin moved there and brought up their two daughters while doing further planning work. In 1958 she was invited to design another house at 12 Lansdowne Road, Cambridge, adjacent to Shawms, in collaboration with a local architect, David Croghan. The later house was demolished in 2003.

ABOVE: Shawms is designed with a practical sobriety favoured by Blanco White's generation of students. The regular bays of the structural frame are readable, although less pronounced than at Serge Chermayeff's Bentley Wood, Halland, East Sussex.

BELOW AND BOTTOM: The house's north side has smaller windows, which light a ground-floor corridor. The stairs become a ladder as they turn upwards to the roof-top study, which has a deep box trellis.

SHAWMS

Conduit Head Road, Cambridge, 1938

The house was originally intended to be built in reinforced concrete, but in 1938 this became hard to obtain since it was required for building new airfields in secret preparation for the War. Timber was used instead. The main living-rooms are on the first floor, where they have better views. The plan is simple and relatively narrow, while the external appearance has similarities to Chermayeff's Bentley Wood, completed in the same year.

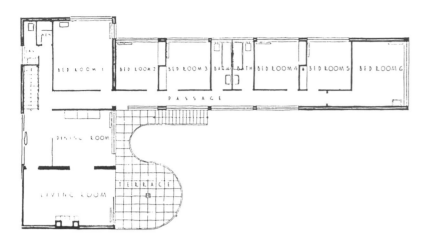

Sea Lane House was commissioned by a bandleader, Mr J. Macnab, and combines a reinforced-concrete slab-and-column structure with load-bearing brick walls. The raised terrace commands a carefully framed view to the sea, while the bedroom wing is continued, rather like the side wings of a stage, by a line of coastguard cottages backed by pine trees. On the right a two-storey 'Sunspan' house had recently been built, and its curved front is echoed in the curves of the balcony.

The kitchen was on the ground floor, with a connecting food lift emerging from a counter in the dining-room above.

Marcel Breuer 1902–1981

Born in Pécs, Hungary, Breuer entered the Bauhaus School at Weimar, Germany, in 1920 and became famous for his chair designs. After completing the Dolderthal flats, Zurich, he moved to London in 1935 to work in partnership with F.R.S. Yorke, until leaving for the United States in 1937. In addition to those illustrated here, Breuer designed two brick houses for schoolmasters at Eton College; interiors at Clifton, Bristol, for Crofton Gane; the bar and restaurant at the Lawn Road flats, London (the so-called Isobar; Breuer also lived in the flats); and the interior of a theatre in Islington. Yorke and Breuer also designed a model of the Garden City of the Future, which was exhibited at the Ideal Home Exhibition in 1936, and again at the MARS Group exhibition in 1938. Jack Pritchard's Isokon company commissioned the famous 'long chair' and other pieces.

The Gane Pavilion is recognized as an important moment of development in Breuer's work, and his confident use of stone was the result of Yorke's experience with the material. In 1937 Breuer's practice in the United States flourished, and he continued with a range of projects, such as the UNESCO building in Paris, until his retirement in 1976.

ABOVE LEFT: The side approach to the front door conceals the view of the sea beyond, although the two ground-floor bays of the narrow wing were originally open, making the two volumes of the house read more distinctly.

ABOVE AND LEFT: The curving balcony on its column support signals Breuer's pleasure in pure architectural form, a trait that became more apparent in his later work.

ABOVE: The first scheme was for a house on three storeys, set back on the site. This was rejected, and the more original built scheme substituted, although the local authority required that the bedroom wing should run down the centre of the plot. The ground beneath the oversailing wing was originally intended to be covered in grass so that the lawn continued uninterrupted.

Marcel Breuer

REFERENCES

Architect

Peter Blake, *Marcel Breuer: Sun and Shadow*, London (Longman) 1956

Christopher Wilk, *Marcel Breuer: Furniture and Interiors*, New York (Museum of Modern Art) 1981, p. 140

Isabelle Hyman, *Marcel Breuer, Architect: The Career and the Buildings*, New York (Harry N. Abrams) 2001

Jeremy Melvin, *F.R.S. Yorke and the Evolution of English Modernism*, Chichester (Wiley–Academy) 2003

Sea Lane House

F.R.S. Yorke, *The Modern House in England*, London (Architectural Press) 1937; 2nd edn, 1944, pp. 88–89

Architectural Review, vol. 85, January 1939, pp. 29–31

Alastair Bruce, 'The Solution of a Mystery by the Sea', *The Independent*, 12 February 1992

Gane Show House

Architectural Review, vol. 80, 1936, pp. 69–70

Architectural Record, vol. 81, May 1937, pp. 40–41

F.R.S. Yorke, *The Modern House in England*, London (Architectural Press) 1937, pp. 58–59

Henry-Russell Hitchcock and Catherine Bauer, *Modern Architecture in England*, New York (Museum of Modern Art) 1937, pls. 2–3

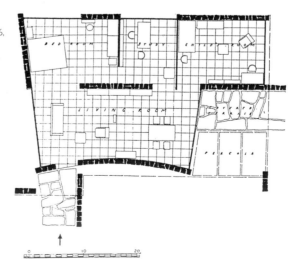

LEFT AND ABOVE: The plan shows the walls forming an abstract pattern, allowing a greater freedom of spatial flow than any real house of the period. The exposed stone walls, previously unknown in British Modernism, would become a familiar feature after the War.

GANE PAVILION
Bristol, 1936

Crofton Gane, the director of a local furniture company, was inspired by Breuer to experiment with Modernism and built this temporary house for the Royal West of England Show. It rained almost continuously during the show, and none of the visiting public ordered any furniture, but, as Peter Blake later wrote, "the little construction of stone, glass and wood represents a major step forward for Breuer and for modern architecture as a whole". There must have been an enveloping warmth of tone in the Cotswold stone and plywood. Breuer himself considered it one of his two most important works, second only to the UNESCO building in Paris.

LEFT AND BELOW: Breuer brilliantly turned the strict geometries of the 1920s into a fresh and playful formal game, showing how indoor spaces could pretend to be outdoors, and vice versa. Since the roof did not need to last more than a week, it could be thin enough to allow the white-painted timber fascia to have the tautness of steel.

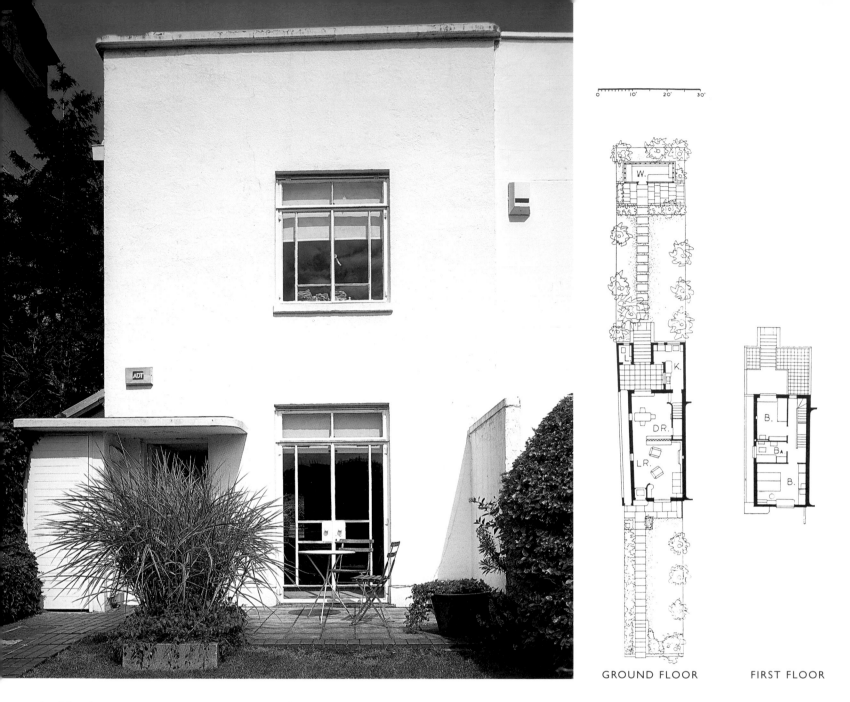

GROUND FLOOR   FIRST FLOOR

Michael J.H. and Charlotte Bunney 1907–1997; [?]

Michael Bunney was a student at the University of Oxford before joining the
Architectural Association course, which his wife, Charlotte, also took. They jointly
designed their own house at 13 Downshire Hill, Hampstead, north London. Later
they lived and worked in the Lake District, where his family originated, but they
appear not to have designed any other Modern Movement buildings in the 1930s.
Michael Bunney's papers are in the Cumbria Record Office at Kendal.

As the *Architect and Building News* commented, at Downshire Hill the architects
"have succeeded in building a modern, non-basement house, with all its attendant
conveniences, in a street of late Georgian terrace houses without striking a
discordant note". This remains true, and the house demonstrates more than any
other how close 1930s Modernism could come to the architecture of a hundred
years before, which in this case is found in the adjoining stucco-faced houses.

The house was originally finished in a pale terracotta render, with the base
plinth in a deeper shade of burnt sienna. It was almost inevitably known to
Downshire Hill residents – including the architects Frederick Gibberd and
Alexander Gibson, and the artists Roland Penrose and Fred Uhlman – as 'the
Bunney hutch'.

ABOVE LEFT: The simple
relationship of window to wall is
satisfying, and the marginal lights
of the metal-framed windows
add to the Regency quality of
the design.

BELOW LEFT: The house needs to be seen in the context of the street, in which it passes almost unnoticed. Forty years later, the architect Michael Hopkins built his own high-tech house in what had previously been Frederick Gibberd's garden on the opposite side of the street.

BELOW RIGHT: The original design included a tradesman's entrance along the left-hand side of the house. This space has been incorporated into the house by the present owners, allowing extra light into the deep, ground-floor open-plan room.

REFERENCES

Architect and Building News,
vol. 148, 16 October 1936,
pp. 78–80
RIBA Journal, vol. 43, 17 October
1936, pp. 1078–82
Architectural Review, vol. 80,
December 1936, pp. 265–68
F.R.S. Yorke, *The Modern House
in England*, London
(Architectural Press) 1937,
pp. 49–51

13 DOWNSHIRE HILL

Hampstead, London NW3, 1935–36

Built of brick, with a smooth render, and steelwork on the top floor, the house replaced the original late Georgian end-of-terrace house in one of London's most attractive streets.

There was no division between front and back rooms, apart from a waist-high sideboard and bookcase unit. A curtain could be pulled between them for winter use, when the settee in the front sitting-room could also be moved from a position near the window to one at a right angle to the gas fire. It was an early example of a 'live–work' space, with an architectural office on the top floor.

RIGHT: The original top-floor office has been extended, but the canopy has been replicated and foldaway windows reused so that the change is almost invisible.

Burnet, Tait & Lorne

SIR JOHN JAMES BURNET, 1857–1938; THOMAS SMITH TAIT, 1882–1954; FRANCIS LORNE, 1889–1963

This distinguished and long-lasting partnership went under this name for most of the 1930s, having been founded by (Sir) John James Burnet, the son of the Glasgow architect John Burnet. The younger John trained at the Atelier Pascal in Paris before working with his father, who died in 1901. Their work was almost entirely in Scotland before 1904, when Burnet was selected to design the King Edward VII Galleries, which formed the northern extension of the British Museum in London, and opened a London office, with Thomas Smith Tait, another Glasgow man, while retaining the Glasgow base. The early work was among the most accomplished and vigorous classical design of its time, although Burnet also designed in Gothic and other styles as the need arose.

Around 1910 Burnet's style changed and became more severely geometrical, for example in Kodak House, Kingsway, London (1910–11). After a quarrel with Burnet, Tait went in 1914 to the USA, where he met Frank Lloyd Wright. He returned to the office and to a partnership in 1918. A series of prominent buildings, such as Adelaide House, London Bridge (1922), moved towards a form of Modernism, in a heroic classical mould, with Egyptian influences derived from the nineteenth-century Scottish architect Alexander ('Greek') Thomson and a

visit to Egypt. Burnet played a lesser role after 1927 and retired in 1935. Tait's Modernist sympathies emerged during these years, although never to the exclusion of classical designs for banks and businesses. Francis Lorne, who had been in the London office before 1914, rejoined as a partner in 1929, having absorbed new practicalities of office management in America. He was also a socialite, good at getting jobs for the firm, in contrast to the shy, retiring Tait. Lorne also recruited new staff, including his brother-in-law, who had worked in New York for Raymond Hood, one of the finest Art Deco skyscraper designers.

The work of this practice shows the gradual emergence of Modernism without a sudden break. Nor is the Modernism based on a classical reductionism, for, while classical in origin, its expression carries some of the visual complexity found in the work of Thomson, which was well known to both Burnet and Tait. Even so, the houses at Silver End, Braintree, Essex, and a few other houses of the same period indicated a sudden development, inspired in part by the client and modelled on Wenham Bassett-Lowke's house New Ways, Northampton, by Peter Behrens, while also showing awareness of work by Robert Mallet-Stevens and André Lurçat in France. The competition designs (1929) for the Royal Masonic

SILVER END
Braintree, Essex, 1926–27

In 1926 F.H. Crittall, whose company made metal-framed windows, developed a factory and garden village at Silver End. The latter included houses by Thomas Tait and his assistant Frederick McManus, with white walls and flat roofs, making it the first substantial cluster of Modernist buildings in Britain. W.F. Crittall (son of F.H. Crittall), who inspired these buildings, wrote: "they are … a very pleasing new dress on a rather humdrum old body, demonstrating that it is not necessary to be eccentric in order to be interesting" ('Silver End', reprinted in Benton and Benton, pp. 197–98). The American critic Henry-Russell Hitchcock argued, however, that the largest of the houses, Le Château, "compares very favourably with the most advanced French, Dutch and German work" (H.-R. Hitchcock, 'Foreign Periodicals', *Architectural Record*, vol. 63, 1928, p. 598).

OPPOSITE: Le Château, built for D.F. Crittall, was the largest house at Silver End, and the most adventurous in its asymmetrical composition.

BELOW LEFT: Wolverton, a detached house for one of the company managers, showing the 'V' window apparently copied from Behrens's New Ways, but which ultimately derived from Frank Lloyd Wright.

BELOW RIGHT: Semi-detached workers' housing in Silver Way, linked by means of ground-floor screen walls to create a more unified street picture.

Hospital, west London, were almost neo-Georgian, but by the time of construction this had changed radically.

It is likely that Tait was impressed by Erich Mendelsohn's dynamic compositions even before he selected Mendelsohn and Chermayeff's design for the De La Warr Pavilion at Bexhill, East Sussex (1934–35), from the competition. The practice was prolific, with healthcare, educational and institutional buildings, such as the government offices, St Andrew's House, in Edinburgh. In 1938 Tait was the chief architect for the Empire Exhibition at Glasgow.

When Tait died, the unnamed obituarist in the *RIBA Journal* (possibly H.S. Goodhart-Rendel, who especially admired Burnet's work) wrote: "Tait seemed able to absorb and reproduce ideas from any source. Although capable of original thought … he seemed to be at home in any manner of design. Yet his work could never be labelled copyist; he often took ideas from others, but gave them the impress of his own personality and sense of design. There was a kind of humility in this – his nature held no trace of self-conceit or arrogance – and he seemed to think of himself as one of a body of architects who held a common stock of ideas from which anyone could borrow."

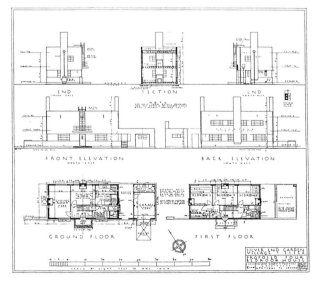

BELOW LEFT: The deeply projecting balconies at the ends of the wings are the most 'modern' feature of the hospital, signalling steel-frame construction placed at the service of fresh air and health.

BELOW CENTRE: The tower-like glazing of the stairs brings light into the building.

BELOW RIGHT: The chapel is severely geometrical and unornamented, apart from the fine original light fittings.

OPPOSITE: In the centrepiece of the courtyard the architecture is composed of interlocking volumes and planes, unified by the dominant rich red of the brick.

ROYAL MASONIC HOSPITAL
Ravenscourt Park, Hammersmith, London W6, 1930–33

In 1929 Sir John Burnet & Partners won the Royal Masonic Hospital competition with a conservative design in a Wren style, but by May 1932 the design had changed radically, with flat roofs and 30-foot (9-metre) balconies at the end of the ward wings, made possible by the steel engineering of Sven Bylander and Oscar Faber.

The Royal Masonic Hospital also retains many aspects of 1920s architecture, with symmetrical elevations suggestive of the American work of Raymond Hood, sumptuous internal finishes and symbolic sculpture by Gilbert Bayes. The operating theatres were air-conditioned, and rooms with up to four beds replaced large wards.

Burnet, Tait & Lorne

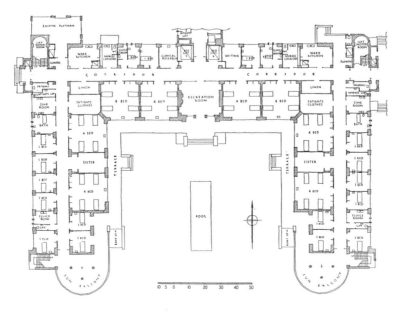

Burnet, Tait & Lorne

BURLINGTON DANES SCHOOL
Wood Lane, Hammersmith, London W12, 1936–37

The school is an ancient foundation, dating from 1699, of the Society for the Promotion of Christian Knowledge (SPCK), which decided to move in 1929 from its building in Boyle Street, by the architect Colen Campbell. Faced with yellowish brick on a reinforced-concrete frame, the teaching block of the school is regular in fenestration, with round windows and a vertical fin of brickwork as its principal architectural signature. The block at right angles to this, fronting Wood Lane and providing a ceremonial entrance, is more elaborate and is one of the most enjoyable abstract compositions by Burnet, Tait & Lorne; its features include brickwork in contrasting stripes.

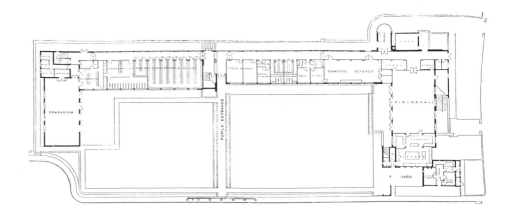

LEFT: The stair tower at the south end makes the most of the building's height and forms a landmark on Wood Lane, a busy local route.

ABOVE: The school bell originally hung from the projecting beam, which was turned into a geometric feature reminiscent of the Dutch De Stijl movement. Building schools with more than two storeys was, however, frowned on as a throwback to bad Victorian days, and C.H. Reilly felt that "it looks more like a warehouse for storing sets of books rather than a place where the child mind could expand and grow in comfort".

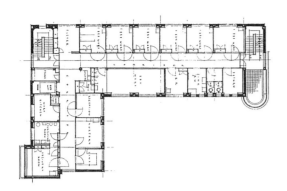

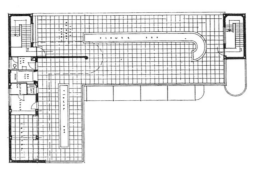

THE GERMAN HOSPITAL
Fassett Square, Hackney, London E8, 1935–36

After a bequest from a Swiss patient the German Hospital, first built in 1845, was extended to provide rooms for private patients, a maternity unit, a children's ward and accommodation for nurses. The structure was steel-framed and faced in yellow sand-lime bricks. Internally, the corridors were lined to dado height with yellow tiles from Germany, and had blue doors.

The façade towards the square is relatively plain, apart from an exaggerated cantilevered canopy over the entrance. Round-ended balconies project from the south-west corner. In 1977 the hospital was closed down and, having been protected by listing, was converted into flats.

Burnet, Tait & Lorne

REFERENCES
Architect
The Architectural Work of Sir John Burnet and Partners, preface by A. Trystan Edwards, Geneva (Masters of Architecture Ltd) 1930
C.H. Reilly, 'Some Younger Architects of Today: Thomas Smith Tait', *Building*, vol. 7, October 1931, pp. 444–50
David Walker, 'Sir John James Burnet', in Alistair Service, *Edwardian Architecture and its Origins*, London (Architectural Press) 1975, pp. 192–215
Thomas N. Fox, 'Francis Lorne, 1889–1963', *Thirties Society Journal*, vol. 6, 1987, pp. 26–32

David Walker, 'Monumental Modernist', *RIBA Journal*, vol. 98, August 1991, pp. 20–25

Silver End
W.F. Crittall, 'Silver End', *Design and Industries Association Journal*, no. 13, 1930, pp. 8–10; reprinted in Tim Benton and Charlotte Benton (with Dennis Sharp), *Form and Function: A Source Book for the History of Architecture and Design, 1890–1939*, St Albans (Crosby Lockwood Staples/Open University) 1975, pp. 197–98
Anthony Cleminson, 'Silver End

Beginnings', *Architectural Review*, vol. 166, 1979, pp. 302–04
David Blake, *Window Vision*, Braintree (Crittall Windows) c. 1989

Royal Masonic Hospital
Architects' Journal, vol. 71, 1930, pp. 20–21 (competition design)
Architects' Journal, vol. 76, 1932, pp. 638–39 (revised design)
Architects' Journal, vol. 77, 1933, pp. 50–53 (lecture on construction by Oscar Faber); vol. 78, 1933: supplement, 3 August, pp. 139–49, 173–81; supplement, 10 August

Architectural Review, vol. 74, August 1933, pp. 51–58
Susan Gold, 'The Royal Masonic Hospital', *Thirties Society Journal*, vol. 2, 1982, pp. 29–34

Burlington Danes School
Architects' Journal, vol. 84, 7 May 1936, p. 693 (perspective by Raymond Myerscough-Walker)
Architects' Journal, vol. 85, 21 January 1937, pp. 137–43
Architectural Review, vol. 81, 1937, p. 5

The German Hospital
Architect and Building News, vol. 148, 30 October 1936, pp. 130–35

Elizabeth McKellar, *The German Hospital, Hackney: A Social and Architectural History, 1845–1987*, London (The Hackney Society) 1991
Elizabeth Robinson, *Twentieth Century Buildings in Hackney*, London (The Hackney Society) 1999

BELOW LEFT: The sheer brickwork of St Saviour's was inspired, like churches from Giles Gilbert Scott's Liverpool Cathedral (begun in 1904) to Basil Spence's Coventry Cathedral (1951–62), by the twelfth-century brick cathedral of Albi in south-west France.

BELOW RIGHT: The side walls with their tall slit windows rise on concrete lintels above low side aisles, a feature based on later nineteenth-century church planning in England.

ST SAVIOUR'S CHURCH

Middle Park Avenue, Eltham, London SE9, 1932–33
(with Herbert Welch and Felix Lander)

St Saviour's is one of the most impressive British churches of the inter-war years, apparently inspired by the sheer defensive brick walls of Albi Cathedral, France, interpreted here through the design language of Rudolf Schwartz or Domenikus Bohm, with perhaps some additional influences from Auguste Perret. The effect at Eltham is especially striking, owing to the narrowness of the nave, the dark colour of the brick and the brilliance of the windows, made from stained glass set in concrete. The roof is of exposed concrete. The cast concrete font and the sculpture in the reredos are by Donald Hastings. The church was comprehensively repaired in the 1990s.

N.F. Cachemaille-Day 1896–1976

Educated at Westminster School and at the Architectural Association, with a gap for war service, Cachemaille-Day was assistant to H.S. Goodhart-Rendel before setting up in practice with Felix Lander in 1928. They were joined by Herbert Welch in 1930, when he had just completed the Crawford's building with Frederick Etchells. The practice was called Welch, Cachemaille-Day & Lander, and Cachemaille-Day is usually assumed to have been the chief designer.

St Saviour's, Eltham, south-east London, was the work of the three partners, following other successful church designs that borrowed from the contemporary German manner of church design in simplifying historic forms to their geometric elements. Other early works include St Nicholas, Burnage, Manchester (1932); St Michael and All Angels, Wythenshawe, Manchester (1937); and the Epiphany, Gipton, Leeds (1938). One of the most prolific church architects of his time, Cachemaille-Day showed an original sense of internal spatial arrangement, as well as a sense of sublime scale. After the Second World War he tended to design with central plans, reflecting the rise of the liturgical movement in Europe, and his exteriors became plainer. Later works include All Saints, Hanworth, Middlesex (1952–58), and St Michael and All Angels, London Fields, east London (1960).

REFERENCES

Architect
Anthony Hill, 'N.F. Cachemaille-Day: A Search for Something More', Thirties Society Journal, vol. 7, 1992, pp. 20–27

St Saviour's Church
Architect and Building News, vol. 134, 30 June 1933, pp. 384–91
Incorporated Church Building Society, New Churches Illustrated, c. 1937, pp. 114–17

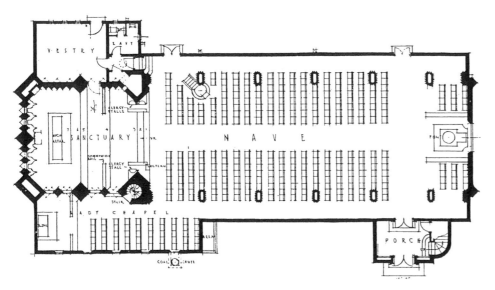

ABOVE: Each bay of the nave is expressed externally by projecting brick 'fins'. The same architectural language transforms the sanctuary area into a version of a Gothic tower. The slight set-back near the top increases the sense of massiveness.

H.T. Cadbury-Brown BORN 1913

After education at Westminster School, Cadbury-Brown entered the Architectural Association School in 1929, before going on to work for Ernö Goldfinger.

In 1936 he was able to establish his own practice after winning a competition for booking offices for British Railways, a newly created administrative consortium of the four private railway companies. Two of these were built in London: one in Queensway (then Queen's Road), Bayswater, which opened in 1937, and one in Aldwych. As a member of the MARS Group, Cadbury-Brown collaborated in the design of the group's exhibition in 1938 and helped to organize the two post-war CIAM conferences held in Britain.

Cadbury-Brown was selected to design the 'Land of Britain' pavilion in the Festival of Britain of 1951, as well as the lighting and landscaping of the important concourse area. In 1959 he began work on the new buildings for the Royal College of Art on Kensington Gore, west London, nominally in collaboration with Sir Hugh Casson and R.W. Goodden. These were completed in 1964 to great acclaim. He has also designed lecture theatres for the University of Essex, as well as Gravesend Civic Centre and a single-storey house at Aldeburgh, Suffolk, for himself and his wife, Elizabeth, who played an important role in the practice.

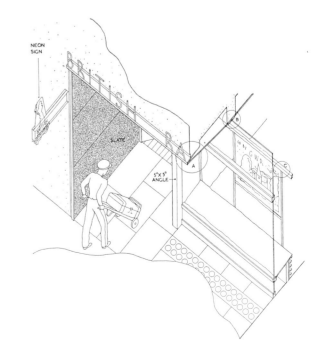

BRITISH RAILWAYS OFFICE

162 Queen's Road (now Queensway), Bayswater, London W2, 1936–37 (demolished)

The brief combined a walk-in booking office and parcel-handling in a converted shop unit. The frontage was faced in zinc-coated steel, and had a coloured glass base and shot-blasted slate inside the framed opening. The window and a panel beside the door were adapted for displaying railway posters, more of which lined the walls of the ticket office inside.

The mixture of materials, combined with the design of a series of frames within frames, is characteristic of the work of Goldfinger, from whom Cadbury-Brown learned a love of expressive materials. The uplighters were produced from Goldfinger's design.

REFERENCES

British Railway Office

Architects' Journal, vol. 84, 1936, pp. 696–97 (competition)

Architectural Association Journal, vol. 53, November 1937, pp. 240–41

Architectural Review, vol. 82, December 1937, pp. 269–70

Architects' Journal, vol. 87, 17 February 1938, pp. 291–92

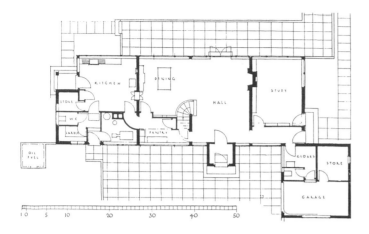

BELOW: It was unusual for modern houses of the 1930s to combine the stair with the main living space, but Checkley made it a distinctive feature of Willow House, where the spatial complexity is closer to European models than many other modern houses in Britain. From a small lobby, the front door brings you straight into the hall and beneath the soffit of a gallery, where the space rises to double height. With a fireplace to one side, this is a convincing reinterpretation in modern terms of a medieval great hall.

OPPOSITE: Willow House is close to being a text-book demonstration of Le Corbusier's architectural principles. Although the plan sensibly avoids raising the house on piloti, it features horizontal windows, a roof terrace and a typical early Corbusian projecting balcony. The addition in the foreground of the main picture was made by Dora Cosens in the 1950s.

George Checkley 1893–1960

Checkley was born at Akaroa, New Zealand, and moved to Britain in 1918, after war service, to study at the Liverpool School of Architecture, where he won the Henry Jarvis Studentship at the British School at Rome in 1922. He began teaching in the School of Architecture at the University of Cambridge in 1928 and built White House in Conduit Head Road in 1930 – one of the earliest Modern Movement houses in Britain, and the first of two in this road to be built by Checkley. It was a concrete-frame structure with brick infill, painted pale yellow and symmetrical in elevation. The local architect H.C. Hughes wrote that Checkley had "built to teach himself to build, a flat-roofed house in the high Corbusier manner. It is on the Madingley Road, set about with trees whose forms pattern its plain surface with their shadows in the winter and shield its long glass windows from the summer heat" (*The Listener*, vol. 6, 23 March 1932, p. 407).

After Willow House, Checkley did no further building. He moved to teach at the Regent Street Polytechnic, London, in 1934–37, and later became head of the Nottingham School of Architecture. He retired in 1948 after suffering from depression as a result of the death of his wife, herself an architect who had studied at the Architectural Association.

WILLOW HOUSE (originally called Thurso)
Conduit Head Road, Cambridge, 1932–33

Willow House was built for Hamilton McCombie, a
University Reader in Chemistry and a Fellow of King's
College, Cambridge.

The engineers Christiani & Nielsen advised on the
concrete-frame design, which helps to produce an effect of
interlocking volumes, where the main bedroom over the
extra height of the hall projects above the main parapet line.
The dining area adjoins the hall but has a lower ceiling, not
unlike the spatial arrangement at Blackwell, Cumbria, by
M.H. Baillie-Scott – a project known to Le Corbusier, who
adapted some of its characteristics, especially at the Maison
La Roche in Paris.

REFERENCES
Architect
Obituary, *RIBA Journal*, vol. 68,
    January 1961, p. 105

Willow House
Architects' Journal, vol. 77, 19 April
    1933, pp. 521–24
Raymond McGrath, *Twentieth
    Century Houses*, London
    (Faber & Faber) 1934,
    pp. 95–96
F.R.S. Yorke, *The Modern House
    in England*, London
    (Architectural Press) 1937,
    pp. 76–77

BELOW: In the Directors' Dining
Common on the top floor
Chermayeff gave a convincing
demonstration of the
compatibility of modern design
with a highly traditional English
company. From the windows the
directors could look westwards
over Regent's Park, although the
grubby life of Camden Town was
carrying on beneath.

OPPOSITE: Having created a
similar effect on the corner of
King's Road, with the Peter Jones
building, C.H. Reilly wrote
admiringly of the way that
Chermayeff "managed to get
the alignment of the streets at
the corner of his building altered
to give him a right-angle corner
and then a pleasant concave
curve". The vertical area of plain
wall at the corner was originally
decorated with the company
name in giant red letters, the loss
of which need not be regretted
since it was not part of
Chermayeff's original intention.

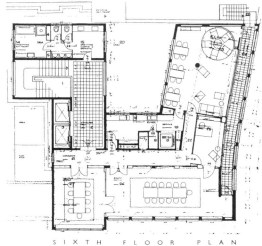

SIXTH FLOOR PLAN

Serge Chermayeff 1900–1996

Born in Grozny, Chechnya, Chermayeff was educated in Britain and worked first
as an interior decorator and stage designer. From 1928 to 1931 he directed the
so-called Modern Art Department at Waring & Gillow and helped to popularize
Modernism. He moved on to design the interiors of the Cambridge Theatre,
London (see p. 15), before simplifying his style still further.

At the end of 1933 Erich Mendelsohn joined Chermayeff in partnership in
London and stayed until the end of 1936. The design for the Gilbey Offices in
Camden Town, north London, had started with Mendelsohn, but Chermayeff took
it over. He had a strong interest in scientific method in design, and considered his
laboratories for ICI Dyestuffs at Blackley, Manchester (1938), to be his most
successful work, because of its integration of practical and technical requirements.
Chermayeff was a colourful figure on the London architectural scene and was
recognized as a fine designer despite his lack of formal training.

By 1940 Chermayeff was more interested in architectural teaching than
practice and moved to the United States, where he became Director of the
Institute of Design in Chicago (1947–51), and later taught at both Harvard and
Yale. He was a prolific writer of articles and lectures, as well as being a painter.

GILBEY OFFICES
Oval Road, London NW1, 1937

The distillers and wine merchants W. & A. Gilbey moved
their head office from Oxford Street to a back street in
Camden Town, where Chermayeff gave them a stylish and
restrained building. To reduce vibration caused by passing
traffic the reinforced-concrete frame rested on cork pads,
while the teak-framed windows were glazed with quarter-
inch-thick glass to keep out the noise from the street, with
full air-conditioning inside. There is a classical echo in the
dark-brown-tiled ground-floor plinth (now overpainted)
and the top-floor loggia for the directors' suite, originally
furnished in restrained luxury.

LEFT: Bentley Wood was carefully sited in relation to existing trees, with a two-sided entrance court to the north and a garden terrace to the south allowing for distant views of the South Downs. The timber was engineered in a sophisticated manner. "Of all the modern country houses I have seen", wrote C.H. Reilly, "this is one of the best as a machine for living in", yet informality was achieved by the close contact between indoors and outdoors.

Serge Chermayeff

REFERENCES

Architect

Richard Plunz (ed.), *Design and the Public Good: Selected Writings and Projects 1930–1980 by Serge Chermayeff*, Cambridge MA (MIT Press) 1982

Alan Powers, *Serge Chermayeff: Designer, Architect, Teacher*, London (RIBA Publications) 2001

Gilbey Offices

Architects' Journal, vol. 82, 15 July 1937, pp. 98–108

Architect and Building News, vol. 150, 30 July 1937, pp. 149–54

Architectural Review, vol. 82, July 1937, pp. 11–12

Building Research Station Notes, no. D814, *Long-term Durability of Buildings*, vol. XV: *The Offices of W. & A. Gilbey, Ltd, Gilbey House, Oval Road, London NW1*, Garston, Watford (Department of Scientific and Industrial Research) July 1962

Bentley Wood

Architects' Journal, vol. 89, 16 February 1939, pp. 293–300

Architectural Review, vol. 85, February 1939, pp. 61–78

Christopher Tunnard, 'Planning a Modern Garden: An Experience in Collaboration', *Landscape and Garden*, Summer 1939, pp. 23–27

Country Life, vol. 88, 26 October 1940, pp. 368–71; 2 November 1940, pp. 390–93

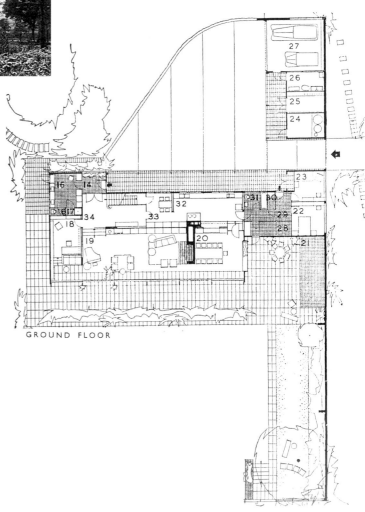

GROUND FLOOR

BENTLEY WOOD
Halland, East Sussex, 1937–38

Chermayeff's first scheme for his own house was contested at a planning inquiry but became a widely admired example of fitting modern architecture into the English landscape.

The timber frame is of jarrah wood, revealed on the garden side of the house and painted white to increase the contrast with the regular openings of the sliding windows. Christopher Tunnard, a rising star of landscape theory, was a consultant for the landscape and planting, although Chermayeff probably played a major role.

The clarity of the original design was lost in post-war extensions. More recently a gradual process of recovery has been begun by more sympathetic hands.

ABOVE AND LEFT: Chermayeff's friendship with such modern artists as Ben Nicholson, Barbara Hepworth and John Piper was demonstrated by works on display in the house, while at the end of the terrace Henry Moore's *Recumbent Figure* (left) in Horton stone (now in the Tate, London) surveyed the distant line of hills. The artwork was specially conceived for this position, and was the only major modern sculpture placed in relation to a modern house in Britain in the 1930s. It remained in place for less than a year before Chermayeff sold the house prior to his move to the United States.

Denis Clarke Hall BORN 1910

Denis Clarke Hall studied at the Architectural Association, where, after "looking at all sorts of traditional styles, while searching for something that really meant something to a young person … I discovered the Modern Movement with its traditional classic proportions, pure logic and beautiful use of form in relation to windows." After working with Clive Entwistle, a former assistant to Le Corbusier, Clarke Hall entered the *News Chronicle* Schools Design competition in 1936, for which he spent three months on research and won the first prize of £500 in Section A. His winning proposal, for a large senior mixed elementary school for 480 children in an urban district, was described by the assessors as "a striking scheme, full of gaiety, movement and thought". His report stressed the child's need for visual and psychological comfort, with the right amount of stimulation from variety of colour. Within a month of the competition results in 1937 Clarke Hall was commissioned to build the girls' high school at Richmond, Yorkshire, which was similar to the *News Chronicle* design.

   After the War, Clarke Hall was the assessor for the Hunstanton School competition in 1949, in which he selected the radical winning project by Alison and Peter Smithson. His later work is characterized by a love of bold shapes.

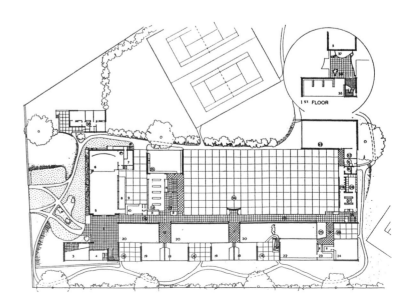

RICHMOND HIGH SCHOOL FOR GIRLS

(now Richmond Upper School)
The Crescent, Richmond, North Yorkshire, 1938–39

The Richmond School combined concrete, painted externally in a mixture of pale grey, grey-pink and grey-blue, with walls of rough local stone. The timber windows were supplied by Kiefer of Switzerland, and nesting chairs and desks were adapted, with permission, from designs by Alvar Aalto. The original colour schemes must have been enchanting, including the use of blue chalk on yellow blackboards to avoid glare.

This is romantic Modernism. As J.M. Richards wrote: "The modern architect had first to exhibit architecture brought back to its essentials; having done that, he can use its legitimate elements for their own sake" (*Architectural Review*, vol. 88, July 1940, p. 27).

REFERENCES
Richmond High School for Girls
Architects' Journal, vol. 92, 25 July 1940, pp. 69–76
Architectural Review, vol. 88, July 1940, pp. 15–27
Architect and Building News, vol. 163, 6 September 1940, pp. 162–67

OPPOSITE: The cobbles in the forecourt, which refer to those in the market place at Richmond, and the concrete paths flanking them are a marriage of old and new that is repeated in other aspects of the design. The school hall is to the left of the main entrance.

ABOVE LEFT AND CENTRE: Along the south side the classrooms extend in a series of pavilions, linked by a corridor. In between are terraces and gardens planted with small trees but suitable for outdoor classes – one of the features of the *News Chronicle* winning scheme.

ABOVE RIGHT: The stairs to the library and roof terrace allow for some bravura concrete construction, set off by the contrasting stone wall behind.

RIGHT: The roof members of the concrete trusses in the hall were pierced with circles to lighten their mass, and to add an element of decoration.

Wells Coates 1895–1958

Wells Coates was born in Japan, where he learned cooking and brush drawing. His academic career was in engineering, but while working as a journalist on the *Daily Express* he developed an interest in planning and architecture, as well as in philosophy and the writing of Wyndham Lewis.

Marriage in 1927 focused Coates's mind, and his career as a designer was launched with the offices for Cresta Silks in Welwyn Garden City, Hertfordshire (1929–30), and their retail shops. With Raymond McGrath and Serge Chermayeff he was involved in the Twentieth Century Group and the interiors for Broadcasting House, Portland Place, London. He was effectively the founder of the MARS Group in 1933–34. Between 1935 and 1939 his assistants included Denys Lasdun, as well as Patrick Gwynne, who designed The Homewood, Surrey, in his office.

Coates served in aircraft production from 1939 to 1945 and after the War became as much concerned with product design as with architecture. He designed the Telekinema at the Festival of Britain of 1951 and projected grandiose plans for a new city in the St Lawrence Seaway, Canada. After teaching at Harvard with Chermayeff (1955–56), Coates moved to Vancouver to develop a mass rapid-transit system but died there of a heart attack while swimming.

ABOVE AND LEFT: The "warhorse" of British Modernism, as John Summerson once called it, has emerged fresh from a much-needed refurbishment. Main access is by the enclosed staircase at the far end. The stark forms of the external stairs and balconies were dramatically lit at night, amplifying the propaganda role of the flats for modern architecture. The flats themselves all look to the opposite side (left), where the ground rises steeply in a small nature reserve.

OPPOSITE: The theory of the plan was that one-room living would be possible with a good enough kitchen, bathroom and dressing-room.

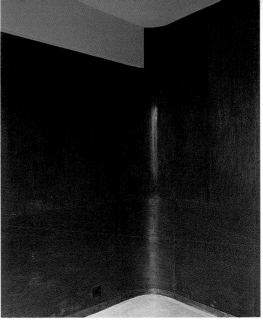

LAWN ROAD FLATS (ISOKON FLATS)

Lawn Road, Hampstead, London NW3, 1933–34

John (Jack) Craven Pritchard was a salesman for the Venesta Plywood Company. With his wife, Molly, a child psychiatrist, he commissioned Coates to design flats with generous bed-sitting rooms and separate kitchens, bathrooms and dressing-rooms.

The construction is concrete-framed, with concrete walls 4 inches (10 cm) thick. Tenants needed to bring only their personal belongings, as the furniture was mostly fitted. The flats are as famous for the people who lived and congregated there as for their architecture: residents included Walter Gropius, Marcel Breuer and Agatha Christie.

A full repair was completed in 2004 by Avanti Architects for the Notting Hill Housing Trust.

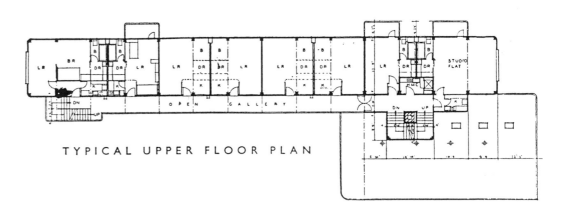

TYPICAL UPPER FLOOR PLAN

EMBASSY COURT

Kingsway, Hove, East Sussex, 1934–35

Embassy Court is a block of sixty-nine flats designed for professional and business people. It has a relatively short sea frontage and a longer return elevation. There was a small communal space in the foyer, decorated with a photo mural by E. McKnight Kauffer (long since lost), and the roof-top was also a shared space.

The structure was intended to be a diagonal beam grid, invented in Budapest, giving a continuous floor of minimum thickness without projecting beams in the ceiling, thus allowing freedom of internal layout. This was vetoed by the authorities, and the lift shafts were used instead to provide strength in the structure. Coates designed special furniture, made by PEL, for use by tenants.

Embassy Court had a history of maintenance problems but was well kept until the early 1990s, when ownership disputes led to severe deterioration. After a long search for solutions a co-operative of individual owners commissioned Paul Zara of Conran Architects to carry out a refurbishment scheme, on site in 2004.

Wells Coates

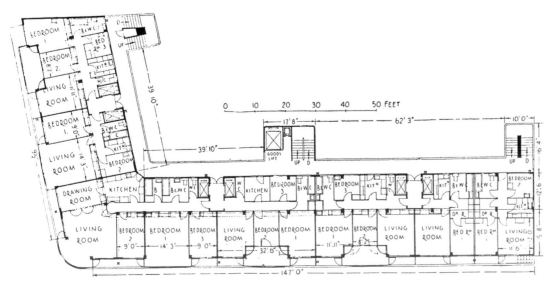

OPPOSITE: The dominant horizontals of Embassy Court disrupt the scale of the neighbouring Regency houses, but C.H. Reilly felt no regrets, writing that he had "seen no big really modern building at home or abroad which, as a whole, satisfies me more". The foldaway windows (top) expressed its outdoor ethos, while heating by "electrical thermal storage" protected residents from winter winds. The roof terrace was set aside as a communal sun deck.

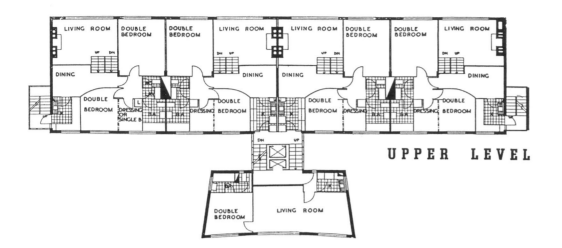

UPPER LEVEL

10 PALACE GATE
London W8, 1937–39

The client, Randall Bell, a relatively young businessman, met Coates at a party in 1936, and was impressed by the theory of the 'three–two' section for flats, in which living-rooms were taller than the bedrooms and kitchen. This scheme had been used at the Narkomfin flats, Moscow, by Moisey Ginzburg (1929), and was adapted by Coates for his own flat in Yeoman's Row, Kensington, in 1935.

The reinforced concrete is faced with artificial stone slabs that were built in as part of the shuttering when the concrete was poured. The main rooms face east and enjoy greater privacy. Compared with Lawn Road, this was a luxury block, and the planning is generous with room size, while the 'three–two' section saved on circulation space.

RIGHT AND FAR RIGHT: The long openings on the west face indicate access corridors at every third level, each of which connects to flats above and below, thus saving space on access. This curving internal staircase shows the extra height of the living-rooms.

Wells Coates

OPPOSITE: The linked block over the main entrance has single-bedroom flats of a more conventional design, and a ramp on the right leads down to a car park. The stone cladding was an unusual feature of the construction.

REFERENCES

Architect

Wells Coates, 'Notes on Dwellings for Tomorrow', in *Flats, Municipal and Private Enterprise*, London (Ascot Gas Water Heaters) 1938, pp. 50–55

J.M. Richards, 'Wells Coates 1895–1958', *Architectural Review*, vol. 124, December 1958, pp. 357–60; reprinted in Dennis Sharp (ed.), *The Rationalists*, London (Architectural Press) 1978, pp. 92–99

Sherban Cantacuzino, *Wells Coates: A Monograph*, London (Gordon Fraser) 1978

Laura Cohn (ed.), *Wells Coates, Architect and Designer 1895–1958*, Oxford (Oxford Polytechnic Press) 1979

Laura Cohn, *The Door to a Secret Room: A Portrait of Wells Coates*, Aldershot (Scolar Press) 1999

Lawn Road Flats

Architect and Building News, vol. 139, 10 August 1934, pp. 154–58

Architectural Review, vol. 76, August 1934, pp. 77–82

Building, vol. 9, August 1934, pp. 310–14

Architects' Journal, vol. 80: 13 September 1934,

pp. 377–78; 20 September 1934, pp. 409–12; 27 September 1934, pp. 496–72; vol. 81, 2 May 1935, pp. 657, 674, 687, 690

F.R.S. Yorke and Frederick Gibberd, *The Modern Flat*, London (Architectural Press) 1937, pp. 153–55

Jack Pritchard, *View from a Long Chair*, London (Routledge) 1984

Embassy Court

Architects' Journal, vol. 80, 23 August 1934, pp. 260–61; vol. 82, 14 November 1935, pp. 741–46

Architectural Review, vol. 77, November 1935, pp. 167–73

F.R.S. Yorke and Frederick Gibberd, *The Modern Flat*, London (Architectural Press) 1937, pp. 70–73

10 Palace Gate

Focus, vol. 2, 1938, p. 65

Architectural Review, vol. 85, April 1939, pp. 173–78

Building, vol. 14, July 1939, pp. 280–87

Architectural Record, vol. 85, November 1939, pp. 34–39

Randall Bell, 'Mechanism of Design: The Client Looks Back', *Architectural Review*, vol. 166, November 1979, pp. 312–13

ODEON CINEMA

Muswell Hill Broadway, Muswell Hill, London N10, 1936

The Odeon at Muswell Hill is one of the most complete
survivals of a cinema of the 1930s, which in American terms
would be called 'Moderne' rather than Art Deco, on account
of the exaggerated streamlined shapes of the foyer and
auditorium. Externally this is a relatively modest cinema,
owing to the presence of a neighbouring church in this late
Victorian suburb in north London. The foyer, by contrast, is
very grand, with its pair of columns flanking the stair to the
balcony and the swooping 'cash register' curves of the ceiling
inside, including a lighting feature in the centre that looks like
a strip of film.

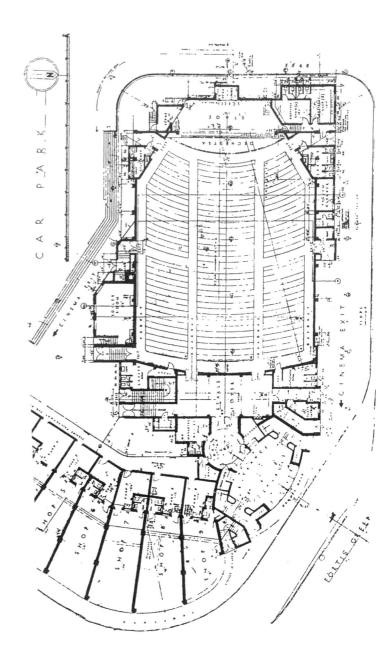

George Coles 1884–1963

George Coles was born in Dalston, east London, and from around 1899 to 1912
was an assistant to Percy Adams, the partner of Charles Holden. Coles's first
cinema, the Popular, Stepney, east London (1912), was designed with Adams. In
1922 he opened his own practice and in 1925 became chief architect to United
Picture Theatres (later Gaumont British). In the period up to 1960 he designed
sixty-five cinemas.

In 1934 Coles began to work with the Odeon chain, founded by Oscar Deutsch.
Harry Weedon was the architect chiefly associated with Odeons, but others were
employed to keep up the pace of new building. The company encouraged a more
modern look than other chains, and Coles rapidly adapted his style accordingly,
designing cinemas in Welling, Kenton and Isleworth, all expanding suburbs of
London. He worked simultaneously on the Odeons in Ipswich, Suffolk, and Muswell
Hill, north London, both of which opened on 7 September 1936. He continued
to work for other companies, however, in the styles they required, so that the
Gaumont State Cinema in Kilburn, north London (1937) – one of the grandest of
its time – is in a stripped classical style. With the decline of cinema building after
the War, Coles's practice never regained the same astonishing productivity.

REFERENCES
Architect
Tony Moss, 'George Coles,
    FRIBA', Picture House, no. 17,
    1991

Odeon, Muswell Hill
*Architectural Design and
    Construction*, vol. 7, March
    1937, pp. 165, 192

ABOVE LEFT: Glazed faience tiles
were a popular material for
cinemas. George Coles used
them for classical and modern
designs alike.

OPPOSITE TOP: Although a
second screen was created
beneath the gallery, the interior
has otherwise remained
unscarred by the subdivisions
that have afflicted many British
cinemas. The wall decoration is
original, although it was not so
strongly picked out in colour.

OPPOSITE LEFT: The foyer is
not only a decorative romp,
but also a clever piece of
planning on a tight site, helping
the audience to change direction
effortlessly on their way through
to their seats.

OPPOSITE RIGHT: The
streamlined lights reflect
the influence of the latest
American designers such as
Donald Deskey.

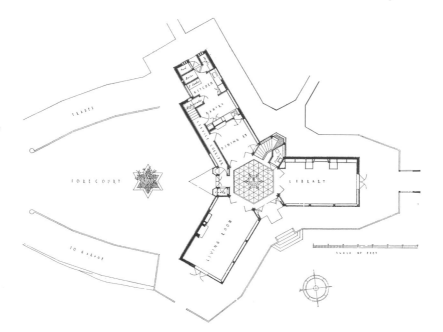

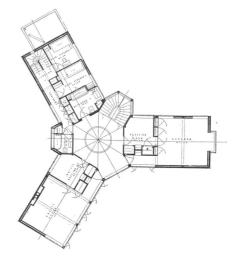

RIGHT AND BELOW: The star plan resembles that of several Edwardian houses, but the elevations are strongly Corbusian. The ground-floor windows were originally as wide as those on the floor above, which run continuously across the whole south side and gave the house a sense of 'lift-off', now sadly lacking.

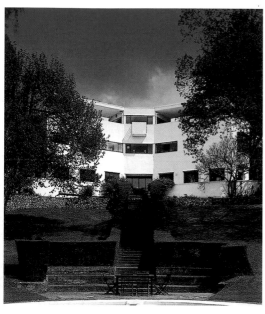

HIGH AND OVER
Amersham, Buckinghamshire, 1928–30

At High and Over three equidistant wings join in a double-height hall, which originally had a fountain placed in the centre. The construction is a reinforced-concrete frame with rendered brick infill. (Connell really wanted monolithic concrete, but the builders were unable to achieve it.) The principal rooms were decorated with striking colours and facings (jade-green cellulose and chromium steel), at odds with the donnish furniture. The roof was fully accessible from the day nursery on the top floor, providing far distant views.

The garden design, some of it by Connell, Ward & Lucas, was one of the best examples of a 'French Cubist' garden, a style that never really caught on in Britain. Most of it has been lost in subsequent development.

Connell, Ward & Lucas   AMYAS CONNELL, 1901–1980; BASIL WARD, 1902–1976; COLIN LUCAS, 1906–1988

Amyas Connell was born to artistic parents in New Zealand and was articled to Stanley Fearn in Wellington. In 1924 he joined Basil Ward to work their passage as stokers to Britain, where they both studied at the classically orientated Bartlett School in London. In 1926 Connell won the Rome Scholarship, and Ward the Henry Jarvis Studentship, the runner-up prize. Connell had a long-standing interest in Modernism, and his time in Europe enabled him to explore it further, so that when the Director of the Rome School, Bernard Ashmole, commissioned a house in 1928, Connell built him the most advanced modern house yet seen in Britain.

Ward returned from a period in Burma and married Connell's sister, so the two men went into partnership for the next house, the White House at Haslemere, Surrey. In 1933 they were joined by Colin Lucas, who had already designed and built several notable concrete houses, using his own construction company. Their executed work was mainly individual houses – the jaunty disregard of these for architectural propriety was inseparable from their creative originality and nearly always provoked controversy. In a radio broadcast of 1934 Connell publicly debated modern architecture with Sir Reginald Blomfield, a great defender of tradition.

After the dissolution of the practice in 1939 Connell went to work in Kenya, producing major buildings with a surprising level of decoration, while Ward formed another partnership. Lucas joined the London County Council Architects' Department, where he promoted younger talent without reasserting his own identity as a designer.

ABOVE: The sloping ground, which covers an old chalk pit, suggested the geometry of the plan. "There is nothing in its clean level lines nor in its whiteness that does not harmonise with the rolling chalk uplands", wrote Christopher Hussey in *Country Life*, at a time when the house stood starkly against the sky.

RIGHT: The walls of the dining-room were described as being "of a rosy orange", an effect reproduced by the current owners. The built-in light is an original feature.

FAR RIGHT: The off-centre fireplace is typical of Connell's interior detailing at this time.

BELOW AND OPPOSITE: In contrast to the simple box shapes of most Modernist houses of the 1930s, the White House is a dynamic architectural composition, offering a series of contrasting views as one moves around its exterior. The stair tower (the glazing bars of which were originally a dark colour) anchors the composition, and the walls play a role as screens on to which shadows are projected. Structurally, the staircase is cantilevered from its central column.

Connell, Ward & Lucas

THE WHITE HOUSE

(formerly known as Alding, and also as Pollard and New Farm), Grayswood Road, Grayswood, Haslemere, Surrey, 1931–32

The White House was built for Sir Arthur Lowes-Dickinson, a seventy-three-year-old accountant. The plan form is one of the most original in British Modernism, spreading out like the fingers of a hand to give different views to the main rooms and described by Raymond McGrath as "more like an invention by Picasso than a house".

Here Connell achieved his aim of building in 4-inch (10 cm) monolithic concrete, using building-board insulation as permanent shuttering. The staircase, boldly glazed on two faces, achieved a transparency unsurpassed in the 1930s and acts as a hinge to the composition at the entrance.

The house was fully repaired by John Allan of Avanti Architects in 1992–93.

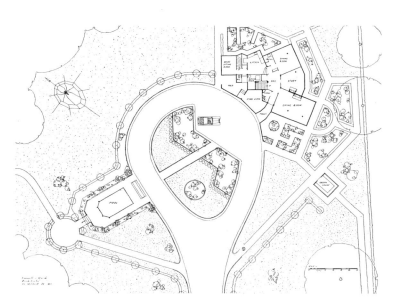

LEFT: Set on a flat site, the White House had an elaborate garden plan that incorporated a turning circle for cars, through which an axis passes from the front door to a pool, and formal bedding around the house itself. Inside, there was originally an unexpected decorative effect created by areas of Persian wall tiles collected by the owner.

Connell, Ward & Lucas

REFERENCES

Architect

Architectural Association Journal, vol. 72, 1956, pp. 94–115

Dennis Sharp (ed.), *Connell, Ward and Lucas: Modern Movement Architects in England, 1929–1939*, London (Book Art) 1994

David Thistlewood and Edward Heeley, 'Connell, Ward & Lucas: Towards a Complex Critique', *Journal of Architecture*, vol. 2, no. 1, Spring 1997, pp. 83–102

High and Over

Architect and Building News, vol. 123, 3 January 1930, pp. 12–13; vol. 126, 26 June 1931, pp. 418, 428–35

Country Life, vol. 70, 19 September 1931, pp. 302–07

Wasmuths Monatshefte für Baukunst, vol. 151, 1931, pp. 466–70

White House

Architect and Building News, vol. 133, 10 March 1933, pp. 314–17

Architectural Review, vol. 73, March 1933, pp. 118–19

Raymond McGrath, *Twentieth Century Houses*, London (Faber & Faber) 1934, pp. 96–97

F.R.S. Yorke, *The Modern House*, London (Architectural Press) 1934, pp. 162–63

Architects' Journal, vol. 199, 16 February 1994, pp. 18–20

66 Frognal

The Times, 9 August 1938, p. 10

Architects' Journal, vol. 88, 27 October 1938, pp. 696–98

Architect and Building News, vol. 156, 28 October 1938, pp. 99–102

Architectural Review, vol. 84, October 1938, pp. 155–58

RIBA Journal, vol. 46, 19 December 1938, pp. 180–85 (text by Geoffrey Walford)

66 FROGNAL

London NW3, 1936–37

Built for a solicitor, Geoffrey Walford, on a tight corner site, this house, designed by Colin Lucas, is one of the most elegant of the firm's later works as well as one of the most controversial.

The house is built of reinforced concrete, with non-structural elements of blue brick. The ground floor was originally largely unenclosed, with the kitchen, living-room and main bedroom suite on the first floor, and the children's bedrooms on the top floor, half of which was originally an open terrace. The external colours were a condition of planning permission and were reinstated in 2002 as part of the restoration by John Allan of Avanti Architects.

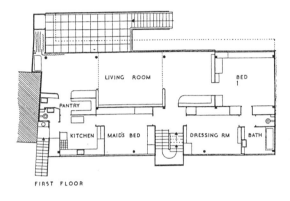

FIRST FLOOR

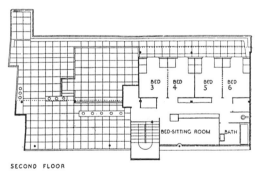

SECOND FLOOR

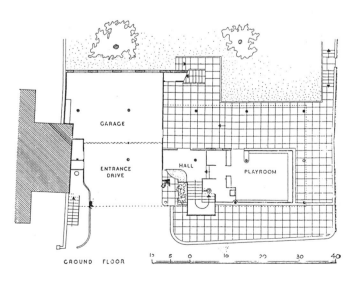

GROUND FLOOR

OPPOSITE: The house turns east to face its garden with a series of terraces. The ground-floor space to the right, now occupied by an indoor pool, was originally a covered open-air play space, and only the left-hand mass of rooms rose above the first floor. The large windows of the living-room were exceptional for this date, owing to the high cost of plate glass on this scale. The windows were fitted with three sets of curtains on a continuous track, giving different effects of light and colour.

ABOVE: The external colours were partly imposed as a planning condition, but were also used by Colin Lucas in other designs of this period to emphasize the contrast of flat planes and interlocking shapes.

BELOW: Composed of architectural elements that had become familiar features of Modernism in Britain by 1937, the house offers changing compositions of window as one moves around it.

9 WILBERFORCE ROAD
Cambridge, 1937

Constructed of rendered brick with concrete roof and roof canopy, the house originally stood right on the edge of the city and still has a large garden with a stream running through it. Unusually for an English Modernist house, its footprint is essentially square, which means that there is a generous amount of roof terrace, with a broad overhanging canopy, and that the main living-room and its connecting dining-room are at right angles to each other, rather than in a straight line. The aesthetic looked back to George Checkley's houses near by, designed five or so years earlier, but this is an assured design, which has survived with little alteration and recently has been lovingly restored.

Dora Cosens

Dora Cosens (her married name) studied at the University of Cambridge School of Architecture, where she probably would have been taught by George Checkley, and lived in Cambridge after she married. In addition to designing, she wrote regular exhibition and book reviews for the *Architects' Journal* that show she was well informed and critical about contemporary developments. Cosens designed an extension to Checkley's Willow House in Conduit Head Road (see p. 73) in around 1944, and apparently lived for only a few more years after this.

REFERENCES
Architects' Journal, vol. 89,
16 March 1939, pp. 448–49

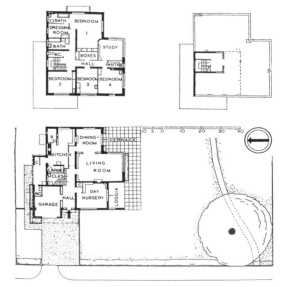

RIGHT: The balcony of the main bedroom, part of a symmetrical arrangement of windows, acts as a focus for the long view down the garden.

BELOW: The entrance from Wilberforce Road, marked by the receding plane of the roof canopy, projects a sense of mystery and expectation. The glazing bars were originally painted black.

LEFT: Swinging elegantly around the corner of Sloane Square and King's Road, Peter Jones was an immediate success with the public, proving that modern architecture need not be controversial. In a 1939 poll of celebrities in the arts taken by the *Architects' Journal* 'Vigilance Committee' for their favourite modern buildings, Peter Jones received the highest number of votes.

REFERENCES

Architect
Peter Richmond, *Marketing Modernisms: The Architecture and Influence of Charles Reilly*, Liverpool (Liverpool University Press) 2001

Peter Jones
J.R. Leathart, 'Current Architecture', *Building*, vol. 10, 1935, p. 188
Architect and Building News, vol. 146, 26 June 1936, pp. 377–83
Architectural Review, vol. 85, June 1939, pp. 291–98

William Crabtree 1905–1991

Born in Cheshire, William Crabtree studied architecture at Liverpool, graduating in 1929 with a fifth-year thesis design for a department store in Oxford Street, London, in a simplified Art Deco style. The head of the school, C.H. Reilly, recommended Crabtree on the strength of this to John Spedan Lewis, the creator of the John Lewis Partnership, who was planning to rebuild the Peter Jones store in Sloane Square. Before going there, Crabtree worked for Joseph Emberton.

Crabtree was employed as a researcher and travelled in The Netherlands and Germany, where he saw Erich Mendelsohn's Columbushaus in Berlin. His pre-war career is virtually synonymous with the story of Peter Jones, although (with P.G. Freeman) he entered the competition for the De La Warr Pavilion, Bexhill, in 1933 and was awarded third prize. He and Reilly began work on a scheme for the rebuilding of the John Lewis store in Oxford Street, but the landlord, the Howard de Walden estate, in any case objected to the amount of glass involved and preferred a design by Arthur Hamilton Moberly, which was completed after the War.

In partnership with Wladyslaw Jarosz, Crabtree designed housing at Heron's Wood, Harlow New Town, and the Kingswood section of Basildon, Essex. He retired from practice in 1960.

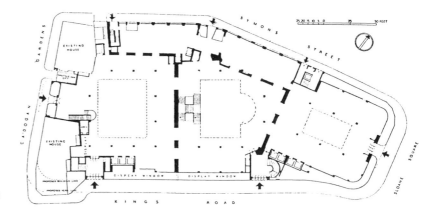

PETER JONES

Sloane Square, London SW3: Cadogan Gardens block, 1934;
Sloane Square corner block, 1935–36; completion of King's
Road range, 1938–39

The architectural scheme for Peter Jones involved the
replacement of earlier buildings on the site, with the
intention of rebuilding the whole island block in phases.
The scheme was developed in association with Reilly and
the experienced department store architects Slater &
Moberly, to add a grounding of practical experience.
(They had recently completed the rebuilding of Bourne
& Hollingsworth in Oxford Street, but, as Crabtree later
recalled, "I took a flat in Berners Street, over Slater &
Moberly's office, and was in a position of control.") The
consulting engineer was B.L. Hurst.

The structure is a welded-steel frame, with 8-foot
(2.5-metre) cantilevers to the edge of the building. A small
experimental section was constructed in 1934 in Cadogan

Gardens, to the rear of the building. It had reinforced-
concrete mullions, and was faced with red-glazed tiles to
the side and a strip of metal on the front. The cornice
was clad in green faience. The concrete took too long to
dry out, and was replaced with a steel mullion system,
continuing the same 4-foot grid. This created a strong
vertical emphasis, which was apparently due to Reilly acting
on the suggestion of Spedan Lewis and contrary to the
original, more horizontal, scheme by Crabtree. Within
this the spandrel panels were fitted with bronze hinged
casements, so that the panels inside could be coloured
by distemper (then the best way of obtaining clear paint
colour) or even by wallpaper. It was suggested that the
mullions could also be painted.

The plan was completed to its existing extent by 1939,
when the complete King's Road elevation was in place,
leaving earlier structures to the west and north that have
remained. Crabtree explained the double curve at the
corner: "The LCC [London County Council] made us slice

a bit off both corners facing Sloane Square, so we sliced
a bit more off the King's Road corner to give it a sort of
movement" ('Historic Pioneers: Architects and Clients',
Architects' Journal, 11 March 1970, p. 597). Two light wells
were placed in the centre of the block. The interior was
relatively plain in style. The continuous display window on
the ground floor, with a deep concrete canopy, a plaster
rather than timber back wall and light introduced from
a clerestory, was considered a successful solution to a
difficult problem.

After 2000 a major refurbishment project was carried
out by John McAslan + Partners, rationalizing floor levels
and 'backstage' spaces. Escalators were introduced in the
west atrium.

This group of three houses, all to a similar design, is built of local yellow brick with monopitch roofs of blue pantile. The architect's parents, early settlers in the nearby Welwyn Garden City, bought the land and were the clients for the central house, while the architect Cecil Kemp, who specialized in building under the Miners' Welfare Scheme, built the one to the east for himself and was a collaborator in the design.

The slope of the roof allowed space for housing the water tank and, while also avoiding the problems of a flat roof, was welcomed by many as a more sympathetic form in the landscape.

Mary Crowley BORN 1907

The daughter of a principal medical officer at the Board of Education and with a Quaker background, Crowley trained at the Architectural Association, among one of the earliest decidedly Modernist cohorts of students. She starred in the Architectural Association pantomimes and visited the Stockholm Exhibition in 1930. In 1934 she collaborated with Ernö Goldfinger on proposals for nursery school classrooms in timber. After the War she joined the Hertfordshire County Council Architects' Department, where important work on school design was carried out under Stirrat Johnson-Marshall.

Mary Crowley was the principal designer for the infants' school at Cheshunt (1946–47) – using the Hills prefabricated steel frame – to which she brought a special understanding of teachers' needs. Andrew Saint calls her "the greatest single influence on planning post-war schools". In 1949 she married a colleague, David Medd, and they moved to the Ministry of Education, where they worked partly on design and partly on research for secondary schools. In 1958–59, in conjunction with Pat Tindale, the Medds designed village primary schools at Finmere, Oxfordshire, and Great Ponton, Lincolnshire: these finally removed the distinction between classrooms and spaces for other activities.

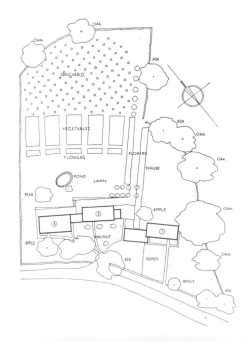

LEFT: The house numbered '1' on the block plan, built for Roland and Grace Miall, relations of the architect, has been sensitively extended.

OPPOSITE AND ABOVE: The monopitch roof brought practical advantages over a flat roof in terms of water run-off, and avoided what one commentator called "the undesirable association with false romanticism that the steep, double-pitched roof of the normal period-style house entails". Mary Crowley later said: "I did not see myself as part of a reaction to the 'International Style' … The very simple plan form seemed best to be expressed by a single pitched roof, lower to the north, higher to the south."

REFERENCES

Architect

Andrew Saint, *Towards a Social Architecture: The Role of School Building in Post-War England*, London and New Haven CT (Yale University Press) 1987

102–106 Orchard Road

Architect and Building News, vol. 146, 26 June 1936, pp. 388–91

Architectural Review, vol. 80, December 1936, pp. 245–48

F.R.S. Yorke, *The Modern House in England*, London (Architectural Press) 1937, pp. 27–30

BELOW AND OPPOSITE: "It is an affair of decks and rails, with windows that survey the estuary and its boats in one broad sweep", wrote the critic of the *Architect and Building News* in 1931. The simple stepped decks of the yacht club, owing something perhaps to sanatorium design, continue to provide an appropriate image for their nautical purpose. The original scheme included large starting numbers along the top balcony railing, but these were omitted.

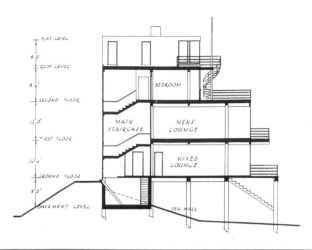

ROYAL CORINTHIAN YACHT CLUB
Burnham on Crouch, Essex, 1929–31

The commission came from the commodore of the club, Philip Benson, the head of a leading advertising agency, who requested "a large three-storeyed ferro-concrete structure of advanced design". The initial design is seen in a perspective drawn by William Crabtree and exhibited at the Royal Academy of Arts, London, in 1930. This is a lower building, with a horizontal emphasis in the broad balcony and continuous banded parapet. It was superseded by a taller design with a smaller footprint, a less emphatic balcony and a stair tower at the eastern end, leading up to a starting box. George Fairweather, at that time an assistant to Emberton, is credited by oral tradition with a major role in the design.

The structure consists of a steel frame on a concrete slab, with panel walls of 4.5-inch brick rendered with white Portland cement. The second floor contained residential rooms for members. There is an oak staircase but little elaboration to the internal fittings.

Hitchcock and Johnson commented that "the large glass area is particularly suitable in a dull, foggy climate", although Burnham has among the highest levels of sunlight in Britain. The yacht club has survived in good condition and remains in its original use.

Joseph Emberton 1889–1956

Emberton belonged to the elder generation of modern architects in Britain. His early career led him, via the Royal College of Art, to a position, after war service, with Burnet & Tait. Their influence can be seen in his early projects, such as Summit House, Red Lion Square, London (1925; in partnership with P.J. Westwood), a bulky if relatively small building with vertical emphasis. In many cases Emberton's clients came from the world of retail and commerce, and his work of the 1920s was typically Art Deco in style. In 1930 he designed the new frontage for the Olympia Exhibition building in west London, in a Modernist streamlined style. The Royal Corinthian Yacht Club at Burnham on Crouch, Essex (1929–31), established him firmly among the Modernists, especially as it was the only British building illustrated in *The International Style*, published by Henry-Russell Hitchcock and Philip Johnson in 1932.

In addition to the projects featured here, Emberton's major designs included Universal House, Southwark Bridge Road (1934; demolished), with glass cladding, and the shop for HMV on Oxford Street (1939; demolished), both in London. Emberton was particularly interested in the solution of engineering problems. There is evidence that most of the designs in his office were made by assistants,

of whom there was a considerable turnover as he did not treat them kindly. To clients, however, he was full of charm.

During the Second World War Emberton worked as Housing Officer to the Ministry of Aircraft Production, architectural adviser on hostels to the Ministry of Works and consultant on the design of steel houses to the Ministry of Supply. After 1945 he worked on several housing schemes in London.

SIMPSONS

203–206 Piccadilly, London W1, 1935–36
Engineer: Helsby, Hamann & Samuely

Simpsons was a new West End store for a successful men's tailor and outfitter, founded in 1894, on the site of the former Geological Museum (designed by James Pennethorne) and running through to Jermyn Street, the street to the rear parallel to Piccadilly.

Simpsons is notable for the 42-foot (12.8-metre) spans of its welded steel framing, which produced one of the most elegant shop interiors of the decade, although the purity of the concept was compromised as a result of interventions by the London County Council. It was faced in Portland stone as required by the landlord.

The Piccadilly elevation has a ground floor of low display windows behind curved (and hence non-reflecting) glass. (László Moholy-Nagy was involved in designing the window displays at the time of opening.) Above this, four storeys rise to a set-back balcony, with a canopy pierced by circular pavement lights. The front was fitted with neon lights, the colours of which could be alternated. The lettering for Simpsons and its proprietary brand, DAKS, was positioned on the first floor. The floor space divides into three zones on each level; a staircase rises through the whole height, with a low, glazed balustrade topped by a Chinese red handrail. C.H. Reilly called it "strong without and elegant within" ('The Year's Buildings', *Architects' Journal*, 14 January 1937, p. 102).

Simpsons remained in occupation until the late 1990s, when the building was bought by Waterstone's booksellers and converted for its new purpose. Despite some slight losses of original fittings as well as most of the external lettering, the general effect remains.

Joseph Emberton

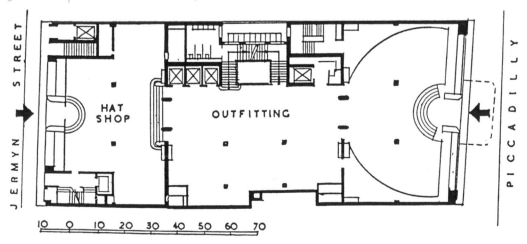

Simpsons' elevation to Jermyn Street (above left), faced in Portland stone and extended to the left at a later date, is a more conventional example of street architecture than the narrower Piccadilly frontage (opposite). In this dramatic intervention into a famous London street, much attention was given to lighting effects. Different sets of coloured neon tubes concealed in the projecting bronze troughs at the head of each row of windows threw light up on to the stone bands above.

BLACKPOOL PLEASURE BEACH
Lancashire, 1935–39

William George Bean returned from New York to his native Great Yarmouth, Norfolk, in 1896, determined to emulate Coney Island. Blackpool proved a better bet, and the Pleasure Beach opened in 1904. Bean died in 1929, and his daughter Doris Thompson (1903–2004) took over this "earthly paradise of a shrewd, hard-working people" with her husband, Leonard; they introduced a crèche as early as 1936. This progressive attitude may explain her employment of Emberton, who was commissioned to rebuild the Pleasure Beach in "a unified modern design", although several of the older rides continued in existence. Artists were employed for painted decorations on the white surfaces. These buildings are a unique example in Britain of modern architecture and mass culture meeting on equal terms.

THE GRAND NATIONAL (1935)

Named after the famous annual steeplechase held at Aintree, near Liverpool, and copying the race's famous jumps, such as Becher's Brook and Valentine's Brook, this was a roller-coaster ride that included a tall pylon feature, reminiscent of the style of the Chicago Century of Progress exhibition of 1933. At ground level riders were taken past the paybox to wait for their car on one of the twin platforms, while riders who had finished exited by a subway without confusing the flow. The curves of the canopy successfully express the sense of movement.

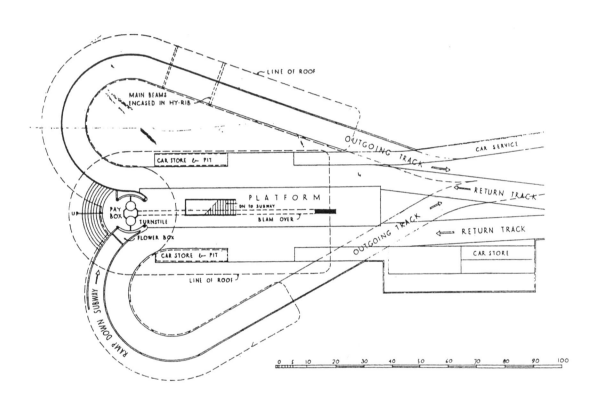

Joseph Emberton

REFERENCES
Architect
Obituary, *Architectural Review*,
    vol. 121, February 1957, p. 82
Rosemary Ind, *Emberton*,
    Aldershot (Scolar Press)
    1983

Royal Corinthian Yacht Club
Architect and Building News,
    vol. 127, 4 September 1931,
    pp. 265–69
Architectural Review, vol. 72,
    November 1932, p. 200

Simpsons
Architects' Journal, vol. 83,
    21 May 1936, pp. 767–72
Architectural Review, vol. 79, June
    1936, pp. 270–71

The Grand National
Architect and Building News,
    vol. 142, 28 June 1935,
    pp. 383–87

The Casino
Architects' Journal, vol. 90, 27 July
    1939, pp. 133–38
Architectural Review, vol. 86, July
    1939, pp. 25–36

THE FUN HOUSE (1935)

In the enclosed space the visitor is exposed to various disorienting physical experiences, such as slides, moving staircases going at different speeds side by side, vertical drops and floors made of rolling barrels with a strong up-draught. The construction was of wallboard on a light steel frame, decorated externally with paintings by Margaret Blundell and internally with a canvas background lit from parabolic reflectors. The night view, with neon lettering and other light features, gives a sense of the excitement. The Fun House was destroyed by fire in 1992.

THE CASINO (1939) (with Halsted Best)

This is not a gambling casino but a multiple restaurant, catering for different social and economic levels, from first-class restaurant and cocktail bar to cafeteria and billiard-room. Each facility is reached by a different door and staircase, although all are linked by the main spiral stair. Colours were co-ordinated on pillars, surfaces and crockery. The Snack Bar had automatic doors, controlled by a photo-electric ray. The kitchens and services are grouped in the centre at each level, from which the public spaces fanned out.

The exterior was marked with a slatted screen to carry neon lettering, flanked by a slender spiral stair similar to that built for the Olympic Stadium at Helsinki. The building used mechanically vibrated precast concrete elements for the first time in Britain and was air-conditioned throughout. An additional storey in a similar style was added after the War.

OPPOSITE AND ABOVE: Hugh Casson, who at the Festival of Britain in 1951 was to achieve a similar marriage of Modernism and fun, commented in the *Architectural Review* that "the architect has been remarkably successful in creating an air of order and unity on the beach without losing the essentially varying characteristics of individual features." The Lancashire holidaymaker, he observed, "patronises the gleaming new bar with its glass and concrete staircase, downs his drink, and goes out again without voicing any comment on the appearance of the place."

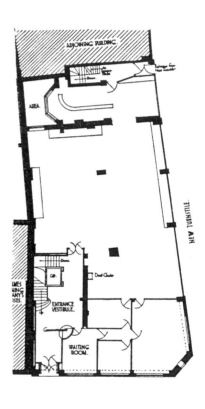

Frederick Etchells 1886–1973

The son of an engineer from Macclesfield, Cheshire, Etchells studied at the Royal College of Art, London (1908–11), where he came under the influence of the Arts and Crafts thinker W.R. Lethaby. He joined the Omega Workshops and then Wyndham Lewis's breakaway group, the Rebel Art Centre. In 1923, after a gruelling war, Etchells decided to become an architect, in partnership with Hugh Macdonald, and established a good connection with the Grosvenor estate in Mayfair, leading to commissions for neo-Georgian and Tudor mews houses.

Etchells's Modernist side was expressed first in 1927, in his translation of Le Corbusier's *Vers une architecture* (as *Towards a New Architecture*), which remains standard, and then in the design of the office building for the advertising agency Crawford's. He designed several flat-roofed houses (including one on the Frinton Park estate, Essex), which show a classical formality of plan and elevation, and later became more interested in church architecture, restoring several churches.

Etchells was a friend of John Betjeman, with whom he shared a love of jokes about architects, particularly the more pompous kind of Modernist. As Betjeman wrote of Etchells in an obituary, "his monologues against all forms of professionalism were a joy to hear".

REFERENCES

Architect

John Betjeman, 'Frederick Etchells', *Architectural Review*, vol. 154, November 1973, pp. 271–72

Crawford's

Architect and Building News, vol. 124, 19 September 1930, pp. 373–79
Architects' Journal, vol. 72, 29 October 1930, pp. 652–54 (text by Sir William Crawford)
Building, vol. 6, November 1930, pp. 500–03
Architectural Review, vol. 69, February 1931, pls. X–XIII

CRAWFORD'S

233 High Holborn, London WC2, 1930
(with Herbert A. Welch)

The poster artist Edward McKnight Kauffer introduced
Etchells to Sir William Crawford as a designer for new offices
for Crawford's Advertising, with Herbert A. Welch to provide
experienced support. The simplicity of the exterior made it
count as the first modern building in London, while the
entrance and lift were a feast of chromed and stainless steel.
Rodney Thomas (1902–1996) added further interiors to the
building, all now lost.

Crawford wrote: "My offices, built round a modern English
business, are modern English. But the attitude towards building
that the new Crawford's typifies is not English; it is not
German, though Berlin may, for the moment, lead; it is a
world-wide attitude."

RIGHT: The argument for
large windows was simple –
the provision of maximum
light – but the architectural
implications still seemed
shocking in 1930, when the
style of the adjoining building
to the left, originally the Times
Furnishing Company, counted
as 'normal' modern architecture.
The magazine *Building*
commented: "Though the
problem is familiar enough, this
building does it whole-heartedly;
perhaps a little ruthlessly".

Rudolf Frankel 1901–1974

Born in Neisse, Upper Silesia, Frankel studied first architecture and then law in Berlin and after 1924 worked independently, with a successful line in cinemas, theatres, houses and flats. Between 1933 and 1937 he moved first to Bucharest and then to London. In an attractive location in the outer suburbs he built his own house, as well as one for a relative on the adjacent plot. He did not have the opportunity for other major work before the War, but continued in practice afterwards, when his work included factories in Birmingham, Congleton in Cheshire and Risca, Monmouthshire, each with an elegant austerity. The Birmingham building, a service station for machine tools, published in the *Architectural Review* in April 1949, is a very elegant and somewhat Germanic building. It has a steel frame enclosing a single internal space, light-coloured brick end walls and continuous glazing flush with the frame. In 1950 Frankel moved to the United States to take up the chair of architecture at the University of Miami.

REFERENCES
House in the Home Counties
Architects' Journal, vol. 92,
    28 November 1940,
    pp. 439–41
Architectural Review, vol. 88,
    November 1940, pp. 136–37

OPPOSITE AND BELOW: The cutaway corner of the house, forming a sheltered outdoor sitting space, is the main feature of the design. It connects to the living-room and dining-room, which are linked internally by a wide opening.

HOUSE IN THE HOME COUNTIES
1938

The house is set well back from the road, in the north-east corner of its plot, with a single-storey garage wing screening the garden as one approaches.

The footprint of the house is relatively square compared with the more elongated rectangles of most contemporary houses, and incorporates a generously proportioned living-room and high ceilings. The house is built of yellow sand-faced brick, with a dark blue brick for the terrace and plinth. The L-shaped terrace runs beneath the corner overhang, giving a pleasing sense of protection and a diagonal view over the garden. It is an assured but undemonstrative design, which has been well preserved, although Frankel's own house adjacent has been altered.

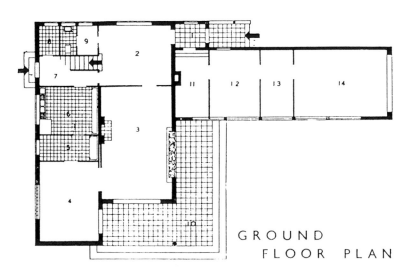

GROUND
FLOOR PLAN

Edwin Maxwell Fry 1899–1987

Born at Wallasey, Cheshire, Fry trained at the Liverpool School of Architecture when it was still in full classical flood under C.H. Reilly. Skilled in drawing and fond of Georgian buildings, he came under the influence of Wells Coates in the later 1920s and began to yearn for Modernism. At Sassoon House, Peckham, Fry made the break and in the same year took Walter Gropius into partnership, although their design approaches differed, and their projects are attributed individually. Fry's office in the 1930s nurtured considerable talent, including Eric Lyons (later the designer of SPAN housing), Edward Mills and Jack Howe.

Fry's concern for housing continued with the Kensal House flats in North Kensington, and he had a close relationship with the housing consultant Elizabeth Denby until the omission of her name in a publication caused a rift. Fry's first marriage was failing, and shortly before 1939 he met the architect Jane Drew. They were married in 1942 and subsequently practised together in Britain, West Africa and India, where they were instrumental in the process of inviting Le Corbusier to design the major buildings at Chandigarh. Fry's own later design work has never been as highly valued, however, as the graceful and elegant products of the 1930s.

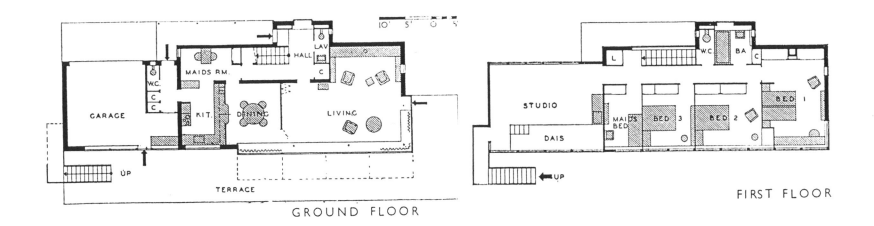

GROUND FLOOR

FIRST FLOOR

LITTLE WINCH

Chipperfield Common, Hertfordshire, 1934–36

Built for the commercial artist G. Butler, the London art director of the J. Walter Thompson advertising agency, Little Winch was planned to incorporate a studio. The first scheme, in reinforced concrete, was rejected under the 1932 Town and Country Planning Act, the purpose of which was to control ribbon development rather than architectural aesthetics. Watford Rural District Council offered a choice between a concrete house with a pitched roof and a flat-roofed house of conventional materials, and the latter course was chosen. Despite these restrictions, which did no more than anticipate the Modernist aesthetic of the later 1930s, Fry produced a comfortable and light house on a flat site.

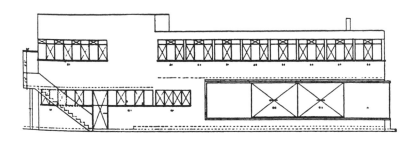

OPPOSITE AND ABOVE LEFT: At a hearing of the Watford Rural District Council to discuss the original proposal by Fry for a concrete house, one member suggested asking for "an antique tiled roof or battlements", while another believed that in ten years' time flat roofs would be standard. Other members seemed chiefly concerned that a flat roof might be used for nude sunbathing. The external stair to the studio at the left-hand end was originally a much smaller structure.

ABOVE RIGHT: The original elevation is shown here, although wisteria has masked the geometric composition of interlocking panels of brick and timber in the executed design, which had a large expanse of glass wrapping around the corner of the ground-floor living-room. The *Architectural Review* called it "an interesting example of modern architecture that is not entirely dependent on 'modern' materials".

LEFT: Fry's early career in town planning may have helped him to understand the potential of the unusual site of Kensal House. The curve of the main block provided its most photogenic aspect, which is visible also from trains travelling to and from Paddington station.

BELOW: In the layout there is one main entrance to the estate, at street level across a bridge where the ground falls away. The circle was the base of a gas holder previously on the site, where Fry and Denby proposed adding a nursery school as one of the most important facilities for the community.

OPPOSITE: The pierced-concrete inset balconies were designed for drying clothes, saving the labour of carrying washing to a drying green or roof. This attention to women's work by Elizabeth Denby was an important but unusual feature of the project. The projecting balconies were made large enough for private gardens, which were encouraged.

Edwin Maxwell Fry

KENSAL HOUSE

1–68 Ladbroke Grove, London W10, 1933–36
(Housing Consultant: Elizabeth Denby; Committee of
Architects: Robert Atkinson, C.H. James and G. Grey
Wornum)

Kensal House was built for philanthropic and promotional
reasons by the Gas Light and Coke Company for the
Capitol Housing Association, on the site of a former
gasworks. Sixty-eight flats were included in two parallel
blocks, with a nursery school. Denby had worked in this part
of London for several years, and, although she preferred
terraced houses, she believed in high-density urban living and
described Kensal House as an "urban village". The kitchens
and bathrooms were equipped with gas heating devices, and
much consideration was given to lightening the burden of
women's work and providing useful clubrooms for men.

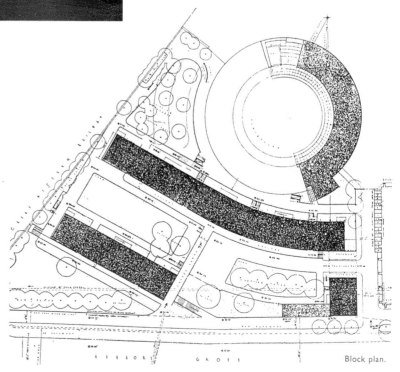

Block plan.

BELOW: This photograph shows additions made in recent years in the building's original style, answering the need to make the small original kitchens of the 1930s into the multi-purpose family rooms of today. The view along the main terrace (below right) looks exactly as it did in 1937, and the projecting sun room gives a satisfying sense of enclosure.

Edwin Maxwell Fry

REFERENCES
Architect
Maxwell Fry, *Autobiographical Sketches*, London (Paul Elek) 1975

Little Winch
Architects' Journal, vol. 80, 20 September 1934, pp. 406–08; vol. 83, 23 January 1936, pp. 170–71
Architectural Review, vol. 79, January 1936, pp. 25–26
F.R.S. Yorke, *The Modern House in England*, London (Architectural Press) 1937, pp. 19, 71–72

Kensal House
Architects' Journal, vol. 85, 18 March 1937, pp. 453,

466–68
Architect and Building News, vol. 149, 19 March 1937, pp. 345, 349; vol. 156, 23 December 1938, p. 323 (trellis)
Architectural Review, vol. 81, May 1937, pp. 207–10
F.R.S. Yorke and F. Gibberd, *The Modern Flat*, London (Architectural Press) 1937, pp. 98–101
E. Maxwell Fry, 'Kensal House' (pp. 56–60), and Elizabeth Denby, 'Kensal House: An Urban Village' (pp. 61–64, 66–71), in *Flats, Municipal and Private Enterprise*, London (Ascot Water Heaters Ltd) 1938

Miramonte
F.R.S. Yorke, *The Modern House*, London (Architectural Press) 1934; 2nd edn, 1935, p. 167 (model)
Architects' Journal, vol. 86, 18 November 1937, pp. 784–87
Architectural Review, vol. 82, November 1937, pp. 187–92
'Early Clients of Maxwell Fry' (letter by Fry of 1979), Appendix A in Lionel Esher, *A Broken Wave*, London (Allen Lane, The Penguin Press) 1981, p. 301

MIRAMONTE
Warren Rise, Coombe, Kingston upon Thames, Surrey, 1935–37

The client, Jerry Brown, made a fortune from speculating in suburban building land, and Fry was delighted by his lack of pretension. Recalling Brown, he commented, "he allowed me to furnish his new estate in life like Sancho Panza's island". The house that Brown commissioned was built to a high specification, and included a separate pavilion for the chauffeur's flat and a swimming pool. The reinforced concrete was painted a cream colour, and the canopies and parapets finished in copper. Special sliding windows were provided throughout, and electric ceiling heating in the bedrooms. Surviving despite the loss of many internal features, Miramonte has been recently repaired and extended by John Allan of Avanti Architects.

ABOVE: The serenity of the
main elevation of Miramonte
has long been a classic image
of Modernism in the 1930s –
apparently made out of standard
elements, but finely tuned and
adapted to the spacious site
with its mature trees.

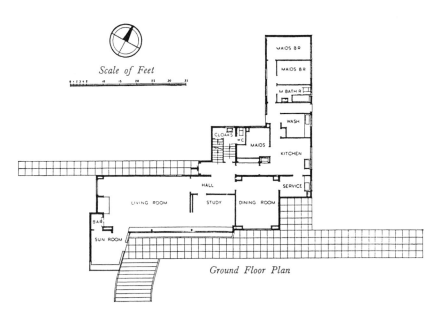

Scale of Feet

MAIDS BR

MAIDS BR

M BATH R

WASH

CLOAKS
WC
MAIDS

KITCHEN

HALL

SERVICE

LIVING ROOM

STUDY

DINING ROOM

BAR

SUN ROOM

Ground Floor Plan

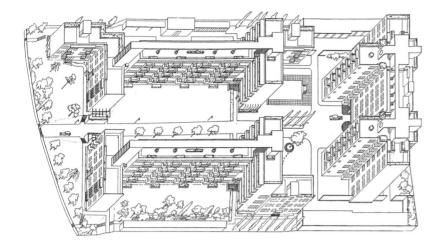

Commissioned from the twenty-seven-year-old architect by a property developer – William Bernstein, who owned the 3-acre site – Pullman Court was built largely to provide flats for single people, with fitted kitchens and refrigerators, and rents from £68 to £130 a year. Gibberd also designed a range of appropriate furniture to offer to tenants.

The reinforced-concrete structure, by L.G. Mouchel, was modular and economic, and overhanging steel rails on the roof-garden spaces were provided to assist repainting of the exterior. Gibberd's sensitivity to landscape is apparent in the preservation of existing trees and the way in which the design encourages use of outdoor space.

ABOVE: The splendid axonometric drawing of Pullman Court recalls the presentation style popular among modern architects in Germany. It shows how Gibberd managed the deep site at Pullman Court, spacing blocks far enough apart to provide good sunlight, yet avoiding the mechanical forms of *zeilenbau*, or parallel blocks. The flats in the long linking blocks face due south.

RIGHT AND FAR RIGHT: The internal angles between the blocks give a pleasant sense of enclosure, while the contrasting shapes and the original colour scheme of warm brown, cream and pale blue added a sense of drama never far from Gibberd's approach as an architect.

OPPOSITE: The deeply projecting balconies, denoting either one- or two-room flats, show off the advantages of reinforced concrete.

Frederick Gibberd 1908–1984

Frederick Gibberd was born in Coventry and attended the Birmingham School of Architecture, in the same class as F.R.S. Yorke. In 1932 they both opened practices at the same address in London, although not in partnership; they subsequently remained close friends. Gibberd's first major building, the Pullman Court flats in south London, was his most representative Modernist work. In the following years his flats at Park Court, Crystal Palace (1936), and Ellington Court, Southgate (1937), were more conservative in structure and appearance. During and after the War he represented a sensitive and romantic attitude to building form, landscape and the use of external spaces. Gibberd was an influential principal of the Architectural Association School (1942–44) and a perceptive collector of paintings, drawings and sculptures by his British contemporaries.

Gibberd was the chief planner for Harlow New Town and made his home there. He planned the Live Architecture exhibition for the Festival of Britain in 1951, which took the form of the Lansbury estate at Poplar, east London. Gibberd also continued to design individual buildings, most famously completing the Roman Catholic Cathedral of Christ the King, Liverpool (1960–67), and the London Mosque in Regent's Park (1969–77).

REFERENCES
Pullman Court
Architectural Review, vol. 79, January 1936, pp. 28–32, 41–44
Architects' Journal, vol. 83, 30 April 1936, pp. 671–72; 14 May 1936, pp. 733–34
F.R.S. Yorke and Frederick Gibberd, *The Modern Flat*, London (Architectural Press) 1937, pp. 46–51
Richard J. Biggins, *Pullman Court: Architecture* [online]. Available: http://web.onetel.net.uk/~rayuela/archi.htm [9 February 2005]

The Covered Way

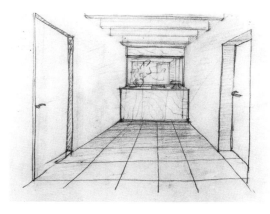

HILL PASTURE
Broxted, Essex, 1936–37 (with Gerald Flower)

Built for Humphrey Waterfield, a painter with a passion for gardening, Hill Pasture was originally a single-storey house, with a change of interior level. A carefully designed entry sequence (above) begins with a narrow, anonymous-looking door in a brick wall, which opens on to the wooden pergola. The covered path leads to the front door, revealing the view to the right. Goldfinger admitted this as perhaps the only moment when his architecture was influenced by Surrealism, although at other times he created unexpected emotional effects.

The upper floor was added after the War by Goldfinger's former partner Gerald Flower. The house was renovated by John Winter in the late 1990s, but because of the addition the exterior no longer resembles the original Goldfinger design.

Ernö Goldfinger 1902–1987

Born in Transylvania, Goldfinger was educated in Budapest before going to Paris in 1920 to study architecture at the Ecole des Beaux-Arts and joining the breakaway atelier of Auguste Perret. In Paris, Goldfinger met leading figures of avant-garde culture, particularly the Surrealists, and enjoyed conversations with the architect Adolf Loos, a formative influence. He began to practise in the later 1920s in an elegant, sparse style. In 1930 he met the artist Ursula Blackwell, whom he married in 1933; that same year, he helped to organize the CIAM Congress, which convened on board the SS *Patras II* and travelled from Marseilles to Athens and back.

Goldfinger and his wife moved the following year to London, where he mostly designed small projects, including prototypes for furniture, exhibition displays and children's toys. His office was an important nursery of talent for H.T. Cadbury-Brown, Ralph Tubbs and others. After the War his schools, offices (in Albemarle Street and at Elephant and Castle) and, finally, two of the tallest residential blocks in London – Balfron Tower, near the Blackwall Tunnel (1965), and Trellick Tower, North Kensington (1967) – were increasingly bold statements of uncompromising but rational design, in which Perret's influence came to the fore in the careful handling of concrete construction.

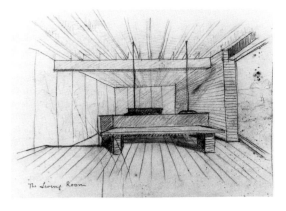

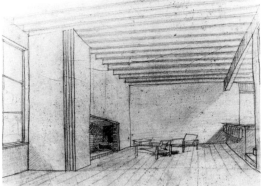

ABOVE: A set of drawings by
Goldfinger shows the sequence
of spatial experiences as one
approaches and enters the
house. A descent of three steps
from the dining-room (left)
leads into the large living-room
(centre), where the fireplace has
a tiny square window.

LEFT: The covered way has been
reconstructed, having been
originally built of telegraph poles.

Ernö Goldfinger

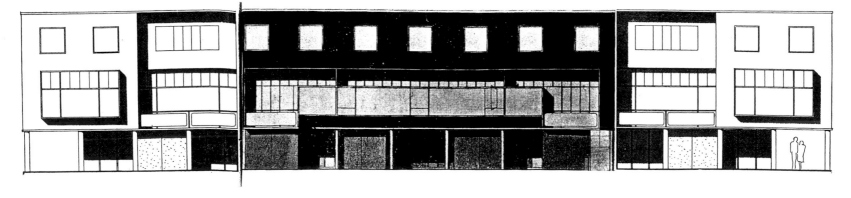

GROUND FLOOR

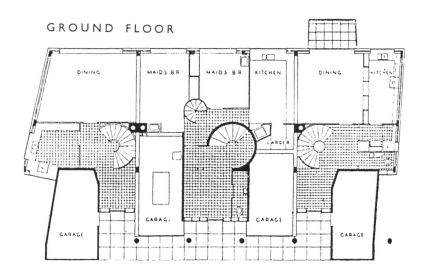

FIRST FLOOR

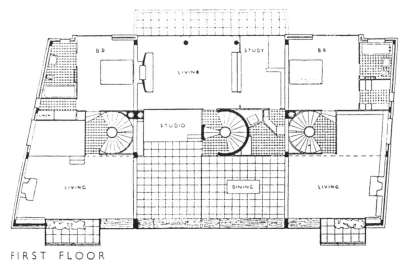

1–3 WILLOW ROAD

Hampstead, London NW3, 1937–39

Funded by Ursula Goldfinger's trust money, in 1935 Goldfinger bought a site overlooking Hampstead Heath. He worked through a series of proposals, beginning with flats, before settling on a terrace of three houses, the largest one in the middle being intended for himself and his family. Construction comprises a concrete frame with concrete floors, and exterior walls in brick. Each of the houses has a concrete spiral stair, and a change of level (Adolf Loos's *Raumplan* in action) on the first floor. Some interior rooms are lined in plywood.

The house at 2 Willow Road was saved by The National Trust as a house museum and repaired by John Allan of Avanti Architects.

OPPOSITE TOP: The street frontage shows Goldfinger's reworking of a London brick terrace in modern form, featuring a contrast of continuous window on the first floor with small square windows above. Narrow garages are neatly tucked beneath the overhang of the upper level.

OPPOSITE BOTTOM: Goldfinger's suggestion for an imaginary extension of the Willow Road elevation to form a terrace of houses.

ABOVE: The change in floor level runs through all three houses, and in Goldfinger's own house provides the studio with a model platform (above right) once the folding doors have shut off the living-room. The studio and dining-room (above left) are also linked through folding doors, and the three spaces were thrown open for parties at the house.

RIGHT: The top of the concrete spiral stair shows the balustrade of looped and tensioned rope beneath the enamelled handrail, with light falling from above into the entrance hall below.

94 WIMPOLE STREET
London W1, 1936

Paul and Marjorie Abbatt were leading makers of educational toys, mostly of wood, for whom Goldfinger also made designs. Their Wimpole Street shop emphasized transparency by the deep insetting of the shop window, and the frameless glass door was one of the first of its kind. Of this design, only the inset I-beam remains visible on the site.

Ernö Goldfinger

REFERENCES
Architect
Architectural Design, vol. 33, January 1963 (Ernö Goldfinger special issue)
Maté Major, *Ernö Goldfinger*, Budapest (Akadémiai Kaidó) 1973
James Dunnett and Gavin Stamp, *Ernö Goldfinger*, London (Architectural Association) 1983
Robert Elwall, *Ernö Goldfinger*, London (Academy Editions) 1996
Passionate Rationalism: Recollections of Ernö Goldfinger, London (British Library/The National Trust) 2004 (recordings made with family and colleagues)

Nigel Warburton, *Ernö Goldfinger: The Life of an Architect*, London (Routledge) 2004

Hill Pasture
F.R.S. Yorke, *The Modern House in England*, London (Architectural Press), 2nd edn, 1944, pp. 56–57
Daily Mail Ideal Home Book, 1956 (two colour photographs)

1–3 Willow Road
Architectural Review, vol. 87, April 1940, pp. 126–30, 149–53
Architects' Journal, vol. 91, 28 June 1940, pp. 427–47
F.R.S. Yorke, *The Modern House in England*, London

(Architectural Press), 2nd edn, 1944, pp. 94–96
Alan Powers, *2 Willow Road*, London (The National Trust) 1996

2 Golders Green Road
Architects' Journal, vol. 83, 18 June 1936, pp. 439–40
Architectural Review, vol. 79, June 1936, p. 272; vol. 80, August 1936, pp. 83–86

94 Wimpole Street
Architectural Review, vol. 81, January 1937, pp. 24–25
Architects' Journal, vol. 86, 2 September 1937, pp. 371–72

ABOVE LEFT: The Abbatt shop window was designed with different areas for the display of different types of goods. Inside the shop was equipped with low tables where children could sit in miniature Thonet bentwood chairs and play. Books, postcards and prints were also on sale, along with the Abbatts' popular climbing frames and indoor slides, one of which was a favourite toy of the Goldfinger children at Willow Road.

OPPOSITE: The Weiss shop was the conversion of an existing shell, and the top storey has been airbrushed out of this period print in order to emphasize the horizontal lines. The main display case formed an island, a traditional feature of drapers' shops. The glass of the display windows sits on sections of steel I-beam, similar to those used by Goldfinger to support sideboards and cupboards.

2 GOLDERS GREEN ROAD
London NW11, 1936

Goldfinger's shop for S. Weiss in Golders Green Road was designed first for a hairdresser's. Its curved corner looks German in character, and the display windows are carefully contrived. Only the broader elements of the building have survived.

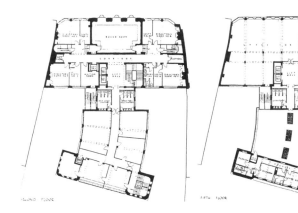

GROUND FLOOR · FIFTH FLOOR

BELOW LEFT: The two main façades are both symmetrical compositions, and the plan conceals the irregularity of the site. Window shapes are differentiated according to use: those facing the river (opposite) are angled so that they can be opened away from the prevailing wind.

BELOW RIGHT: The internal surfaces at St Olaf House are also decorated with geometric patterns.

OPPOSITE: The decorative sculpture by Frank Dobson, which Goodhart-Rendel likened to a tapestry hanging, forms a panel around the board room and main offices. The bold gilded lettering is one of the delights of this highly individual building.

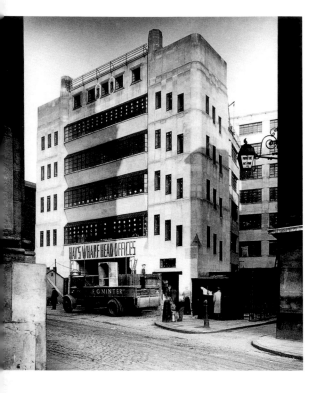

ST OLAF HOUSE
Hay's Wharf, Tooley Street, London SE1, 1930–31

Built as head offices for a major import trading company, St Olaf House incorporated a working quayside, hence its elevation on piloti. Goodhart-Rendel answered the challenge of Modernism by rationalizing the frame construction and cladding, and reinventing ornament from basic geometry in a version of Art Deco derived from medieval Gothic.

One critic wrote that "Mr Goodhart-Rendel, within functional limits, has 'let himself go'". The architect himself wrote at this time that "the five orders have been packed away in a box, and we are playing with new toys now, rather hard and cornery, perhaps, but sensible and strong". Hay's Wharf was among the first batch of inter-war buildings to be listed, in 1971.

H.S. Goodhart-Rendel 1887–1959

Goodhart-Rendel had twin passions for architecture and music. He worked for a church architect, Sir Charles Nicholson, before starting his own practice in 1910, although he had designed buildings from his teens onwards. He was one of the cleverest and most articulate architects of his generation, who believed that plans and construction had to be rational, although style could take its cue from history or surroundings. He never accepted Modernism and as Architectural Association Director of Education came into conflict with students in 1937–38. He revived intelligent interest in Victorian architecture, and his own work was an attempt to pick up the abandoned potential of nineteenth-century architecture in Britain and France that Modernism had bypassed in its search for a new style. Hay's Wharf, beside the Thames near London Bridge, can be seen in this context, as well as being a critique of the early Modernist office buildings of the 1920s, such as Adelaide House, also at London Bridge, by Burnet, Tait & Lorne.

Although removed from commercial pressure by inherited wealth, Goodhart-Rendel was a prolific architect, whose work got better as he went on until in the post-war years, when he seemed completely out of step with the times, he produced most of his best buildings.

REFERENCES
Architect
Alan Powers, *H.S. Goodhart-Rendel, 1887–1959*, London (Architectural Association) 1987

H.S. Goodhart-Rendel, *English Architecture since the Regency: An Interpretation*, London (Constable) 1953; reprinted with introduction by Alan Powers, London (National Trust Classics, Century Hutchinson) 1989

St Olaf House
Architect and Building News, vol. 118, 2 September 1927, p. 389; vol. 125, 20 February 1931, pp. 278–79; vol. 129, 5 February 1932, pp. 190–95

Architectural Review, vol. 71, February 1932, pp. 49–53

BELOW: The tall windows in the saloon were designed to light the sculptures as the sun moved during the day, and still serve the same purpose.

DORICH HOUSE

Kingston Vale, London SW15, 1935–36 (with Henry Cole)

Dorich House is unlike any other Modern Movement building in Britain. The accommodation was vertically arranged so that the residential flat on the top floor could have the best views. The plan is compact, with a stair rising in the projecting tower. The semicircular windows are matched by a completely circular door between the dining-room and living-room, and arched openings, initially without doors, between the first-floor rooms.

Muriel Barron wrote of Dora Gordine in *Country Life*: "She knew what she wanted in house and studio, and, more uncommon knowledge, why she wanted it. Consequently her home and studio have realized her needs perfectly."

Dora Gordine 1906–1991

Dora Gordine was a sculptor, born in Russia of a Scottish architect father, who made her reputation in Paris in the 1920s before moving to London and marrying the Hon. Richard Hare, later a professor of Slavonic art, in 1936. In Paris she commissioned a studio from Auguste Perret in 1929, and the Hares originally tried to build in Hampstead, to a scheme by Godfrey Samuel. When this was turned down by the landowner, they found a site in Kingston upon Thames, overlooking Richmond Park, and designed their house and studio themselves. They selected materials at the Building Centre, then recently established in New Bond Street, and employed subcontractors directly.

Gordine continued her career as a sculptor, specializing in life-size bronze figures with an archaic Greek and classical serenity, similar in some respects to the work of Aristide Maillol. She lived in the house until her death, having left it and its contents in trust. The house was taken by Kingston University, which has a campus near by, and restored in the mid-1990s after falling into disrepair. It now houses a range of educational activities and is open occasionally to the public. There is a display of Gordine's sculpture in her first-floor studio, and items from her collection of Russian art and decoration furnish the house.

REFERENCES
Dorich House
Muriel Barron, 'Dorich House, Kingston Vale', *Country Life*, vol. 84, 5 November 1938, pp. 456–57
Brenda Martin, *Dorich House Guidebook*, London (Kingston University) 1998
Architects' Journal, vol. 201, 8 June 1995, p. 20; vol. 204, 12 September 1996, pp. 41–42

ABOVE: Many of the stylistic features of Dorich House, such as the round-headed windows, were not generally used by modern architects, but this was nonetheless a strongly original house design. The brick garden wall is the boundary of Richmond Park.

RIGHT: The main studio connects across the central stair landing with the saloon, making a fine suite of spaces.

BELOW LEFT: The tonal contrast between the red cedar boarding and the fascias of the roof was less pronounced in early photographs, but the latter seem always to have been painted white. Internally, Gropius welcomed the idea of a fireplace flanked by local flint, but the decoration was provided by J. Duncan Millar, whose furnishing of the living-room included "a large settee and two easy chairs in a grey and white striped tweed … and plain scarlet, dark green and chrome face-cloth cushion covers", combined with a grand piano and a Regency sofa table.

OPPOSITE : The plan should be read as a key to understanding the photographs. The projecting day nursery shares a terrace with the adults, and the design features two levels of loggia at the corner, the upper one originally extending all the way to the back of the house, but later mostly enclosed to serve as an extra bedroom.

THE WOOD HOUSE

Shipbourne, Kent, 1936–37

Commissioned by Jack and Frances Donaldson, a left-wing intellectual couple with a practical interest in farming (Jack Donaldson put his inherited money into funding the Peckham Health Centre, London), The Wood House was controversial locally despite its modesty and the use of cedar cladding on a structural timber frame, with teak corner posts.

Although never widely celebrated, the building was an important marker in the romantic and regional turn of modern house design in Britain. It shares many features (such as the deep projecting porch and the external stair) with the house that Gropius designed at Lincoln, Massachusetts, on his arrival in the United States.

Walter Gropius 1885–1969

Walter Gropius was an acknowledged leader of modern architecture in Germany before 1914, when his Fagus factory (1910) and the exhibition buildings at Cologne (1914; both with Adolf Meyer) initiated a new level of rational transparency, derived in part from Frank Lloyd Wright. After the War came the foundation of the Bauhaus at Weimar in 1919, and the new building to house the school at Dessau in 1925; shortly afterwards Gropius retired from teaching in order to practise, which he did successfully until the rise of Nazism.

After arriving in London in October 1934, Gropius went into partnership with Maxwell Fry, but declared that he would not try to found another Bauhaus. He had almost no money and, initially, little command of English. In 1937 he went to Harvard, where he remained until his death, although he was, rather bizarrely, the consultant architect to the Playboy Club in Park Lane, London, in the 1960s.

Gropius's book *The New Architecture and the Bauhaus* was published in 1935 in a translation by Philip Morton Shand, and drew attention to Gropius as an ideological balance to Le Corbusier, who encouraged technical and social research in architecture. Of his three principal buildings in Britain, 66 Old Church Street, Chelsea, is omitted here, having been much altered.

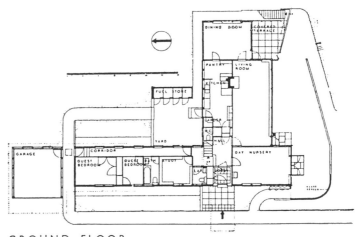

GROUND FLOOR

Walter Gropius

REFERENCES

Architect

Reginald Isaacs, *Gropius: An Illustrated Biography of the Creator of the Bauhaus*, Boston MA (Little, Brown & Co.) 1991

The Wood House

Architectural Review, vol. 81, February 1937, pp. 61–63
Country Life, vol. 83, supplement, 26 February 1938, pp. xi–xii
Country Life, vol. 120, 17 July 1956, pp. 132–33
Frances Donaldson, *A Twentieth Century Life*, London (Weidenfeld & Nicolson) 1992

Impington Village College

Architects' Journal, vol. 87, 7 April 1938, pp. 587, 591
Architectural Review, vol. 86, December 1939, pp. 224–34
Harry Rée, *Educator Extraordinary: The Life and Achievement of Henry Morris*, London (Longman) 1973

ABOVE: The bay windows of the curved adult wing at Impington, containing the suite of games rooms and the common room, add a domestic touch to a building that tried not to be 'institutional'. These windows were intended to "give a more intimate character to the interiors". Note the darker bricks of the plinth, which give an almost classical sense of hierarchy.

BELOW: The promenade has a wide opening onto a three-sided courtyard. The main classroom wing (below right) was designed so that lessons could easily move out on to the grass in warm weather. The projecting room in the foreground is the original science laboratory, and the five other classrooms stretch in line beyond.

BOTTOM: The plan shows the pinwheel arrangement, which became common for post-war schools in place of the previous preference for symmetry. The public entrance to the assembly hall is closest to the main entrance to the site, but there was also a side entrance to the adult wing, which housed a branch library.

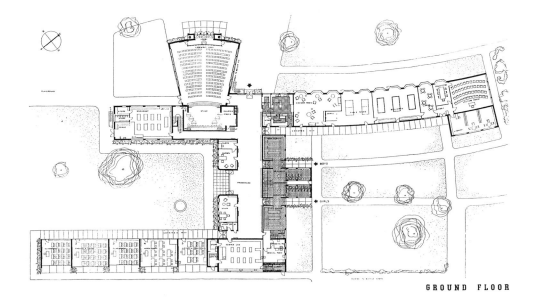

GROUND FLOOR

IMPINGTON VILLAGE COLLEGE
Impington, Cambridgeshire, 1937–39

The 'village college' was the brainchild of Henry Morris, Director of Education for Cambridgeshire, as a means of combining a school with a centre for adults' activities after hours. Impington was the fourth such project to be built, after Jack Pritchard introduced Morris to Gropius. Features of earlier designs persisted, but Gropius configured the layout at Impington around existing trees, making a comfortable pattern of indoor and outdoor space, branching from a wide central corridor known as the 'promenade'.

Extra funds were raised from benefactors, and construction began only after Gropius had left Britain; it was left to Jack Howe to reduce the cost without loss of quality. Impington is the least spectacular of buildings, showing how Gropius internalized English reticence.

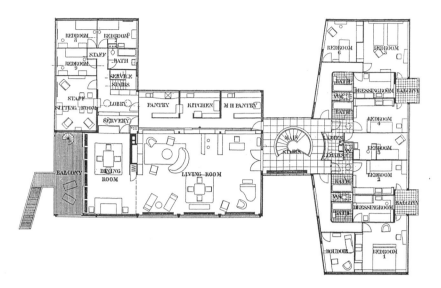

THE HOMEWOOD
Esher, Surrey, 1937–38

During the 1920s Gwynne's parents lived in a Victorian house in Esher, with a large garden of pools, trees and azaleas, close to the Portsmouth Road. By the mid-1930s the traffic noise was becoming unbearable and justified the building of a replacement house at the far corner of the site. The budget was generous, and Patrick Gwynne was able to plan what he called a "two-storey bungalow", raised up to get the best views of the garden and provide outdoor space below. The main rooms of the house are therefore all on one level, with the staircase making a hinge point between the living block and smaller bedroom wing. The plan is dominated by the large living-room, the space of which was carefully structured by the positioning of the furniture.

Patrick Gwynne 1913–2003

The son of a naval officer, Patrick Gwynne was educated at Harrow and fell for modern architecture on a sketching trip to Amersham, Buckinghamshire, where he saw the newly completed High and Over (see pp. 88–89). He was an articled pupil and then joined Wells Coates as an assistant, working alongside Denys Lasdun and launching the commission for The Homewood, Surrey, from the Coates office; he completed it shortly before the War.

After service with the RAF in Canada, Gwynne lived at The Homewood and ran his small practice there, specializing in one-off houses, of which he produced some of the most individual and delightful post-war examples. Each was carefully tailored to the site and the client's needs, with occasional rather baroque gestures.

Gwynne also designed two restaurants in Hyde Park, London, of which only the smaller remains, and the foyer addition to the Theatre Royal, York. In 1992 he offered The Homewood to The National Trust, remaining in occupation while extensive works were carried on around him under the direction of John Allan. The house opened to the public in the spring of 2004.

REFERENCES
Architect
Neil Bingham, 'The Houses of Patrick Gwynne', *Twentieth Century Architecture*, no. 4: *Post-War Houses*, London (Twentieth Century Society) 2000, pp. 30–44

The Homewood
Architectural Review, vol. 86, September 1939, pp. 103–16
Neil Bingham, *The Homewood*, London (National Trust) 2004

ABOVE LEFT AND TOP: The bedroom wing (shown on the right of the first-floor plan) also acts as a *porte-cochère* for the main entrance.

ABOVE: At one corner, the grid of the façade encloses a terrace rather than a room, and an external staircase leads down to the pool and the garden.

ABOVE AND RIGHT: The narrow link that connects the bedroom wing to the main block of the house, which is largely filled by the living-room, can be made out between the trees. The living-room (right) in turn opens into the dining-room.

P.J.B. Harland 1900–1973

Peter Harland studied at the Architectural Association and stayed on as a teacher there, submitting an entry for the RIBA building competition in 1932. At this stage he was not a committed Modernist, but when the composer Arthur Bliss and his wife, Trudy – whom Harland knew through Grace Lovat Fraser, the widow of his cousin the artist Claud Lovat Fraser – wanted to build a weekend and holiday house, he concurred in their desire for a modern building. The composer Gerald Finzi saw and admired Pen Pits but asked Harland to build something more traditional for him at Church Farm, Ashmansworth, Berkshire, in 1938–39.

Harland's main work was in the design of two hospitals: the Tolworth Isolation Hospital, Surrey (1936), and the South Middlesex Isolation Hospital, Isleworth (1936–38). The latter was a major complex, in a middle-of-the-road brick style, and was demolished in the early 1990s. The buildings at the former have been much altered. After the War, Harland was never able to re-establish his practice successfully, although a painting of Pen Pits by Edward Wadsworth, the only country house portrait of its kind by a major British artist, hung in his office as a reminder of better days.

REFERENCES

Pen Pits

Architect and Building News, vol. 143, 16 August 1935, pp. 194–97

F.R.S. Yorke, *The Modern House in England*, London (Architectural Press) 1937, pp. 68–70

Alan Powers, 'Harmonious Mansions: Two Composers' Houses of the 1930s', *Country Life*, vol. 178, 29 August 1985, pp. 559–63

PEN PITS

Penselwood, Somerset, 1934–35

The site was found by the Blisses after searching for a year and takes its name from the Iron Age quern quarries near by. Only a cottage existed on the site, which allowed for the creation of a sizeable garden, now very much matured, and a study for Arthur Bliss in the woods, some distance from the house.

The structure was brick, rendered and painted white, with orchestrated colour in the window frames and curtains. Trudy Bliss was born in California, and the chief feature of the house was the broad first-floor terrace, equipped for sunbathing with curtains along the rails and an outdoor shower. The house was originally lit with oil lamps, as there was no electricity supply.

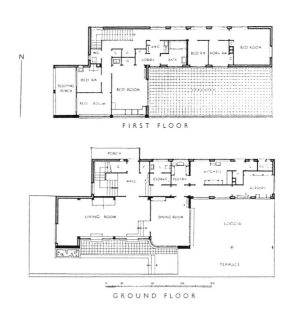

FIRST FLOOR

GROUND FLOOR

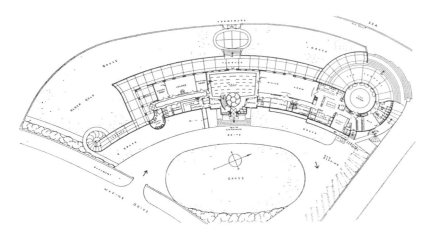

LMS MIDLAND HOTEL
Morecambe, Lancashire, 1932–33

A replacement for a Victorian hotel, the Midland was conceived to boost seaside leisure in Britain during the slump. It was inspired in part by a hotel at St Tropez: Latitude 43, by Georges-Henri Pinguisson, finished in 1932.

The Midland was built with a steel frame and rendered in white cement, with the soffits of the overhanging ledges coated in a sparkling green-coloured render of ground bottle-glass. The interior was sumptuously lined with terrazzo floors, Marion Dorn rugs and plywood walls. The original artworks were outstanding, including a variety of reliefs in stone and plaster by Eric Gill, decorative motifs in the floors, and murals by Eric Ravilious, the last sadly lost to damp at an early date. In 2004 the much-decayed hotel was awaiting restoration by its new owners, the development company Urban Splash.

Oliver Hill 1887–1968

After studying at the Architectural Association, Oliver Hill began practice in 1912 and after the War became one of the most conspicuous eclectic architects, working in a series of fashionable modes including neo-Georgian and vernacular. His interest in Modernism was sparked in Stockholm in 1930 and suited his unconventional lifestyle and love of open air and sun. By 1933 he had completed the LMS Midland Hotel, Morecambe, Lancashire, and a handful of houses, had organized the important design exhibition at Dorland Hall, London, and was planning a modern seaside development at Frinton Park, Essex.

Hill never ceased to design in other styles, but his Modernism matured through projects for schools (of which only one was built). The houses at Hampstead and Poole were a consummation of his learning process. He designed the British Pavilion for the Paris Exhibition in 1937 and played a major role in organizing its displays, in which polite Modernism was joined with wit to traditional craftsmanship. After the War he found it difficult to get work again and built mainly in a classical style, although was still interested in Modernism as seen from his own, primarily aesthetic, viewpoint. He was friendly with many artists and found ways to use their work in his buildings, regardless of style.

The entrance to the Midland Hotel (opposite) was surmounted by stylized carved seahorses by Eric Gill, whose stone relief of Odysseus being received out of the waves by Nausicaa (above) will soon return to its original home after many wanderings. The circular café (above left), with murals by Eric Ravilious, was designed for use by non-residents.

Oliver Hill

ABOVE AND LEFT: The mature Victorian landscape provided Joldwynds with a setting of deep green, while the stepped profile aligned with the distant Leith Hill. The curve of the entrance front is one of Hill's most dramatic compositions, the shadows of which are richly portrayed in this original photograph, which would have been closely supervised by Hill himself.

JOLDWYNDS
Holmbury St Mary, Surrey, 1931–32

The original house on the site, built by Philip Webb in 1891, was bought by the lawyer Wilfred Greene, a former client of Oliver Hill who subsequently became Master of the Rolls. The Webb house was demolished, and a replacement, Hill's first major Modernist venture, was built on the site, closer to the brow of the hill. The body of the house is broken up with terraces and loggias, not otherwise found so extensively in English Modernism, and the curves of the entrance front on plan are reproduced in flights of garden steps. C.H. Reilly wrote: "There must still, in the most ascetic of universes, be a few baroque folk with whom one would hope to spend an occasional weekend. For such an occasion I confess I should prefer Joldwynds to the strictest Corbusier–Connell rectangularity" (C.H. Reilly, 'The Year's Work', *Architects' Journal*, vol. 81, 10 January 1935, p. 69).

The Greenes found, however, that the external render crazed and fell off in places, while the hard surfaces of the interior were uncomfortable. Having pursued Hill for compensation, they sold the house and built another, designed by Tecton with a pitched roof, higher up the site.

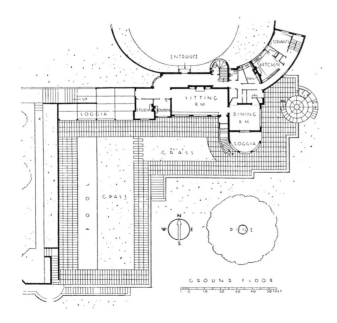

GROUND FLOOR

ABOVE: Inside there were few rooms. The living-room was furnished with paintings by Ivon Hitchens, then scarcely known as a modern landscape artist; he was commissioned by Hill, who also designed the furniture. The dining-room features a succession of spaces that lead back into the kitchen area behind, giving the illusion of perspective.

LEFT: The plan shows Hill's flair in extending the house into the garden with various forms of terracing and levels, in which devices developed by Sir Edwin Lutyens in the Edwardian period were translated into Modernist forms. "I believe the strictest sect of new-worlders does not admit his jolly curved rooms and terraces, clearly designed more for a leisured and rather lazy life than for hard thinking, to be sufficiently puritanical", wrote C.H. Reilly.

LEFT: Curves were a feature of most of Hill's designs, as seen in an original photo of brave purchasers of the first houses enjoying summer activities.

BELOW: The Round House on Cliff Way (bottom) served originally as the information and sales office for the new estate, so Hill commissioned a picture map in mosaic for the floor from the artists Clifford and Rosemary Ellis, which shows the building itself, amid boldly projected new streets.

Oliver Hill

FRINTON PARK ESTATE
Essex, 1934–38

The South Coast Development Company was founded by Francis Arnatt, working with the builder Frederick Tibbenham, who introduced Oliver Hill to the scheme. They hoped to build a complete Modernist settlement to the north of Edwardian Frinton for owners of holiday houses keen to "escape the typical English seaside resort". Hill drew up ambitious plans for a civic centre (of which a fragment was constructed) and a hotel that, if built, would have eclipsed the Midland with its sheer simplicity.

About twenty modern houses were built, the majority to designs by Hill, the remainder by Etchells, Sisson and other lesser-known Modernists, and a similar number to designs by the builders. The buyers usually, however, rejected flat-roofed houses. By 1935 the company was facing bankruptcy, and Hill resigned. The remaining land was sold to local estate agents, but the losses were never fully recovered.

THE PROSPECT INN

Minster-in-Thanet, Kent, 1936–39

The Prospect Inn stands on a busy road junction, near Manston Aerodrome, and was one of the more successful Modernist pub designs of the 1930s. Hill's interest in planning with curved forms is apparent not only in the main oval of the building but also in the flanking wings to the rear. A mast rises from the 'prow' of the upper storey, with an electric star, while a delightful curvy name sign stood originally on the serpentine dwarf wall by the roadside. In the bars decorative linoleum floors showed giant leaf patterns.

Although the Prospect Inn remains standing, much of the fine detailing has been lost over the years.

TOP: There were many architect-designed pubs in the 1930s, a few of them modern in style, but none more ingenious than the Prospect Inn, with its coloured floors of inlaid linoleum featuring giant foliage (as seen in the original saloon bar), and PEL furniture in tubular steel.

ABOVE AND RIGHT: Hill's love of irregular curves, seen in the exterior views and the plan, was similar to developments in South American architecture during the 1940s.

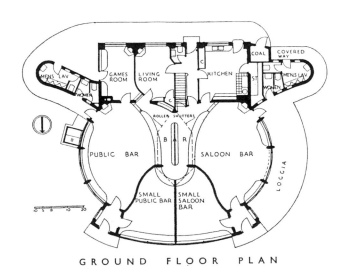

GROUND FLOOR PLAN

LEFT AND OPPOSITE: The peculiar features of the Hill House site brought out the architect's ingenuity, and it resembles no other house of its period. The brick portico was part of a bull-nosed form at each end of the building, and draws together the approaches to the house from the street below and from the garden terrace in a theatrical but graceful gesture.

BELOW: The living-room, separated from the study by sliding doors, shows a contrast of surface materials in which Hill, whose roots were in the Arts and Crafts movement, relished the new expressiveness that was developing in Modernism.

Oliver Hill

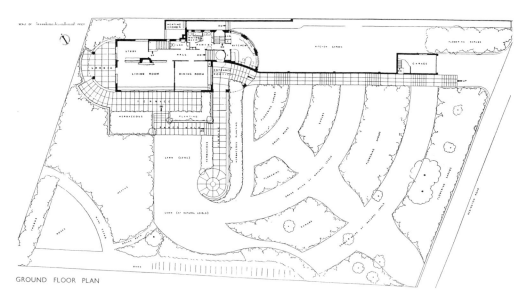

GROUND FLOOR PLAN

THE HILL HOUSE

Redington Road, Hampstead, London NW3, 1936–38

Commissioned by Gerald Schlesinger, who was also involved in Raymond McGrath's St Ann's Hill at Chertsey, Surrey (see p. 184), this house stands on one of the highest points in London. Hill placed it at the top of the site and chose brick construction, which expressed, in Nikolaus Pevsner's words, "that keen sense of joy which goes through all his houses in whatever phantastic disguise it may have appeared in the past" (Nikolaus Pevsner, 'The Modern Movement', MS, 1939, Getty Center, Los Angeles).

The house was approached up a long flight of steps through a bull-nosed portico; another internal stair reached the main rooms, linked to face south across a levelled lawn with a bastion-like retaining wall. The gardens were laid out by Christopher Tunnard.

ABOVE: The approach to the Hill House is now much altered, and, although poor-quality later additions have been replaced by two coherent upper levels designed by John Allan, this distant view up the slopes of the lower garden is no longer obtainable.

Oliver Hill

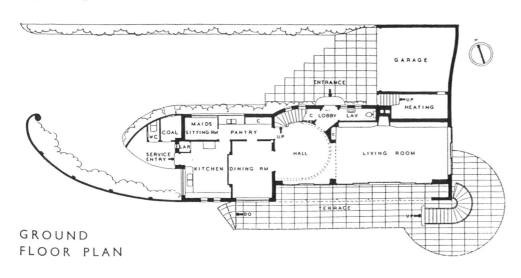

GROUND FLOOR PLAN

LANDFALL
Crichel Mount Road, Poole, Dorset, 1936–38

Commissioned by a young documentary film director, Dudley Shaw Ashton, Landfall is set among pine trees, overlooking Poole Harbour. Ashton had previously interviewed Erich Mendelsohn and Berthold Lubetkin but preferred Hill's approach and made a film of the construction process. The house is set end-on to the road, with the main rooms laid out in a line along the south front, partly recessed behind a double veranda with a balletic external stair at the far end. A hall, positioned between the living-room and dining-room, has a circular ceiling pattern that guides the ascent of the stair.

The construction was of rendered brick. Timber frames were used for the main ground-floor sliding doors, and metal windows elsewhere, painted green.

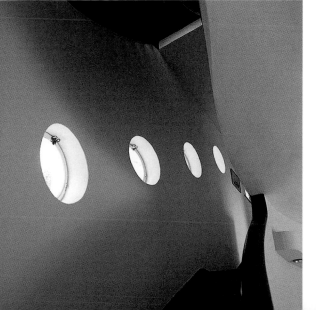

REFERENCES

Architect
Oliver Hill, *Fair Horizon: Buildings of Today*, London (Collins) 1950

Alan Powers, *Oliver Hill: Architect and Lover of Life*, London (Mouton Publications) 1989

LMS Midland Hotel
Architecture Illustrated, vol. 7, August 1933, pp. 72–101

Architectural Review, vol. 74, September 1933, pp. 93–99

Country Life, vol. 74, 18 November 1933, pp. 539–43

The Builder, vol. 145, 1933, pp. 378, 380–83

Alan Powers, 'The Stone and the Shell: Eric Gill and the Midland Hotel, Morecambe', *Book Collector*, vol. 47, 1998, pp. 43–66

Joldwynds
Architecture Illustrated, vol. 6, June 1933, pp. 170–74

Country Life, vol. 76, 15 September 1934, pp. 276–81

Architectural Review, vol. 76, October 1934, pp. 115–16

Frinton Park estate
The Builder, vol. 147, 7 September 1934, pp. 382–87; vol. 155, December 1938, p. 788

Building, vol. 9, 1934, pp. 482–87

Country Life, vol. 78, 17 August 1935, pp. 182–83

F.R.S. Yorke, *The Modern House in England*, London (The Architectural Press) 1937, pp. 38, 104–05

RIBA Journal, vol. 86, November 1979, pp. 496–99

The Prospect Inn
Architects' Journal, vol. 88, 24 November 1938, pp. 856–59

Architect and Building News, vol. 157, 6 January 1939, pp. 7–9

The Hill House
Country Life, vol. 85, 28 January 1939, pp. 96–97

Architectural Review, vol. 85, April 1939, pp. 187–89

The Builder, vol. 156, 1939, pp. 427–29

Architects' Journal, vol. 215, 9 May 2002, pp. 36–43 (restoration by John Allan)

Landfall
Architectural Review, vol. 85, May 1939, pp. 224–25

Country Life, vol. 86, supplement, 25 September 1939, pp. xxxv–xxxvii

Hoar, Marlow & Lovett HAROLD FRANK HOAR, 1909–1976; ALAN F. MARLOW; W.F.B. LOVETT

In September 1933 Morris Jackaman bought an existing airfield, on the railway line midway between London and Brighton, that had the potential for handling commercial flights. According to legend, the young Jackaman was puzzling late one night in 1934 how to achieve a terminal building with a limited budget when his father, a building contractor, came into the room, and said, "Oh! For Heaven's sake, go to bed, you're just thinking in circles." This accidentally prompted the idea of a circular terminal, which then formed part of the brief to the architects. Alan Marlow was the chief designer involved in making the drawings, but little information is recorded about this practice. Jackaman patented the idea of the telescopic jetty, which meant that, by using a subway from the railway station, passengers could board their planes without needing to go outdoors.

Difficulties with draining the site delayed the work by a year, and the terminal was opened in May 1936 for use by British Airways Ltd. In 1956 the 'Beehive', as it was called, closed for passengers. In 1958 the new Gatwick Airport opened, further to the north, to a design by F.R.S. Yorke's new practice, Yorke, Rosenberg, Mardall, leaving the 'Beehive' as an office building.

THE 'BEEHIVE' TERMINAL

Beehive Ring Road, off Gatwick Road, Crawley, West Sussex, 1934–36

The main construction is in reinforced concrete, with floors supported on two ring beams, 38 feet and 80 feet in diameter. The ring beams are supported at six points where they meet the ground-level entrance and the five 'fingers' that extend into the airfield. The remainder is built with a steel frame infilled in brick. The subway (now shut off) emerged on the east side of the main concourse, which had a central island of shops. A restaurant on the first floor could seat eighty, with a hundred more on the terrace outside.

The interiors were mainly designed by a Mrs Arnold of Reens-Arta Ltd, Mayfair, who used a colour scheme of green and pink.

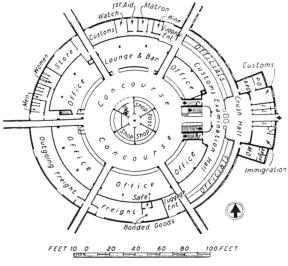

FEET 10 0   20   40   60   80   100 FEET

GROUND FLOOR PLAN

REFERENCES

The 'Beehive' Terminal

Architect and Building News,
    vol. 145, 6 March 1936,
    p. 295; vol. 146, 5 June 1936,
    pp. 270–71
Architects' Journal, vol. 83, 4 June
    1936, pp. 368–73
Architectural Review, vol. 80, July
    1936, p. 32
John King, 'Gatwick's Beehive:
    A Forgotten Development',
    Thirties Society Journal, no. 2,
    1982, pp. 25–28

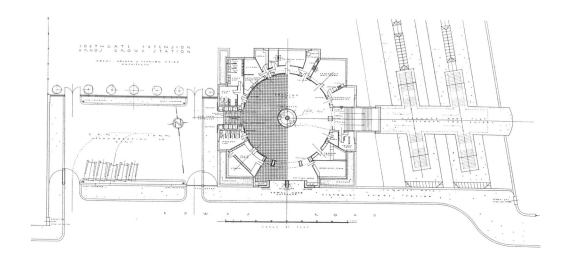

LEFT: The circular plan of Arnos Grove is partly explained when one sees that it acts as a junction for three pedestrian routes, skilfully encouraging separate pathways from the car park, the street or the platform.

BELOW AND OPPOSITE: Internally, the exposed concrete is softened by the panels of brick, while the height, as in most of Holden's stations, gives a sense of dignity. Thanks to protection by listing, this station has been spared some of the insensitive alterations that have damaged the legacy of Pick and Holden since the Second World War.

ARNOS GROVE UNDERGROUND STATION
Bowes Road, London N11, 1932

The prototype station for the Piccadilly line extension was Sudbury Town (1930), which established the brick box form with a projecting concrete lid, making a high booking hall within, lit from a continuous clerestory that acted like a beacon at night.

The roughness of the reddish brick added a rustic quality to the designs, in which a simple palette of brick, tile and concrete was deployed to avoid monotony within the carefully controlled design formula. At Arnos Grove the tight drum shape of the booking hall recalls Gunnar Asplund's much larger but similar Stockholm Public Library of 1928.

Charles Holden 1875–1960

Charles Holden was brought up in straitened circumstances in St Helens, Lancashire, and was articled as an architect in Manchester. He showed a talent for architecture and friendship with artists, and was inspired by Walt Whitman's poetry.

After moving to London, Holden worked for C.R. Ashbee before joining Percy Adams, a hospital architect, in 1899, when his austerely handsome but inventive massing and elevations accompanied Adams's knowledgeable plans. With the Central Reference Library, Bristol (1905–07), Holden emerged as one of the finest younger architects in Britain. Lionel Pearson became a third partner in 1913. An incipient Modernism can be found in early work by Holden and reappeared in the 1920s with his first Underground stations, on the Northern line. His Continental journey in 1930 with Frank Pick was a further turning-point: he took ideas from Sweden, Germany and The Netherlands but remixed them into a London style that contributed to London Underground's wide-ranging design strategy, extending, as Nikolaus Pevsner put it, "from teaspoons to trains".

After the stations, no work by Holden created such electricity again, and his buildings for the University of London, although highly skilled, are restrained to the point of coldness.

SOUTHGATE UNDERGROUND STATION
Southgate Circus, London N14, 1932–33

A broader, flatter drum than Arnos Grove, Southgate is a
transport interchange for trains and buses, which occupied
their own co-ordinated building next door. The ground level
is ringed with shops, with three entrances, and a pair of
escalators descending that still retain their distinctive period
uplighters. A column rises at the centre, forming a decorative
turret with a ball on top, a Modernist adaptation of the
traditional cupola.

LEFT: One stop beyond Arnos
Grove, Southgate is an
interchange for buses and tubes,
with more than the usual
number of lettable shops
forming a 'parade' on Station
Road. The finial on top of the
circular station concourse and
the multi-branched light near by
both have a sense of quirky
humour that often lightens the
mood of the Underground.

OPPOSITE: Close up, the quality
of the brickwork, laid in warmly
coloured sandy mortar, is
typical of Holden's Arts and
Crafts roots.

Charles Holden

REFERENCES
Architect
Charles Hutton, 'Dr Charles
   Holden', *Artifex*, vol. 3, 1969,
   pp. 35–53
Christian Barman, *The Man
   who Built London Transport:
   A Biography of Frank Pick*,
   Newton Abbot (David &
   Charles) 1979
*Charles Holden: Architect,
   1875–1960*, exhib. cat. by
   Eitan Karol and Finch
   Allibone, London, Heinz
   Gallery, 1988
David Lawrence, *Underground
   Architecture*, Harrow (Capital
   Transport) 1994
M.T. Saler, *The Avant-Garde in
   Interwar England: Medieval*

*Modernism and the London
   Underground*, New York and
   Oxford (Oxford University
   Press) 1999

**Arnos Grove Underground
   Station**
Architects' Journal, vol. 76,
   28 December 1932,
   pp. 819–26

**Southgate Underground
   Station**
Architects' Journal, vol. 77,
   26 April 1933, pp. 553–56

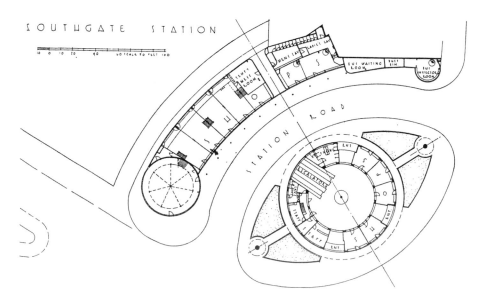

SOUTHGATE STATION

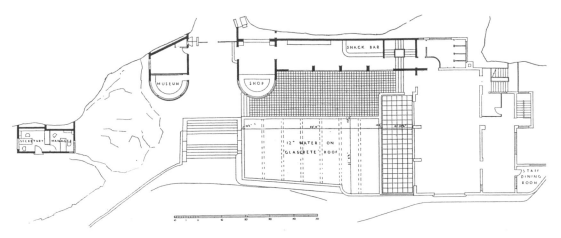

BELOW: "Anything with a pitched roof would have looked absurd in this position", wrote C.H. Reilly when the Caveman Restaurant was first published. These two photos show the initial phase, with open-air seating between the two arms of the building.

OPPOSITE: The infilling of this space with a restaurant for parties of 300 had not been anticipated; the glass roof was primarily a functional requirement owing to the lack of height and the need for lighting and cooling in the space below, rather than a sought-after visual effect.

Geoffrey Jellicoe 1900–1996

Geoffrey Jellicoe studied at the Architectural Association. His formative experience was a study tour of Italian gardens undertaken in 1924 with J.C. Shepherd, which resulted in the publication of *Italian Gardens of the Renaissance* (1925). Jellicoe also taught at the Architectural Association from 1929 and designed a garden for the furniture maker Gordon Russell at Chipping Camden, Gloucestershire. The commission for the Caveman Restaurant in 1933 was the catalyst for Jellicoe's change to Modernism, working with Russell Page, a garden designer, although he continued to carry out garden work in a simplified historic style.

Having been Principal of the Architectural Association at the beginning of the War, Jellicoe had a post-war practice divided between architecture and landscape, creating the War Memorial Gardens at Walsall and the water gardens at Harlow New Town. The J.F. Kennedy Memorial at Runnymede (1965) was his breakthrough to a more symbolically loaded approach to landscape design, which occupied the long remainder of his career and established him as the sage of landscape theory through such designs as Sutton Place, Guildford, begun in 1980. With his wife, Susan, he was author of *The Landscape of Man* (1975). He was a founder member of the Institute of Landscape Architects in 1929, and later its president.

REFERENCES
Architect
Michael Spens, *Gardens of the Mind: The Genius of Geoffrey Jellicoe*, Woodbridge (Antique Collectors Club) 1992
Michael Spens, *The Complete Landscape Designs and Gardens of Geoffrey Jellicoe*, London (Thames and Hudson) 1994

Caveman Restaurant
Architects' Journal, vol. 79, 28 June 1934, pp. 922, 929–31
Architect and Building News, vol. 138, 29 June 1934, p. 371
Architectural Association Journal, vol. 50, October 1934, pp. 118–27

Architects' Journal, vol. 81, 30 May 1935, pp. 831–34
Henry-Russell Hitchcock and Catherine Bauer, *Modern Architecture in England*, New York (Museum of Modern Art) 1937, no. 33
Russell Page, *The Education of a Gardener*, London (Collins) 1962
Alan Powers, 'In Search of the Caveman Restaurant', *Thirties Society Journal*, no. 5, 1984, pp. 18–23

CAVEMAN RESTAURANT

Cheddar Gorge, Somerset, 1934, extended 1935 and 1936
(with Russell Page)

The management of the Cheddar caves, a popular tourist
attraction, reverted in 1930 to their owner, the 4th Marquess
of Bath, whose heir, Viscount Weymouth, took them over.
A new building was needed for food, drink and visitor
facilities. The first phase consisted of two ranges at right
angles to each other. The space between was turned into
another restaurant, with a glass roof of pavement lights,
above which goldfish swam in a shallow pool. More additions
in subsequent years have lost the clarity of the original
concept and involved removing the pool. There was a mural
by Eliot Hodgkin and furniture by Gordon Russell Ltd.

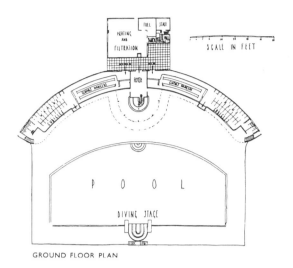

HEATING AND FILTRATION

SCALE IN FEET

POOL

DIVING STAGE

GROUND FLOOR PLAN

BELOW AND OPPOSITE:
The sinuous line of the balcony, combined with the centrepiece in the style of Erich Mendelsohn, gives Saltdean prime place in lido architecture. The site faces south, where the valley broadens towards the sea, encouraging the symmetrical approach that lido designers happily adopted in order to balance male and female changing rooms around central facilities.

LEFT: The diving stage noted on the plan has, like almost all others of its type, long been demolished for safety reasons.

R.W.H. Jones 1900–1965

Saltdean is a few miles east of Brighton, East Sussex, where a valley drops down through the chalk downs. The lido at Saltdean was part of a larger development planned by Jones, including a hotel on the hilltop, which, when seen from the road, resembles the LMS Midland Hotel at Morecambe, Lancashire (see pp. 136–37). Among the houses built in the valley in the 1930s were three designed by Connell, Ward & Lucas.

REFERENCES
Saltdean Lido
Architectural Design and Construction, vol. 8, September 1938, p. 342

SALTDEAN LIDO
Saltdean, East Sussex, 1938

The open pool with a café provided for five hundred bathers. It is separated from the beach by an elevated roadway but linked to it via a tunnel. Construction is of reinforced concrete, with a symmetrical plan adapted to the triangular site, and the building is wrapped in an embrace around the pool.

Among the many open-air pools (traditionally called lidos) built in the 1930s, Saltdean was always one of the most attractive. Fortunately it has survived to become a listed building when others have been lost, although its future is not permanently assured.

BELOW: The Bata factory was
built to the same pattern,
developed by František Gahura,
in the company towns
established all round the world.
Together with the 'Bata Hotel',
originally a workmen's hostel,
it rises above the flat landscape
of south Essex.

BATA ESTATE
East Tilbury, Essex, 1933–c. 1950

The British Bata Company was established in 1933 and
began building a company town at East Tilbury, with its own
railway halt. The layout followed Gahura's model for Zlin,
which provided family houses with gardens rather than
apartments for all married workers, and dormitory 'hotels'
for the single. This housing attracted workers to the
otherwise rather bleak and isolated settlement from the
more traditional centres of shoe manufacture in the
Midlands. The factory of 1933 was a five-storey rectangular
block, the same height as the hotel of 1936. Most of the
remainder of the town consists of a grid of residential
streets, with flat-roofed concrete houses.

Vladimir Karfik 1901–1996

Karfik studied at the Technical University in Prague and in Paris with Auguste
Perret, André Lurçat and Adolf Loos; he also worked for a few weeks for
Le Corbusier. Karfik travelled to the United States in 1925, and, after experience
with Holbird & Root in Chicago, worked for Frank Lloyd Wright but returned
home in 1930, having met Jan Bata in Chicago. His skill in languages, combined
with a thorough technical training, was useful to the company, and Karfik followed
František Gahura as the company's chief architect at the company town of Zlin
in central Czechoslovakia. Gahura had already pioneered a standardized concrete
skeleton system with round columns, which Karfik continued to use in the
seventeen-storey administrative block at the Bata factory, with a movable office for
Jan Bata. His overseas work at this time included Bata factory towns at Belcamp
in the United States and Borovo in Yugoslavia, as well as East Tilbury in Britain.

Under Communism, Karfik taught at Bratislava in the Slovak Technical University
and after his official retirement in 1971 continued to lecture at the Old University
at Valletta, Malta, where he also designed the president's residence. In 1993 he
published his autobiography, *An Architect Reminisces*, and was awarded a gold medal
by President Václav Havel.

REFERENCES
Architect
Vladimir Slapeta, *Czech
 Functionalism*, London
 (Architectural Association)
 1987
Vladimir Slapeta, *Bata,
 Architectura e Urbanismus*,
 1910–50, exhib. cat., Zlin,
 State Gallery, 1991

Bata Estate
Jane Pavitt, 'The Bata Project',
 Twentieth Century Architecture,
 no. 1: *Industrial Architecture*,
 London (Twentieth Century
 Society) 1994, pp. 32–44

ABOVE AND RIGHT: The repetitive flat-roofed houses have little about them to indicate that they are in England – apart, perhaps, from the individualism of the paint colours. They have evidently proved themselves adaptable and serviceable during a period of more than sixty years.

46A DICK PLACE
Newington, Edinburgh, 1932

The house was built by Kininmonth for himself, around
the time of his marriage in 1934. He lived there for the
rest of his life. The structure is brick, and this was originally
lime-washed a light buff colour. This showed the texture
of the material, with the horizontal joints raked out, and
harmonized with yellow paintwork on the timber windows
(it was known locally as 'the ice-cream house').

The dining area was separated only by a tweed curtain
from the large living-room, which had a wide opening into
the hall. There were solid upholstered armchairs, but tubular-
steel upright chairs by Marcel Breuer. The stairs use Lutyens's
trick of black treads and white risers.

BELOW AND OPPOSITE: By
keeping his living-room as a
single-storey volume, Kininmonth
succeeded in making a dynamic
composition out of a small
house, centring it around the
pivot of the living-room chimney
threaded through the canopy of
the second bedroom. These
compositional devices probably
derive from the widespread
influence of Erich Mendelsohn.
The separation of the garage
from the main house on the
plan indicates an unusual
awareness of the value of spaces
between buildings at this period.

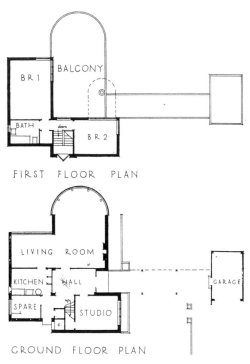

William Kininmonth 1904–1988

William Kininmonth was articled to an architect in Leith and attended evening
classes at Edinburgh College of Art and Heriot-Watt College, Edinburgh. He then
worked for Sir Rowand Anderson & Paul in Edinburgh, and for a short period in
London with Sir Edwin Lutyens on the design of New Delhi. Kininmonth accepted
a partnership with Balfour Paul, setting a condition that his friend Basil Spence,
already noted as a brilliant draughtsman, should come with him. It was agreed,
provided they shared one drawing-board in the office. They worked essentially as
separate entities, however, and Spence's post-war international fame far
outstripped Kininmonth's, although the latter sustained a considerable practice after
the War, as Sir William Kininmonth, Anderson & Paul (he was knighted in 1972).

Both Kininmonth and Spence experimented with Modernism in the early years
of the decade (including a house in 1932 for Dr King at 11 Easter Belmont Road,
Edinburgh, which was contemporary with Kininmonth's own house) but reverted
to more traditional styles, often with a strong regional flavour. As Kininmonth
later recalled: "We rather prided ourselves on being able to work in any style"
(quoted in Charles McKean, *The Scottish Thirties*, Edinburgh (Scottish Academic
Press) 1987, p. 36).

REFERENCES
46A Dick Place
Architect and Building News,
vol. 144, 11 October 1935,
pp. 40–41

32 NEWTON ROAD
London W2, 1937–38

The building at 32 Newton Road was designed as a studio house for the artist F.J. Conway in a street of early Victorian stucco villas. (It was later owned by Ronald Searle.) Derivation from Le Corbusier's Maison Cook, Boulogne-sur-Seine, Paris (1926), has always been recognized but is tellingly – in view of Lasdun's later liking for the monumental – made into an axial composition. The brown tiles of the façade are similar to Berthold Lubetkin's Highpoint II (see p. 171) in Highgate, north London, as was the ironic incorporation of a nineteenth-century French Rococo fireplace in the main living-room.

Lasdun stressed the urban context of the house when publishing it in the *Architectural Review*, showing how the street could hypothetically be completed with a row of similar houses.

BELOW: These two original photos were staged to show how the living-room could equally well be furnished with a client's antique pieces as with modern items, thus providing "a demonstration of the principle that … good examples of any period combine well provided that they have character in common, character being a design attribute rather than a chronological one". The salvaged Victorian fireplace was considered to work well with both arrangements.

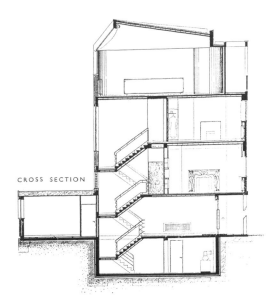

CROSS SECTION

Denys Lasdun 1914–2001

Educated at Rugby and the Architectural Association, Lasdun visited Le Corbusier's Paris buildings when a student. He worked with Wells Coates and, having completed the studio house in Newton Road, London, with Lubetkin and Tecton, became a partner in the firm in 1946–50, after completing a distinguished war service. He completed the Hallfield estate, Paddington, London, a project begun with Lubetkin, and the Hallfield School marked a new stage of his development towards sculptural building forms with dramatic effect. Lasdun was then a partner with Maxwell Fry in Fry, Drew, Drake & Lasdun, and headed the firm's work in Britain while Fry and Jane Drew were working overseas.

After Lasdun had set up his own practice in 1959, when his Royal College of Physicians building in London was completed, the 1960s were the peak years of his activity, when he built the University of East Anglia, college buildings in Cambridge, and the School of Oriental and African Studies Library and Institute of Education for the University of London. Most of these projects use some version of a raked profile, capable of linear extension and heavily constructed in concrete. The National Theatre, London, a scheme begun in 1963, was opened in 1975 and has become a much-loved, if controversial, building.

REFERENCES
Architect
Denys Lasdun & Partners, *A Language and a Theme: The Architecture of Denys Lasdun & Partners*, London (RIBA Publications) 1977
Denys Lasdun (ed.), *Architecture in an Age of Scepticism*, London (Heinemann) 1984
William J.R. Curtis, *Denys Lasdun: Architecture, City, Landscape*, London (Phaidon) 1994

32 Newton Road
F.R.S. Yorke, *The Modern House in England*, London (Architectural Press), 2nd edn, 1944, pp. 98–102
Architects' Journal, vol. 89, 30 March 1939, pp. 539–41
Architectural Review, vol. 85, March 1939, pp. 119–32

OPPOSITE: The studio originally had a solid, curved screen wall, which formed a background for models and sitters internally, beneath the balcony trellis, since the light came from sloping glazing towards the north. The three supports for the balcony panel were painted a dark colour in order to give the impression that it was floating. Beneath the windows the original matt brown tiles have been painted over. Such details of colour are important in transmitting the architect's intentions.

The pool was built on the site of earlier defensive works, to provide swimming facilities on an otherwise rocky beach, with spectacular views towards St Michael's Mount. The pool filled at every high tide, and the water was originally floodlit at night, with the intention of holding concerts. Dressing boxes and a café are built into the side walls, which are wide enough to allow for sunbathing.

Having been threatened with various redevelopment schemes, the pool was listed in 1993. The local authority then carried out repairs, which recovered the pool's understated elegance. The architect M.J. Long has been involved in making proposals for generating more income without spoiling the building.

Frank Latham

As Borough Engineer for Penwith District Council, Cornwall, Captain Frank Latham was the designer of the Jubilee Pool, Penzance, completed in 1935 and named to commemorate the Silver Jubilee of George V. The local newspaper reported:

Jutting out into the sea, exposed to the full violence of the south-easterly and southerly gales, ... the interior of the pool is not only a fine piece of engineering – it is also a work of art ... there are graceful curves and pleasing lines – an adaptation of Cubism to the terraces and diving platforms which enhances the effect and makes the whole so pleasing to the eye.

REFERENCES
Jason Orton, 'The Great
    Outdoors', *Blueprint*, no. 197,
July 2002, pp. 62–67

ABOVE: The narrow openings to the side of the pool are the individual changing spaces common in more old-fashioned English pools, both indoor and outdoor.

OPPOSITE: The Jubilee Pool may represent a form of accidental Modernism, deriving from an engineer's direct approach to structure and materials combined with some residual classical details – an example being the curving steps, which add to the design's natural, unpretentious elegance. As a result, the pool has many supporters both locally and further afield.

William Lescaze 1896–1969

Born in Switzerland and educated in Geneva and Zurich (under the first-generation Modernist Karl Moser), Lescaze went to the United States in 1920 and established his own practice in 1923 in New York. In 1929, having become a naturalized US citizen, he went into partnership with George Howe. The joint names in the partnership persisted, although Howe dropped out in 1932. During this time they designed and completed the Philadelphia Saving Fund Society building in Pennsylvania, the first Modernist skyscraper in the United States, and Lescaze built the smaller but still influential Oak Lane Country Day School (1929), from which the English head, W.B. Curry, was headhunted to lead Dartington Hall School in Devon. Curry took Lescaze as architect for High Cross House (although too late for Lescaze to design the school itself) and a number of other buildings on the Dartington estate.

After disappointing sales of speculative seaside houses by Lescaze at Churston Bay, Devon, Dartington Hall's building company reverted to more traditional architects, but his work in the United States picked up, and he was designer of the Swiss Pavilion at the 1939 World's Fair in New York.

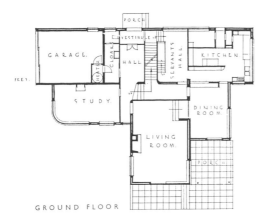

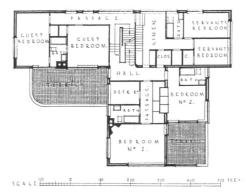

GROUND FLOOR

FIRST FLOOR

SCALE

OPPOSITE: The angle between the living-room and the study makes a strong composition of planes.

RIGHT: These views show clearly the blue colouring of the rearmost volume of the house. This bold contrast had been lost for many years, but was restored by John Winter.

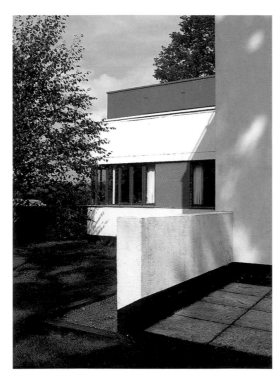

RIGHT: The generous American scale of the house is seen in the opening between the dining-room and living-room, now furnished as far as possible with the original pieces of the 1930s. The house is normally open to the public on afternoons from Tuesday to Friday between May and October (for details, see www.dartingtonhall.org.uk/pages/heritage_and_buildings/highcrosshouse.html).

HIGH CROSS HOUSE
Dartington, Devon, 1930–32

High Cross is a substantial house in rendered brick, designed for the headmaster of the progressive Dartington Hall School, founded by Leonard and Dorothy Elmhirst as part of their project for rural regeneration. Letters record the commissioning process in great detail, including the attempts to make the kitchen a demonstration of ergonomics. The inexperience of the builders caused problems, however, although these were solved in later Modernist buildings at Dartington.

High Cross was widely publicized when new, and again in 1995, when it reopened as a gallery and archive centre, following a restoration by John Winter.

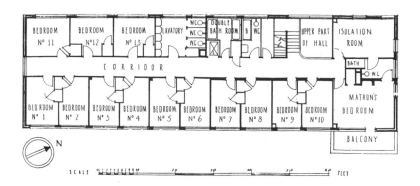

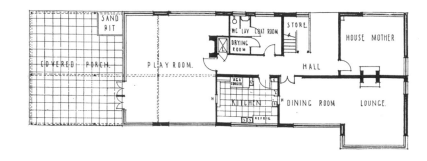

SCALE 0 10 20 30 40 50 60 FEET

William Lescaze

REFERENCES

Architect

Christian Hubert and Lindsay
    Stamm Shapiro, *William
    Lescaze*, New York
    (IAAS/Rizzoli) 1982
Lorraine Welling Lanmon,
    William Lescaze: Architect,
    Philadelphia (Associated
    University Presses) 1987

High Cross House

Country Life, vol. 73, 11 February
    1933, pp. 144–49
Architects' Journal, vol. 78,
    12 October 1933,
    pp. 443–45
F.R.S. Yorke, *The Modern House
    in England*, London

(Architectural Press) 1937,
    pp. 64–65
Lawrence Wodehouse, 'Lescaze
    and Dartington Hall',
    *Architectural Association
    Quarterly*, vol. 8, 1976,
    pp. 2–14
Michael Young, *The Elmhirsts of
    Dartington*, London
    (Routledge) 1982
Architects' Journal, vol. 198,
    22 September 1993,
    pp. 32–33; vol. 201,
    9 February 1995, pp. 24–25
Country Life, vol. 189, 3 August
    1995, pp. 50–53
Maggie Giraud (ed.), *House for
    Mr Curry*, Dartington
    (Dartington Hall Trust) 1995

Boarding Houses

Architectural Review, vol. 75,
    April 1934, pp. 119–22

ABOVE: "Functional architecture is
happier in the country than in the
town", wrote the psychologist
Gerald Heard in the *Architectural
Review* in response to these
buildings. "It keeps its surface
brightness unsmirched by soot
and, as a design, how suited, with
its great extent of window and
its large space of porch leading
straight into the woodland, is it
for children of an outdoor age,
an age which is beginning to
understand that the country may
now lead the town and not the
town the country." The boarding
houses' interiors were delicately
coloured and originally furnished
with modern pieces similar to
those at High Cross.

BOARDING HOUSES

Dartington Hall School, Devon, 1933–35
(with Robert Hening)

The boarding houses consist of three almost identical blocks,
built in echelon formation in successive summer holidays
and originally set among birch trees. Dartington believed in
mixed-gender houses, containing individual rooms for pupils
on the upper floor and communal spaces below. Each house
included accommodation for a 'house parent'.

    The construction problems of High Cross were overcome,
and these light concrete buildings proved their economic
value. The later addition of fire escapes could not fail to spoil
the clean lines.

The Penguin Pool is one of the most popular Modern Movement buildings; its sculptural forms, derived from Russian Constructivism, dramatized the walking, swimming and diving of the penguins. Ove Arup's engineering was crucial to the design of the ramps, which are invisibly supported by massive abutments.

The pool was comprehensively repaired, with some original features re-created, through a collaboration between John Allan of Avanti Architects and Lubetkin in 1987. In 2004 the zoo announced that the pool would not in future be used to house penguins, since the birds mated more successfully in less exposed surroundings.

Berthold Lubetkin 1901–1990

Born in Tbilisi, Georgia, Berthold Lubetkin witnessed the Russian Revolution at first hand, including the experimental art training that was instituted in its wake. In 1922 he travelled to Berlin, where he studied, before moving on to Warsaw and later to Paris, where he studied in the Atelier Perret. He began to practise in Paris in 1927 but moved to London in 1931 with the prospect of a private house commission. The following year he founded Tecton, with Anthony Chitty, Lindsay Drake, Michael Dugdale, Valentine Harding, Godfrey Samuel and Francis Skinner, all recent Architectural Association graduates, several of them with good social connections that brought in jobs. Lubetkin was the chief creative force, although collaborators were named for various projects, and Ove Arup played a key role as structural engineer.

From the London Zoo buildings of 1933–34 onwards, through the Highpoint flats in Highgate, north London, and concluding with the Finsbury Health Centre, London, Lubetkin and Tecton's buildings are among the most immediately appealing, as well as culturally and technically the richest, of the decade. Most of them redefined the agenda for modern architecture in some respect, with a conspectus of early, middle and late styles coming rapidly after one another. After

1936 several of the founder partners left to work independently, leaving Drake and Skinner, along with an office containing a wide variety of home-grown and émigré talent, not least Lubetkin's wife, Margaret Church, but also including Denys Lasdun, Peter Moro and Gordon Cullen. The MARS Group and later the Architects' and Technicians' Organization were centred on the Tecton office.

During the War, Lubetkin lived in Gloucestershire and farmed, but in 1943 he resumed work on housing projects for the London district of Finsbury. The first of these, Spa Green, was completed in 1950, and shows the continuing sophistication and impact of his work. Tecton was formally dissolved in 1948, although Lubetkin continued to work with Skinner, Drake, Lasdun and Douglas Bailey, separately or in combination, until the 1960s, almost entirely on housing in London. Lubetkin's appointment to plan a new town at Peterlee, Co. Durham, in 1948 was abortive, and he resumed his farming career before achieving a renewed architectural fame in his last years, culminating in his being awarded the RIBA Gold Medal in 1982.

OPPOSITE: The Penguin Pool was the second of Lubetkin's buildings at London Zoo, and followed the Gorilla House of 1933. "It uses our beloved concrete in a way which opens up new vistas for us all", wrote C.H. Reilly, recapturing the dour quality associated with Modernism that could now be convincingly disproved. The colours, which were an important feature of the original design, were recovered in 1987, although even Lubetkin himself only vaguely remembered the originals.

BELOW: The play of curves was a leading motif in most of the buildings at Dudley Zoo, including this entrance canopy. Five shallow S-curves interlock in a gentle descent, retaining their original signage. The apparent floating of solid objects was a recurrent design theme in Lubetkin's work of the later 1930s.

DUDLEY ZOO

Castle Hill, Dudley, West Midlands, 1935–37

The Earl of Dudley developed a new zoo in the grounds of the partly ruined Dudley Castle, standing above an industrial town in the Black Country. Lubetkin and Tecton had eighteen months in which to design and build a large number of structures. The philosophy of displaying animals remained unchanged from that of London Zoo, but the site brought a drama of its own.

Berthold Lubetkin

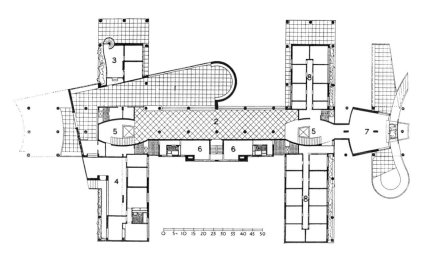

HIGHPOINT I

North Hill, Highgate, London N6, 1933–35

Perhaps the single most celebrated Modernist building of the 1930s in London, and praised even by Le Corbusier, Highpoint I was commissioned by Sigmund Gestetner, an industrialist with a strong interest in the social role of Modernism. The footprint developed as a Cross of Lorraine, with equal arms, each containing a single flat, reached from two stair and lift cores at the intersections. The building is entered beneath the projecting end of the long axis, and the ground-floor plan bends and flows in contrast to the more rigid geometry overhead, leading to the stairs and through to the gardens beyond.

The construction in monolithic reinforced concrete was a collaboration with Ove Arup and was facilitated by lifting the shuttering by stages to form the walls. The details of services and fittings were meticulously thought through, producing some novel alternative solutions.

LEFT AND ABOVE: The ground-floor plan of Highpoint I is drawn with artistic freedom, while the elevations (above, left-hand building) show the rigour and consistency of the scheme. Highpoint II (above, right-hand building) presents a symmetrical front to the shared gardens, with a distinct elevational system for the duplex flats in the middle.

ABOVE: Lubetkin's penthouse in Highpoint II has been lovingly restored, and now includes some original furniture, such as the cowhide chair and the wall lining of rough pine. The door into the main room is covered with an enlargement of a microscopic study of plankton, a reconstruction of the original.

ABOVE RIGHT: The oval staircase linking the levels in the duplex flats signals in its travertine treads the luxury nature of the development. On public view since 1938, the casts of ancient Greek caryatids have puzzled passers-by, as Lubetkin, who published an elaborate but still elusive justification, intended they should.

HIGHPOINT II

North Hill, Highgate, London N6, 1936–38

When Gestetner bought the site adjoining Highpoint to the south, a further block was planned, but there was greater difficulty in obtaining permission. Only one fifth the number of flats could be included, and Highpoint II had to emphasize the value of luxury, with flats accessed directly from the two lifts, and double-height living-rooms in the maisonettes in the centre block. Other requirements led to a formal and symmetrical scheme, featuring a variety of surface materials within a concrete frame, richer in effect than Highpoint I and rounded off with the puzzling reproductions of the Erechtheion caryatids holding up the entrance canopy.

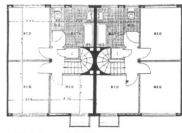

SECOND FLOOR

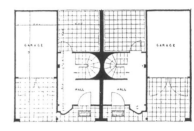

FIRST FLOOR

GROUND FLOOR

Berthold Lubetkin

85–91 (ODD NUMBERS) GENESTA ROAD

Plumstead, London SE18, 1933–34 (with A.V. Pilichowski)

Ranged along a suburban street, these houses have distant
views to the north, far over the Thames estuary. They were
among the first attempts to redesign the traditional English
terrace house with the benefits of concrete construction,
and the plans and spatial arrangements have many graceful
points, chiefly resulting from the compact spiral stair in the
centre of each house. There is room for a garage below
street level, and the main living area is on the first floor. The
little bedroom balconies appear again at Highpoint I.

Lubetkin was the chief designer, although Pilichowski did
significant solo work elsewhere, now either sadly destroyed
(Whittinghame College, Brighton, 1933) or altered (Highfield
Court, Golders Green, London, 1935).

ABOVE: The Genesta Road
houses offer a preview of
Highpoint I's diminutive balconies
in their 'cyma' double-curved
fronts, a form explained by the
natural posture of someone
leaning their elbows on the
top ledge. In the plan corridors
are eliminated and stair landings
are the only circulation spaces
needed. If these houses were
in fashionable Hampstead
rather than Plumstead, they
would surely be better known
and offer lessons for
contemporary designers.

BELOW: The garden elevation emphasizes the double-height central hallway facing the garden with a typical Tecton concrete lattice. The unusual position of the service wing on the right was dictated by covenants on the site imposed by a previous owner.

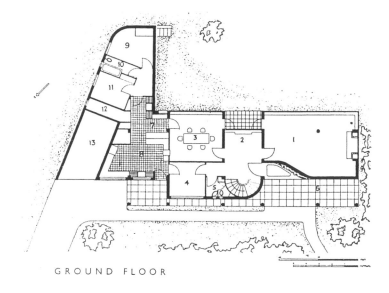

GROUND FLOOR

SIX PILLARS

Crescentwood Road, London SE26, 1934–35
(Valentine Harding and Tecton)

Designed for the headmaster of Dulwich College Preparatory School, Six Pillars lacks the simple elegance of Harding's own house in Buckinghamshire but compensates with ingenuity and the kind of complexity found in later projects by Tecton members, such as the interweaving of brick and concrete. The brick was a concession to the conservatism of the Dulwich College trustees, on whose land the house stood. Six Pillars was repaired by John Winter in the 1990s.

ABOVE RIGHT: Strongly Corbusian from the street, with its strip of corridor windows and eponymous six pillars (originally white rather than blue), the house's use of London brick was an original improvisation in the spirit of Le Corbusier.

RIGHT: The staircase makes three half-turns as it rises to the roof-top study and exercise terrace.

HILLFIELD ('BUNGALOW A')
Dagnall, Buckinghamshire, 1933–35

Lubetkin planned his own 'dacha' on the edge of a steep chalk slope, cutting away the hillside and forming a terrace. The plan resembles the shape of a glider about to launch. (Many actually fly from the nearby London Gliding Club, designed by Christopher Nicholson; see pp. 198–99.) Because of this topography, the main elevation is seen only obliquely, with its external shelter including an outdoor fireplace. Small though it is, Hillfield is as subtle and complex as any other Lubetkin design, introducing the 'shadow gap' (a recessed zone just above the ground) to give the impression of floating, and experimenting with tapering corridors. The entrance is dramatized by a Corbusian patio with a curved back wall and a concrete pergola. Lubetkin's published statement of intent concerning the building subverted all the naturalistic and functional assumptions of modern architecture. He used the building for only a short time before giving it to a friend.

The 'dacha' was restored in the early 1990s by its owner, Mike Davies, of Richard Rogers Partnership.

Berthold Lubetkin

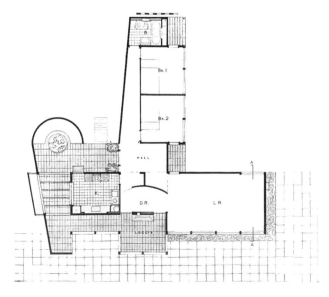

LEFT: Despite the simplicity of the brief, Lubetkin managed to incorporate layers of practical experiment and aesthetic meaning in the bungalow. The extension of the house itself with garden walls and trellis (on the left-hand side of the plan) makes the visitor's contorted approach to the final revelation of the view a delightfully complex episode.

ABOVE: Lubetkin published an ironic text to explain why he had adapted the sloping site to the building rather than the other way round, and replaced the literal demands of Functionalism with a broader metaphorical approach. "It is not a 'Modern House', a 'Shelter', which according to professors, should be self-obliterating, unselfconscious and insignificant in its hygienic anonymity", he began.

HOLLY FRINDLE ('BUNGALOW B')
Whipsnade Park, Dunstable, Bedfordshire, 1933–36

Holly Frindle is a smaller version of Hillfield sited within the zoo compound and built for a staff member. Wallabies regularly visit the garden.

The photograph above shows the 'shadow gap' at the base of the building that Lubetkin was beginning to introduce at this time, and which had a considerable effect on 1950s design. The panels below the windows were originally filled with Thermolux, an opaque coloured glass, which would have given greater unity to the elevation.

ABOVE: Seen here in its freshly restored condition, Holly Frindle was originally planned to have a more extended garden terrace, where kitchen herbs would be grown in a grid of square beds.

Berthold Lubetkin

REFERENCES

Architect

Peter Coe and Malcolm
    Reading, *Lubetkin and Tecton:
    Architecture and Social
    Commitment*, London (Arts
    Council) 1981
John Allan, *Architecture and the
    Tradition of Progress*, London
    (RIBA Publications) 1992
Berthold Lubetkin and Sacha
    Lubetkin, 'Lubetkin: The
    Untold Story', *World
    Architecture*, vol. 24, 1993,
    pp. 64–77
John Allan (with photography
    by Morley von Sternberg),
    Berthold Lubetkin, London
    (Merrell) 2001

Penguin Pool

Architectural Review, vol. 74,
    July 1933, pp. 17–19
Architect and Building News,
    vol. 138, 1 June 1934,
    pp. 254–55
Architects' Journal, vol. 80,
    14 June 1934, pp. 856–59
RIBA Journal, vol. 95, February
    1988, pp. 30–32

Dudley Zoo

Architects' Journal, vol. 86,
    4 November 1937,
    pp. 717–22
Architect and Building News,
    vol. 152, 5 November 1937,
    pp. 166–77; 12 November
    1937, pp. 201–07
Architectural Review, vol. 82,
    November 1937, pp. 177–86

Highpoint I

Architects' Journal, vol. 81,
    17 February 1935,
    pp. 113–19; 2 May 1935,
    pp. 660–64
Architect and Building News,
    vol. 145, 10 January 1936,
    pp. 49–55
Architectural Review, vol. 79,
    January 1936, pp. 5–16

Highpoint II

Architects' Journal, vol. 88,
    8 September 1938,
    pp. 383–84; 13 October
    1938, pp. 601–07, 625;
    1 December 1938,
    pp. 907–08
Architect and Building News,
    vol. 156, 14 October 1938,
    pp. 30–31, 35–41

Architectural Review, vol. 84,
    October 1938, pp. 161–76;
    vol. 86, July 1939, pp. 41–50
    (penthouse)

85–91 Genesta Road

Architectural Review, vol. 80,
    1936, pp. 302
F.R.S. Yorke, *The Modern House
    in England*, London
    (Architectural Press) 1937,
    p. 112

Six Pillars

Architects' Journal, vol. 81,
    21 February 1935,
    pp. 301–02; 4 April 1935,
    pp. 523–24
Architectural Review, vol. 77,
    February 1935, pp. 51–56
F.R.S. Yorke, *The Modern House
    in England*, London
    (Architectural Press) 1937,
    pp. 136–37

Hillfield

Architect and Building News,
    vol. 149, 5 February 1937,
    pp. 174–79
Architects' Journal, vol. 85,
    18 February 1937,
    pp. 299–303
Architectural Review, vol. 81,
    1937, pp. 60–64
F.R.S. Yorke, *The Modern House
    in England*, London
    (Architectural Press) 1937,
    pp. 126–28

Holly Frindle

F.R.S. Yorke, *The Modern House
    in England*, London

(Architectural Press) 1937,
    p. 129

Finsbury Health Centre

Architects' Journal, vol. 89,
    12 January 1939, pp. 47–53
Architect and Building News,
    vol. 157, 13 January 1939,
    pp. 66–74
Architectural Review, vol. 85,
    January 1939, pp. 5–22
Architects' Journal, vol. 201,
    16 February 1995,
    pp. 22–23

FINSBURY HEALTH CENTRE
Pine Street, London EC1, 1935–38

Finsbury, a borough adjoining the City of London, contained many early nineteenth-century streets and squares in a run-down condition, where tuberculosis and other infectious diseases were rife. Dr Katial, an Indian who in 1938 became Mayor of Finsbury, had seen a scheme by Tecton, from 1932, for a tuberculosis clinic. He commissioned a new health centre, a developing genre of municipal building, in this instance including scope for housing tenants prior to relocation, and providing health education.

The architectural solution was modest in scale, with clearly articulated entrance, lecture hall and wings. The project was distinctive for the attention given to the provision of mechanical and electrical services, not only in first installation, but also – and unusually for Modern Movement buildings – in terms of ease of access at a later date.

The health centre still serves its basic original function. Part of the building was repaired by John Allan of Avanti Architects in 1994–95.

OPPOSITE AND TOP RIGHT: The main entrance shows how tiles had become Lubetkin's preferred concrete finish by this date. The specially created lettering recalls early Victorian signage, and, like several other aspects of this project, anticipates the flavour of Modernism prevailing in the Festival of Britain in 1951.

BELOW: The plan of the centre is broadly symmetrical, showing Lubetkin's willingness to use pre-Modernist devices when they suited his purpose – in this case, the easy navigation of a multi-function building.

BELOW RIGHT: The waiting area originally had bright red columns, a pale blue ceiling and brown floor tiles, with furniture designed by Alvar Aalto.

RIGHT: The spandrel panels of the wings continue the use of Thermolux from Hillfield, backed on this occasion by coloured spun silk. Since this material was no longer available, John Allan devised a lookalike replacement in the restoration. These panels were intended to be simple to remove so that pipework behind them could be replaced easily.

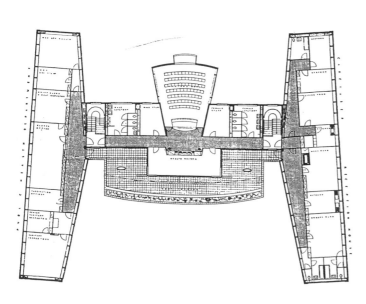

J. Leslie Martin and Sadie Speight 1908–2002; 1906–1992

By 1939 Leslie Martin was recognized as a figure whose importance went beyond his buildings. As its head, he had expanded and consolidated Hull School of Architecture in five years. As a joint editor of the book *Circle* (1937), he was well connected with British and overseas modern architects and abstract artists.

Martin studied at Manchester and completed a doctorate with a study of the Spanish Baroque. In collaboration with his wife, Sadie Speight (they married in 1935), he built three new private houses before 1939; made additions to another, for the art collector Helen Sutherland; and was responsible for the nursery school at Northwich, Cheshire. After his wartime work on prefabrication prototypes with the LMS Railway, he joined the London County Council in 1948 as Deputy Chief Architect to work on the Royal Festival Hall, taking over the top job from Robert Matthew in 1953. In 1956 he became head of the Cambridge School of Architecture, where he remained until 1973, creating a blend of Arts and Crafts morality and Scandinavian influences. He was an important adviser to institutional patrons on their choice of architect and was knighted in 1957.

Sadie Speight was a member of the Design Research Unit, and worked as a designer of interiors and products in the post-war years.

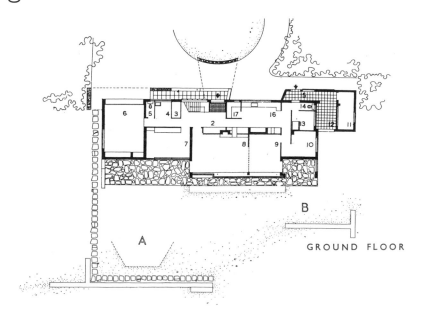

GROUND FLOOR

BRACKENFELL
Brampton, Cumbria, 1936–37

Brackenfell was designed for Alistair Morton, a textile manufacturer in the family company, Morton Sundour, and an abstract painter. It was built of brick with elements of stone, notably the curved wall of the *porte-cochère*, which sets a late-Corbusier/Lubetkin tone for the design as a whole. The living-room and dining-room are generous spaces; the other rooms are relatively tight. A studio for Morton was provided over the garage. The colour scheme by Morton included white and pale grey walls in the living-room, a primrose ceiling and chairs upholstered in bright yellow and red, with a grey haircord carpet throughout the house.

RIGHT: The stair shows the thoughtful detail of the design with a built-in seat in the hall, above which originally hung an abstract painting by Ben Nicholson.

BELOW LEFT AND OPPOSITE: The projection of the colonnade has been made much deeper in the reconstruction of the school, as a comparison with the original plan (below) demonstrates, but the space is clearly put to good use.

BELOW: The form of the curved timber screen of the *porte-cochère* has been reproduced, although the original was painted white and created a stronger feeling of floating. The plan was devised so that, in theory, a second set of classrooms could be joined on to the central service spine, which could itself be extended as far as required.

J. Leslie Martin and Sadie Speight

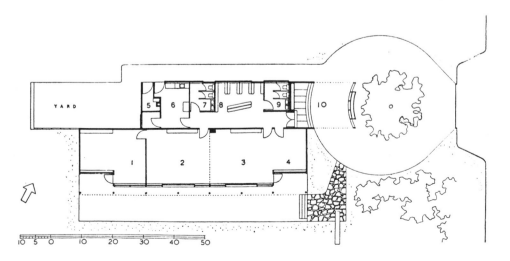

NURSERY SCHOOL

Bradburn's Lane, Hartford, Northwich, Cheshire, 1938

Commissioned by a local Quaker benefactor, this project typified Martin's later thinking, since it was conceived as a prototype, in this case for timber unit construction, with a plan form that could be expanded sideways and lengthways. The elements were extremely simple and elegantly handled, and included another curved entrance screen, this time in open timber, and timber post columns supporting an overhanging roof to shade the classrooms. The doors from classrooms leading on to the terrace were bright yellow, and the front door 'pot red'.

The original building was destroyed by fire and has been completely reconstructed (as the Sir Leslie Martin Nursery School), with the main structure in brick and a deeper overhang.

REFERENCES

Architect

Ben Nicholson, Naum Gabo and J.L. Martin (eds.), *Circle: International Survey of Constructive Art*, London (Faber & Faber) 1937

J.L. Martin and S. Speight, *The Flat Book*, London (Heinemann) 1939

J.L. Martin, *Buildings and Ideas, 1933–83*, Cambridge (Cambridge University Press) 1983

P. Carolin and T. Dannatt (eds.), *Architecture, Education and Research: The Work of Leslie Martin: Papers and Selected Articles*, London (Academy Editions) 1996

Brackenfell

Architectural Review, vol. 86, July 1939, pp. 13–15

Richard Calvocoressi, *Alastair Morton and Edinburgh Weavers: Abstract Art and Textile Design, 1935–46*, exhib. cat., Edinburgh, Scottish National Gallery of Modern Art, 1978

Nursery School

Architectural Review, vol. 86, 1939, pp. 127–28

Raymond McGrath 1903–1977

Born in Gladesville, a suburb of Sydney, McGrath was a brilliant architecture student, with gifts for words and for drawing. He travelled to London in 1926 on a scholarship. His friendship with Mansfield Forbes, a Fellow of Clare College, Cambridge, and one of the founders of the university's English faculty, led him to enrol and study there as a postgraduate, his subject being 'The Architecture of Entertainment'. The thesis was never completed because Forbes propelled McGrath on his career by commissioning Finella.

McGrath's book *Twentieth Century Houses* (1934) was more inclusive and historically based than F.R.S. Yorke's rival *The Modern House* of the same year. The imaginative and poetic side of McGrath's personality resulted in his producing several buildings that, with hindsight, seem among the most forward-looking of their time. His last major house, Carrygate, Galby, near Leicester (see p. 26), is equally fascinating for its reuse of Elizabethan bricks and its timber superstructure.

McGrath compiled (with A.C. Frost) a large and lavish book on *Glass in Architecture and Decoration* (1937). In the summer of 1939, driven by personal and professional crises, he accepted a job as Deputy Chief Architect to the Office of Works, Dublin, where he spent the rest of his life but lacked opportunities to build.

FINELLA

Queens' Road, Cambridge, 1928–29

Mansfield Forbes rented Finella (originally called The Yews) from
another college, and converted its dowdy late Victorian
interiors into a Modernist fantasy of glass and reflective copper.
The project fulfilled three ambitions: to create a showcase for
modern building materials; to apply them poetically rather than
practically, with a loose mythical iconography; and to act as a
place for entertaining and promoting new ideas in the arts. The
story was of Finella, the Scottish queen who discovered glass
and met her death by being thrown down a waterfall – hence
the presence of Pictish images, glass and (by implication as well
as actual presence) water.

The results were spectacular, and Forbes became an unlikely
catalyst for the development of Modernism before his death in
1936. Finella was restored by Christophe Grillet for Gonville
and Caius College in the early 1980s.

ABOVE: The entrance corridor
at Finella is in large part a
reconstruction, but still conveys
the excitement felt by early
visitors. The ceiling was formed
from slabs of glass, until it
reached the foot of the stairs,
where it became a plywood
groin vault covered in silver foil
(substituted by aluminium foil
from chocolate wrappings in
the restoration). The floor of
inlaid Induroleum contains
'Pictavian' iconography, including
a serpent guarding the threshold
of 'South Pink'.

LEFT AND BELOW: The circular living-room provides a panorama of the garden and connects with the dining-room beyond. On the first-floor landing the curve of the main stair meets the upper flight leading on to the roof (bottom). The dramatic intersecting concrete roof beams are more typical of contemporary Rationalist architecture in Italy by Giuseppe Terragni, or the work of Richard Meier in the 1970s, which was inspired by such sources.

Raymond McGrath

REFERENCES

Architect

Raymond McGrath, *Twentieth Century Houses*, London (Faber & Faber) 1934

Raymond McGrath (with A.C. Frost), *Glass in Architecture and Decoration*, London (Architectural Press) 1937, revised 1962

'Rhapsody in Black Glass', *Architectural Review*, vol. 162, 1977, pp. 58–64 (interview with Raymond McGrath by Brian Hanson)

Alan Powers, '"Simple Intime": The Work of Raymond McGrath', *Thirties Society Journal*, no. 3, 1983, pp. 2–11

Donal O'Donovan, *God's Architect: A Life of Raymond McGrath*, Bray, Co. Wicklow (Kilbridge Books) 1995

Finella

Architects' Journal, vol. 70, 25 December 1929, pp. 974–81

Architectural Review, vol. 66, December 1929, pp. 265–72

Country Life, vol. 67, 22 March 1930, pp. 437–40

Hugh Carey, *Mansfield Forbes and his Cambridge*, Cambridge (Cambridge University Press) 1984

St Ann's Hill

Architectural Review, vol. 82, October 1937, pp. 117–22

ST ANN'S HILL

Chertsey, Surrey, 1936–37

On a hilltop above the Thames valley, the eighteenth-century politician Charles James Fox owned a villa with an elaborate garden, which was later the site for McGrath's outstanding contribution to the 1930s corpus of houses. The cylindrical form, tracking the path of the sun, had been projected by Raymond Myerscough-Walker in a published project of 1934, while the 'Sunspan' design by Wells Coates embodied the same idea.

Working with the landscape architect Christopher Tunnard, the cohabitee of the client, Gerald Schlesinger (see the discussion of Hill House, Hampstead, by Oliver Hill, p. 143), McGrath responded sensitively to the landscape, incorporating, for example, an existing wisteria.

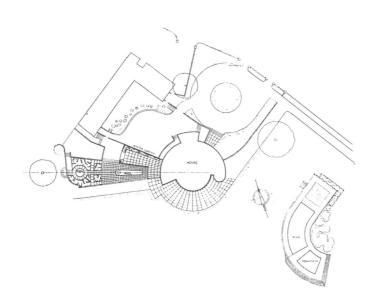

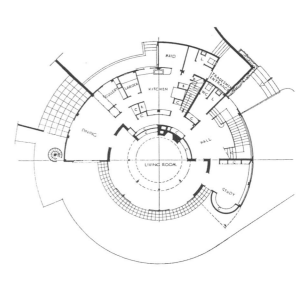

BELOW AND RIGHT: From the sloping lawn the house appears, in McGrath's words, like a cheese with sections cut away. The site plan shows how the old stable block to the rear remained as service accommodation, while the swimming pool below the house provided a complementary curve.

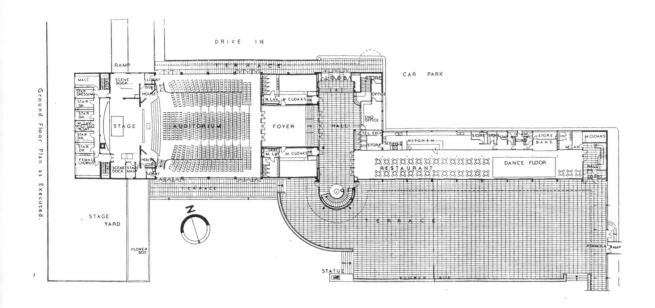

LEFT: The ground-floor plan shows the tight but effective use of space for cultural and leisure purposes. The theatre appears on the left of the foyer, and the restaurant on the right

BELOW LEFT AND OPPOSITE: The exterior was awaiting comprehensive repair when this photograph was taken. The broad, blank wall of the theatre makes a telling contrast with the stair tower (opposite), which encourages visitors to ascend in order to overlook the English Channel.

Erich Mendelsohn 1887–1953

Mendelsohn was born in the historic town of Allenstein, east Prussia, the son of a merchant father and musician mother, and studied architecture in Berlin and Munich. Although he built nothing before the War, in which he served on both fronts, Mendelsohn developed an interest in German Expressionist art and experimented with the possibility of translating music into architecture. On war service he made small pencil sketches of imaginary buildings, usually massive in scale and industrial in purpose, and the Einstein Tower, Potsdam (1920), an experiment in sculptural form, repeated these.

Through the 1920s Mendelsohn became one of the most prominent figures in German architecture and one of the most frequently admired in Britain, designing department stores, factories and the Woga complex in Berlin (1929), which combined housing with the Universum cinema.

After Mendelsohn moved to London with his wife and daughter in 1933 as refugees from Nazism, he soon discovered better opportunities in Palestine, and began dividing his time between the two countries. His partnership with Serge Chermayeff was dissolved at the end of 1936, but he built no more in Britain thereafter and left for the United States.

ABOVE: The library has long vanished, but epitomizes the building's ideal of space and leisure for everyone. The chairs were from the 'Plan' range adapted by Chermayeff from originals by Knoll of Stuttgart and marketed by him in Britain.

RIGHT: The theatre was carefully
considered for acoustics and
harmonious colouring.
C.H. Reilly called the pavilion
"a revelation from another
planet in the stucco redness of
that terrible town".

DE LA WARR PAVILION

Marina, Bexhill, East Sussex, 1934–35 (with Serge
Chermayeff)

A project won in a contentious competition, the pavilion
was the brainchild of the left-wing politician the 9th Earl
De La Warr, to regenerate a sleepy seaside town. The
welded steel frame, designed by Felix Samuely, carried an
immaculate white skin, from which the glazed stair tower
projects, punctuating the long seaward elevation. Inside,
the spaces flow with an assurance rare in British Modernist
architecture. A mural by Edward Wadsworth and furniture
by Alvar Aalto made the interiors, in Chermayeff's charge,
an elegant public space.

The pavilion, in public ownership and supported by the
efforts of a charitable trust, has benefited from a phased
programme of restoration by the architect John McAslan
over ten years, and has become a landmark of its period.

SHRUB'S WOOD

Chalfont St Giles, Buckinghamshire, 1934–35
(with Serge Chermayeff)

A house in a park-like setting for a businessman with a
Texan wife who knew Geoffrey Bazeley, Shrub's Wood is
understated, indicating Mendelsohn's rapid assimilation of
an English aesthetic. The construction is reinforced concrete,
with continuous rows of windows on both the long elevations
and a typical Mendelsohn stair. Chermayeff put his mark on
the simple wooden fitted cupboards and wardrobes.

Shrub's Wood has been fortunate in its later owners,
who included Dame Bridget D'Oyly Carte and then a well-
known architect.

BELOW AND OPPOSITE: The
clarity of the building's forms
has become blurred by luxuriant
planting but can be read from
the plan, which shows a simple
L-form. The stairs form a hinge
in the composition when
viewed from the entrance front,
and are smoothly expressed
by Mendelsohn, as one expects
in his work. The long continuous
line of bedroom windows
indicates his interest in finding
dynamic horizontals.

Erich Mendelsohn

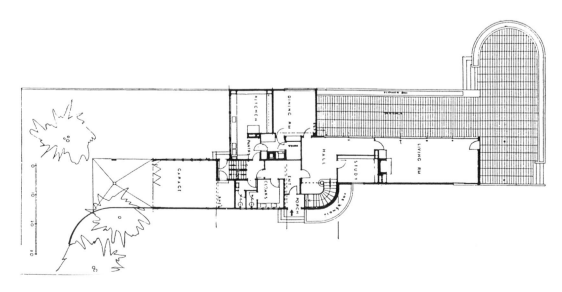

Erich Mendelsohn

REFERENCES

Architect

Arnold Whittick, *Eric Mendelsohn*, London (Leonard Hill) 1956

Jeremy Brook *et al.* (eds.), *Erich Mendelsohn 1887–1953*, London (Modern British Architecture) 1987

Bruno Zevi, *Erich Mendelsohn: The Complete Works*, Basel (Birkhäuser) 1999

De La Warr Pavilion

Architect and Building News, vol. 137, 2 February 1934, pp. 161–64; 9 February 1934, p. 196; vol. 144, 20 December 1935, f.pp. 322, 352; 27 December 1935, f.p. 372

Architects' Journal, vol. 79, 8 February 1934, pp. 197, 205–06, 213–17; vol. 82, 12 December 1935, f.p. 352; 27 December 1935, f.p. 372

Architectural Review, vol. 80, July 1936, pp. 19, 21–28, 50; pl. iii

Alastair Fairley, *Bucking the Trend: The Life and Times of the Ninth Earl De La Warr, 1900–1976*, Bexhill (The Pavilion Trust) 2001

Alastair Fairley, *The De La Warr Pavilion*, London (Merrell) 2006

Shrub's Wood

Architectural Review, vol. 78, November 1935,

pp. 174–78; vol. 80, December 1936, pp. 299–301

Architects' Journal, vol. 83, 2 January 1936, pp. 9–14

F.R.S. Yorke, *The Modern House in England*, London (Architectural Press) 1937, pp. 109–11

64 Old Church Street

Architects' Journal, vol. 84, 24 December 1936, pp. 872–74; vol. 87: 2 June 1938, pp. 945–46; 9 June 1938, pp. 985–86; 16 June 1938, pp. 2025–26; 23 June 1938, pp. 1065–66

Architectural Review, vol. 80, December 1936, pp. 254–55

F.R.S. Yorke, *The Modern House in England*, London (Architectural Press) 1937, pp. 36–37

R. Myerscough-Walker, 'Two Houses in Chelsea', *Building*, vol. 14, January 1938, pp. 15–19

64 OLD CHURCH STREET

Chelsea, London SW3, 1935–36 (with Serge Chermayeff)

Built for Dennis Cohen, a publisher (with the Cresset Press), this house was co-ordinated architecturally with its neighbour, which had been designed by Walter Gropius and Maxwell Fry. The Cohen house, built of rendered brick, opens up towards the garden, where the main rooms make an enfilade, from the bow-ended drawing-room through a library and dining-room to a squash court, built into the basement and overlooked from the dining-table. The need to incorporate this feature gave Mendelsohn difficulties with the design.

The generous terrace extends along the garden front and echoes the bow, returning to the narrow south elevation. Here Cohen first built a modest if inappropriate conservatory, later superseded by a much larger structure designed by Norman Foster.

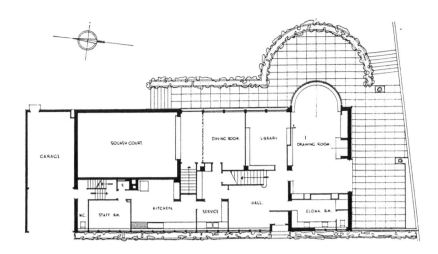

GROUND FLOOR

OPPOSITE: The street view of the house is dominated by the conservatory added in the early 1990s. Originally, as the right-hand (south) end of the plan shows, the end of the building was marked by a rounded 'full stop', a device often used by Mendelsohn.

ABOVE LEFT: The eastern front, facing the garden, has been less severely altered. Only a framework for temporary awnings has been added.

ABOVE RIGHT: The stairs rise in straight flights, unusually for Mendelsohn. The broad landing window forms the main outlook on to the street.

LEFT: The sequence of rooms along the garden front, with the living-room and dining-room divided by sliding partitions, enhances the feeling of space. Chermayeff was responsible for the high standard of internal finishes.

Peter Moro 1911–1998

Born in Heidelberg, Moro was the son of a professor of paediatrics and studied architecture in Stuttgart and Berlin. He was expelled from Germany by the Nazis (although he was raised as a Catholic, his grandmother was Jewish) and completed his studies under Otto Salvisberg at Zurich.

In 1936 Moro moved to Britain and joined the Tecton office, where he claimed to have begun finally to learn architecture properly. He completed only one pre-war project, which landed by luck in the lap of Moro and his then flatmate Richard Llewelyn-Davies, who was still a student at the time. After a brief internment Moro began teaching at the Regent Street Polytechnic, London, where he influenced a rising generation of students whom he recruited in 1947 to work with him on the design of the Royal Festival Hall, under Leslie Martin. In 1952 he opened his own office and became a specialist in theatre design, working on older buildings and also on several completely new theatres in Nottingham, Hull and Plymouth. His own house, in Blackheath, south-east London (1956), was a classic of its time, filled with Moro's own paintings and reliefs, and furniture by his friend Robin Day.

REFERENCES

Architectural Review, vol. 89, April
    1941, pp. 63–70
Architects' Journal, vol. 93, 22 May
    1941, pp. 339–40
Peter Moro, 'Harbour Meadow,
    Birdham, Sussex', *Twentieth
    Century Architecture*, no. 2:
    The Modern House Revisited,
    London (Twentieth Century
    Society) 1996, pp. 8–14

ABOVE: The outer walls of the main portion of the house were originally in unpainted pale brick, with the inner wall painted dark brown for contrast. A 'flash-gap', or recessed, darkened base, was designed to make the house appear to float a little above the grass. The square window on the right was a surrealist joke contributed by Gordon Cullen, later famous as the author of *Townscape*. It was glazed with yellow glass and fitted internally with a plaster rococo frame, thus presenting the view over Bosham Creek as a 'living picture'. The glass bay window was equipped with two Isokon long chairs designed by Marcel Breuer.

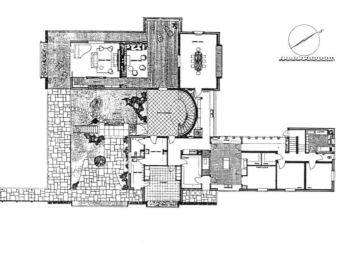

BELOW AND LEFT: This photograph shows the house as if viewed from the top of the plan. On the other side, a complex area of 'hard' landscaping and planting marked the entrance and a two-storey window to the staircase (bottom), the elegant curve of which could be seen at night. The side wall was intended to be covered in William Morris wallpaper. Also out of view, a single-storey screen wall of rubble masonry stood forward from the main block of the house, while a long covered way extended to the garage.

HARBOUR MEADOW

Birdham, West Sussex, 1938–40 (with Richard Llewelyn-Davies)

This expansive house, close to a tidal harbour beloved of yachtsmen, was built by a Scottish steel magnate and his wife, who dropped into the Architectural Association looking for an architect and were charmed by the then inexperienced pair. (Llewelyn-Davies was an important post-war figure, better known as an architectural administrator than as a designer.) Built of load-bearing brick, Harbour Meadow is a pinwheel plan centred on the graceful staircase. Externally there are reminiscences of Tecton (including curves in the plan and some architectural jokes) and a flavour of post-war architecture still to come. Kiefer timber windows, popular at the end of the 1930s, were imported from Switzerland.

193

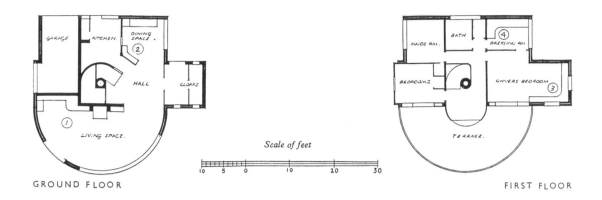

GROUND FLOOR

Scale of feet

FIRST FLOOR

GARAGE | KITCHEN | DINING SPACE ② | HALL | CLOAKS | ① LIVING SPACE.

MAIDS RM. | BATH | ④ DRESSING RM. | BEDROOM 2 | OWNERS BEDROOM ③ | TERRACE.

10 5 0 10 20 30

LEFT AND OPPOSITE: For a house with an element of fantasy, the plan is perfectly practical and makes good use of space. The depth of the upper terrace, although apparently wasteful, makes it more usable than the majority of such outdoor spaces provided in modern houses, and the top terrace, where the stairs rise to a glass enclosure, is equally appealing.

Raymond Myerscough-Walker 1908–1984

Born in Yorkshire, Myerscough-Walker was taken up by a rich guardian, who took him sketching abroad. He first wanted to become a jazz musician but instead chose architecture and in 1928 was able to go to the Architectural Association on a scholarship. His drawing skills revealed themselves, as well as his independent and pleasure-loving character, and he grew a beard, then a rarity. (Basil Ward also had one.) He worked mainly as a perspective artist – his drawings were 'set up' by another talented but impoverished Architectural Association student, the photographer Edwin Smith – and also designed film sets and wrote architectural journalism. The house in Nottingham was his principal executed building, although he also designed a penthouse in Ladbroke Grove, London (in a block by Maxwell Fry), in 1938, for the developer and art patron Charles Kearley. After the War, Myerscough-Walker decided to 'drop out' and live with his wife and five children in a caravan, working as a freelance perspective artist.

REFERENCES

Architect

Gavin Stamp, *Raymond Myerscough-Walker: Architect and Perspective Artist*, London (Architectural Association) 1984

35 Hallams Lane

Architect and Building News, vol. 139, 28 September 1934, pp. 382–83 ("'Murus', A House to be Built in Yorkshire")

Architect and Building News, vol. 150, 25 June 1937, pp. 398–401

F.R.S. Yorke, *The Modern House in England*, London (Architectural Press) 1937, pp. 66–67

LEFT: The handrail appears to be a later replacement for a simpler original. The stair rises around the flue of the living-room fireplace; this view shows the upper flight, which rises to the roof.

35 HALLAMS LANE
Chilwell, Nottingham, 1936–37

The house was commissioned by R.J.T. Granger, who had seen a speculative published design by Myerscough-Walker for a completely circular house, from 1934. He wanted to try to build one, but the original conception had to be cut down because of budget constraints. It is nonetheless an extraordinary house, with a well-considered, compact plan and a dramatic use of the simple geometric idea. The core of the house is the flue of the fireplace in the 'living space' on the ground floor, around which the stairs wind. The house is built of brick, but the broad canopy over the first-floor terrace – enjoying uninterrupted views to the south, where the land slopes sharply away – is made of concrete.

BELOW LEFT: The curved west-facing window of the studio makes it especially adaptable for ordinary domestic living.

BELOW RIGHT AND OPPOSITE: The deep concrete lintels and rough brickwork are more reminiscent of an industrial building than a 'polite' one.

STUDIO
Fryern Court, Fordingbridge, Hampshire, 1933–34

Augustus John, a notable British portrait painter, lived in the country in bohemian style with his wife, Dorelia. Axially aligned to a formal garden near the main house, the studio was raised on a concrete frame to first-floor level to provide more light and was reached by an external stair. The walls are of painted brick, and the design constructed to modular dimensions. The first floor originally consisted of a single room reached through a lobby, with a small picture store on the ground floor. The studio interior was provided with three generous window seats along the north-east side.

Christopher Nicholson 1904–1948

The younger son of the painter William Nicholson and the brother of Ben Nicholson, also a painter, Kit Nicholson (as Christopher was always known) studied architecture at the University of Cambridge and discovered Modernism under his brother's influence. He returned to Cambridge to teach in the early 1930s, when he met his wife, E.Q. Myers, a notable textile artist. His father's long-standing friendship with Augustus John produced Kit's first substantial commission, which was followed by a small number of notable buildings, including the house at Kit's Close, Fawley, Oxfordshire, in 1936. His strangest work was for the young art patron Edward James, who transformed a house by Edwin Lutyens on his estate at West Dean in West Sussex into a private Surrealist fantasy, involving Nicholson and his assistant Hugh Casson in discussions with Salvador Dalí. In 1937 James bought the stones from the façade of the Oxford Street Pantheon, London, by James Wyatt, and commissioned Nicholson to design a house reusing them, which included a proposal for abstracted caryatids by the artist John Piper.

Nicholson joined the Fleet Air Arm in the War and afterwards became design consultant to British European Airways. Hugh Casson rejoined him, and worked with him until Nicholson's death in a gliding accident in northern Italy.

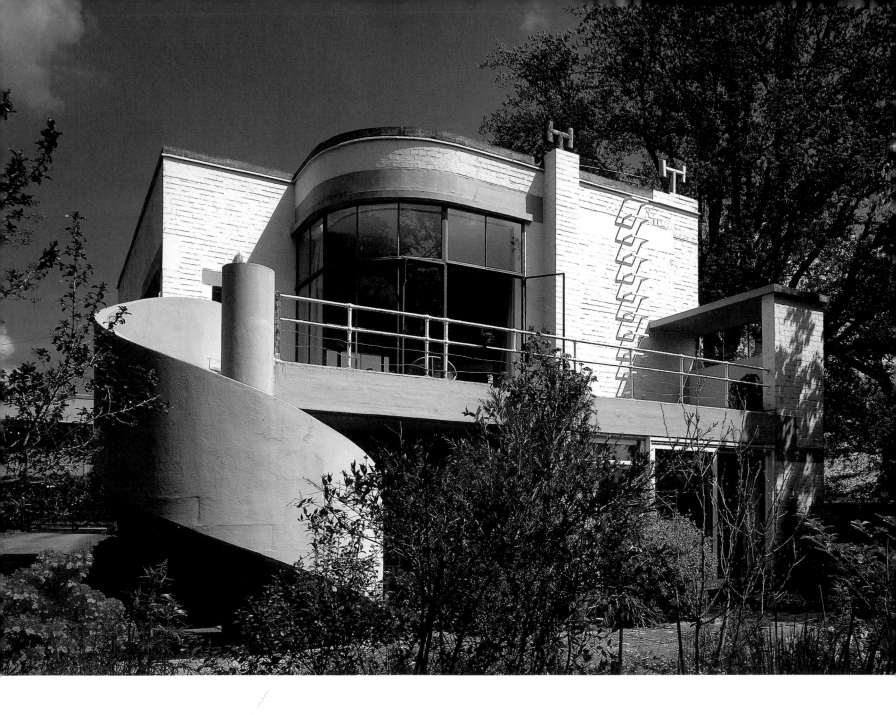

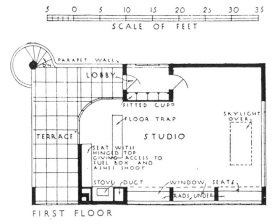

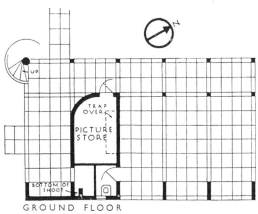

5 0   5   10   15   20   25   30   35
SCALE OF FEET

PARAPET WALL

DN

LOBBY

FITTED CUPD

FLOOR TRAP

SKYLIGHT
OVER

TERRACE

STUDIO

SEAT WITH
HINGED TOP
GIVING ACCESS TO
FUEL BOX AND
ASHES SHOOT

STOVE DUCT

WINDOW SEATS

RADS. UNDER

FIRST FLOOR

N

UP

TRAP
OVER

PICTURE
STORE

BOTTOM OF
SHOOT

GROUND FLOOR

ABOVE AND LEFT: Without a
washbasin, and with only a
ground-floor lavatory, the studio
was surprisingly spartan in its
practical provision, although
the indoor and outdoor spaces
are generously scaled. The
spiral stair was designed in
collaboration with an engineer
from Nottingham University, and
used an ingenious prefabricated
shuttering for the concrete.

197

Christopher Nicholson

REFERENCES

Architect

Neil Bingham, *Christopher Nicholson*, London (Academy Editions) 1996

Studio

Architectural Review, vol. 77, February 1935, pp. 65–68

London Gliding Club

Architects' Journal, vol. 83, 11 June 1936, pp. 915–19

Architectural Review, vol. 79, June 1936, pp. 353–62

ABOVE: Gliders can emerge from the hanger on to the apron prior to launching from the grass. Behind the narrow frontage building, the square-shaped hanger was designed to take about twenty-five fully-rigged gliders. Above, the window of the lounge and dining-room, 27 m (90 ft) long, gives the best view to the maximum number of members and guests. The whole building was conceived and executed on a very tight budget. The original colour has now been restored.

OPPOSITE: The axonometric drawing, originally published in the *Architectural Review*, reveals how areas for different functions interlocked tightly . For example, a dormitory with three pairs of bunk beds was squeezed into the ground floor at the edge of the hanger.

LONDON GLIDING CLUB
Dunstable Downs, Bedfordshire, 1935

Nicholson was an enthusiastic follower of gliding and a member of the club, and he replaced its wooden huts with one of the most stylish sports buildings of the decade, which remains in its original use. The hangar occupies most of the space, and a deep steel-plate girder was concealed behind a brick face to support the lounge and restaurant, with its continuous bank of windows. In the projecting wing by the entrance there is a ground-floor bar in an original colour scheme of pale blue, terracotta and black, with a tea terrace overhead.

LEFT: The ground-floor bar in the single-storey wing retains its original metal-framed doors, although other features of the interior have changed. The colour scheme, described above, was devised by E.Q. Nicholson, the architect's wife.

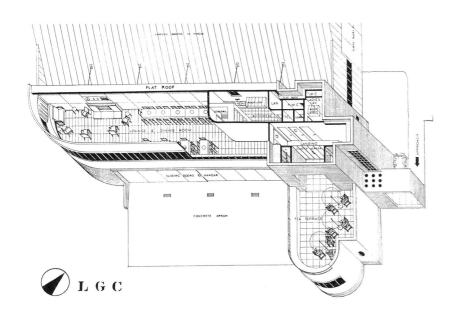

LGC

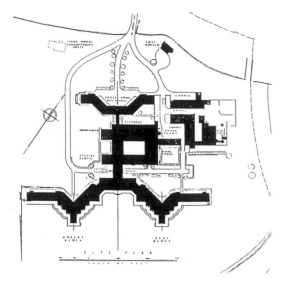

William A. Pite 1860–1949

The son of an architect, and brother of the better-known A. Beresford Pite, William Pite began practice in 1884 and initially specialized in hospitals, designing King's College Hospital on Denmark Hill, Camberwell, and the Middlesex Hospital, both in London. He was joined by H.W. Fairweather, and his son, Robert A. Pite, in 1919. Pite, Son & Fairweather, as the firm was then called, won the competition for the King Edward VII Welsh National Memorial in 1931, but the design was considerably revised before construction began in 1932 and emerged with a more pronounced Modernist character in its white walls and larger windows.

Hospital design, with its focus on practicality and rational planning, was in several instances a way by which modern architecture became accepted without argument about taste. This was especially so with tuberculosis sanatoria, such as Sully Hospital, South Glamorgan, after the discovery of the curative properties of sunshine and fresh air, which operated reciprocally with modern architecture. J.M. Richards commended Sully Hospital in the *Architectural Review* for the way its "sensibly large-paned windows, carefully organized into simple patterns, allow the direction and massing of the whole to make its effect without any artificial monumentality".

REFERENCES
Sully Hospital
Architects' Journal, vol. 74, 11 January 1931, pp. 710–13 (competition design)
Architectural Review, vol. 80, October 1936, pp. 139–46

SULLY HOSPITAL

Hayes Farm, South Glamorgan, 1931–38

The flat site overlooks the Bristol Channel, between Cardiff and Barry. The symmetrical site layout is dominated by the balancing men's and women's ward blocks (some rooms having four beds, others only one) on one side and the similar configuration of the nurses' home on the other.

The building is mainly of load-bearing brick, rendered in a cream colour, although the ward blocks are steel-framed with brick panel walls. Having served as a general hospital in the post-war years, Sully Hospital was closed in the 1990s but protected by listing. After a long period of uncertainty about its future, it was converted to housing by Countryside Homes in 2004.

BELOW: "One of the most arresting images in British architecture", is Gavin Stamp's opinion of Dell & Wainwright's original photo of Ramsgate Aerodrome, seen from beneath the wing of a twin-engined Short 16 Scion Junior on the grass runway.

BOTTOM: The aerodrome's plan was extremely compact, but allowed for an axial extension, which would have made it even more plane-like. The whole style of the building speaks of flying as a privileged and leisured pursuit. Sadly, this building was demolished soon after the closure of the airport in 1968.

RAMSGATE AERODROME
Ramsgate, Kent, 1936–37 (demolished)

In 1935 Whitney Straight, the son of Dorothy Elmhirst of Dartington, founded the Straight Corporation to acquire and develop small municipal airfields for light-aircraft training and private use. He commissioned a series of Modernist buildings, many of them from Robert Hening (for example at Exeter and Ipswich), and for Ramsgate chose Pleydell-Bouverie, who produced the most elegant of the series. It has a 90-foot (27-metre) range of folding teak doors and a wing-like canopy, providing a metaphor of flight perfectly captured a famous image by the photographers Dell & Wainwright.

David Pleydell-Bouverie 1911–1994

A grandson of the 5th Earl of Radnor, Pleydell-Bouverie was a typical upper-class rebel of the 1930s, hating the brutality of his father and his public school, Charterhouse. He was a pupil of the architect Walter Sarel before becoming the partner of Wells Coates in 1932. His interiors at 43 Prince's Gate, London, were widely published, and he also designed the Second Feathers Club in Norland Gardens, London, in 1934, as part of a project by the then Prince of Wales to assist the urban poor.

Pleydell-Bouverie's few works were all distinctive, including (in addition to those described here) a row of quarrymen's cottages (1936) for Sir Michael Assheton-Smith at Dinorwic, Gwynedd, which had pitched roofs and a carefully considered plan.

In 1937 Pleydell-Bouverie emigrated to the United States, where he married Alice Astor and settled on a ranch in Sonoma County, California, creating the Bouverie Audubon Reserve to teach children how to appreciate nature. He designed his own simple buildings for the ranch and also a house for the writer M.F.K. Fisher. He moved in social and literary circles, both in California and in New York, where he spent the winter.

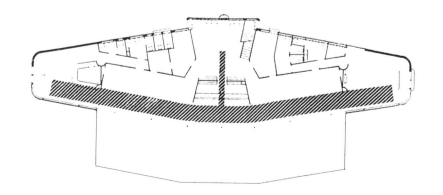

LEFT: The photo of the roofs achieves a slightly surreal sense of contrast with the more traditional seaside architecture in the distance. Architecturally, the Foreshore tried to bring back long-lost Georgian and Regency decorum.

BELOW: The long shelter of glazed bricks scalloped into bays gave a sense of personal space, protected the new boating pool from the wind off the sea, and provided a setting for the domed 'rotunda'.

FORESHORE DEVELOPMENT
Folkestone, Kent, 1937 (demolished)

Much of Folkestone is owned by the earls of Radnor, hence Pleydell-Bouverie's involvement in this improvement scheme consisting of a restaurant, shelter, fun-fair and boating pool. The domed concrete structure for the fun-fair was engineered by Felix Samuely and had circular glass lights let into it. The outer surface was covered in asphalt, with ground blue glass colouring. Inside, the walls and roof were white, and the floor red.

The other buildings, although more modest, helped to define a comfortable leisure space, similar to the kind of modern-style park and resort building more common on the Continent than in Britain.

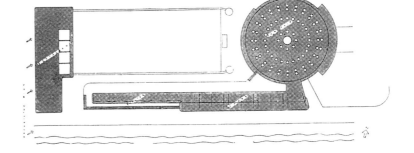

REFERENCES
Ramsgate Aerodrome
Architectural Review, vol. 82, July 1937, pp. 3–6
Gavin Stamp, 'Lost C20th Buildings: Ramsgate Aerodrome', *Twentieth Century Society Newsletter*, Spring 2003, pp. 8–9

Foreshore Development
Architectural Review, vol. 83, January 1938, pp. 23–26

KIRKBY HOUSE
Kirkby Overblow, North Yorkshire, 1931

Designed for a Mr McLaren, Kirkby House is a large building of rendered brick on an attractive sloping site in a small village. The *Architects' Journal* reported that "at the outset, the usual 'Battle of the Styles' in its minor form was pleasantly fought, and, after a mild struggle, the Germanic prevailed over the locally favoured Tudor and Queen Anne".

The projecting dining-room and main bedroom above it provide a centre to the almost symmetrical composition, where the house rises above garden retaining walls of rough stone, a contrast of texture that appealed to Raymond McGrath.

BELOW LEFT: This photograph of the entrance shows the way the two main chimney stacks were used to flank the roof-top sunroom. The entrance was originally beside the garage, but is now through the former kitchen, below the projecting bay of the original maid's bedroom – a solution that seems to agree better with the symmetry of the composition.

REFERENCES
Architect
Obituary, *The Builder*, vol. 161,
    5 September 1941, p. 217

Kirkby House
Architects' Journal, vol. 74,
    14 October 1931,
    pp. 500–01
Raymond McGrath, *Twentieth
    Century Houses*, London
    (Faber & Faber) 1934,
    pp. 94–95

OPPOSITE: The house and its gardens enjoy fine views over Wharfedale, encouraging the use of a Modernist glass-roofed balcony to the main dressing-room, despite the northern latitude and the comparatively early date of the house. The balcony was designed not to be overlooked, and was probably intended for the outdoor physical exercises popular at the time. The original metal-framed windows have been replaced. The gardens, which are in a simplified Lutyens style, are extensive.

John Proctor 1882–1941

Proctor was the son of a professor at the University of Leeds, and was educated at the Quaker school at Bootham in York. His brother was the painter Ernest Proctor. John Proctor studied architecture at the University of Leeds, and his career was locally based in West Yorkshire, apart from war service, for which he was awarded the Military Cross. Apart from the suggestion in his family background of a liberal outlook, there is no clear indication of what drew Proctor to modern architecture at such a relatively early date for Britain, although he was one of several regional architects (William Walter Wood of Torquay, Devon, was another) who seem to have been 'ahead' of their London contemporaries.

Apart from two or three houses, Proctor's other buildings, including pubs and university buildings in Leeds, were stylistically mainstream.

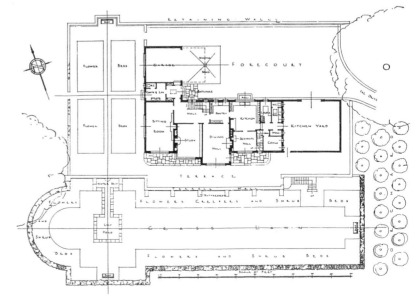

Sevenoaks Way, Sidcup, Kent, 1938

Built as Chislehurst and Sidcup County Grammar School for
Boys, the buildings have a spacious site on the fringes of
London that was already in use as playing fields. Because
of this, the school was built up to three storeys high, with a
courtyard plan of two storeys, and extra height to the south –
the public face of the building. The construction, for which
the consulting engineers were Christiani & Nielsen, was a
reinforced-concrete frame with brick facings. The metal-
framed windows were fitted directly to the columns, and
the rounded staircase cantilevered from the central duct.

W.H. Robinson *c.* 1876–1950

Wilfred Harold Robinson joined the staff of Kent County Council as a surveyor
under the Director of Education in 1904, then became Education Architect for the
county and, in 1929, County Architect. His work was classical in style. The Kemnal
Manor building was actually designed by John W. Poltock ARIBA, who joined the
county council in 1933 and was publicly credited as Assistant Architect under
Robinson. Poltock designed new buildings for Victoria College, Cairo, at Digla,
Maadi, in 1948, although the college was dissolved in 1956.

   The lack of information about both figures highlights the secondary status
accorded to local authority architects, something that the members of the Modern
Movement hoped to change in order that architecture could take on its role as
a social service without lagging behind the latest development. Other county
architects of this period, such as S.E. Urwin in Cambridgeshire, G.E. Stillman in
West Sussex and W.T. Curtis in Middlesex, all of whom were prominent in the
design of schools, had proved that they were open to new architectural ideas, but
Robinson's long career shows how, once in post, they stayed as long as possible.

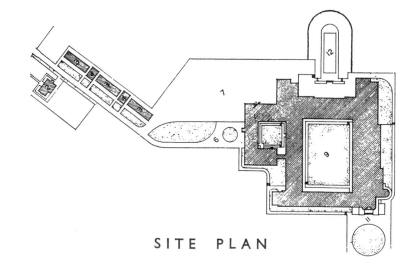

SITE PLAN

OPPOSITE AND ABOVE: Only the front range of the school rises to a height of three storeys, but this provides a rationale for the fine glazed stair tower – its architectural pedigree probably comes from Willem Dudok via Burnet, Tait & Lorne. The whole building, protected by listing in 1982, has remained largely unaltered.

RIGHT: The school hall introduces streamlined concrete columns, unusual among the puritanical majority of Modern Movement architects.

REFERENCES

Architect
Obituary, The Builder, vol. 178, 24 March 1950, p. 398

Kemnal Manor College of Technology
Architects' Journal, vol. 89, 19 January 1939, pp. 109–13
Architectural Review, vol. 85, March 1939, pp. 145–46

BELOW: The chief feature of the house is the large living-room, seen here with its original furniture at the time of completion. It was probably unique in Britain as a combined living-room and bedroom by choice rather than expediency. The plan shows that a folding partition was available for use, passing just this side of the grand piano.

The bed folds down from the central section of the wall (behind the piano) so that the panel above (fitted with wooden handles) becomes the foot of the bed, and the seat folds back into the recess. The other items of furniture were not quite so ingenious, but each occupied a particular place in the room.

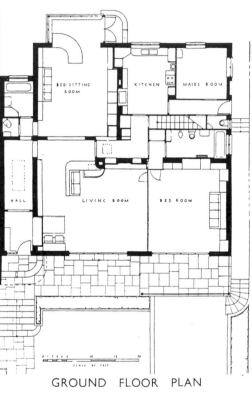

GROUND FLOOR PLAN

Fritz A. Ruhemann 1891–1982

Ruhemann was born in Berlin and worked in the offices of Bruno Paul and Peter Behrens, before running his own practice in Berlin from 1918 to 1936, when he emigrated to Britain. There he initially formed a partnership with Michael Dugdale, one of the founder members of Tecton. The principal work of this practice was 2 South Parade, Chiswick, and, although Ruhemann continued an active career during and after the War, he was known principally as an engineering consultant and specialist in old buildings.

REFERENCES
Architectural Review, vol. 85, February 1939, pp. 88–89
Architect and Building News, vol. 157, 3 March 1939, pp. 274–76

ABOVE: Because the main bedroom is downstairs, the only upstairs room was a guest room, which allowed for a generous roof terrace. The main living-room connects with the bed-sitting room overlooking the rear garden (right).

2 SOUTH PARADE

Bedford Park, Chiswick, London W4, 1937–38

The site, with a house by Norman Shaw, was bought by Leo Neumann, a German refugee, who wished to live on a single floor level, in the manner of an apartment with three rooms capable of being opened into a single space. His sketch plan was published in the *Architectural Review* and was more or less adhered to in the project. The house is remarkable for its ingenious built-in and folding furniture, all carefully positioned in the space – particularly the double bed, which can be transformed into a settee, with its headboard becoming part of the panelling of the room.

The house remained almost unaltered to the time of its listing in 1991. A new room was later added on the roof terrace to a design by Patrick Gwynne, to increase the conventional bedroom accommodation.

Rudolf Otto Salvisberg 1882–1940

Born in Switzerland, Salvisberg studied in several German cities and became an associate of the architect Otto Brechbühl in Berlin and afterwards in Basel. He was cautious in his initial take-up of Modernism and was considered conservative by the German and Swiss avant-gardes of his time. The Lory Hospital at Bern was, however, influential in its T-plan form. Salvisberg liked to use conventionally proportioned upright windows in plain white rendered walls, although he was also able to express the dramatic horizontal balconies of the hospital. In 1929 Salvisberg succeeded Karl Moser as head of the ETH School of Architecture in Zurich, where Peter Moro was one of his students.

At Basel, Salvisberg designed the headquarters of the Roche Pharmaceutical Company, built between 1935 and 1940, which led to his work in Britain.

REFERENCES
Architect
Articles by Stanislas von
    Moos, Claude Lichtenstein,
    Dennis Sharp et al. in
    Werke/Archithese, vol. 64,
    no. 10, 1977

Roche Pharmaceuticals
Architects' Journal, vol. 89,
    19 January 1939, pp. 126–27
Architectural Review, vol. 85,
    April 1939, pp. 193–96

ABOVE: C.H. Reilly was from the same generation as Salvisberg, and his desire to reconcile Modernism and classicism was satisfied by the Roche factory. He wrote, "Salvisberg's building is thoroughly modern in that from its masses and fenestration it could only be a ferro-concrete structure, yet it gives to the material a finish and an elegance which we are not accustomed to in this country." These qualities were consistent in Salvisberg's work, and indicate the existence of a tradition of moderate Modernism in Europe, sometimes called 'Das Andere moderne' or 'the Other Modern' to distinguish it from the avant-garde.

BELOW LEFT: The use of
repeated simple elements, such
as the windows or the 'joists'
over the *porte-cochère*,
contributes to the elegance.

BELOW RIGHT: The spiral stair,
backed by a semicircular bay of
glass bricks set in concrete, was
the most sensational aspect of
the Roche offices. Sadly, the
window has been replaced by
conventional glazing owing to
the problem of thermal
expansion in the concrete
cracking the blocks.

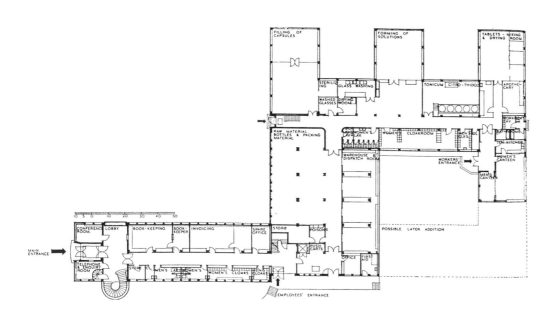

ROCHE PHARMACEUTICALS

Broadwater Road, Welwyn Garden City, Hertfordshire,
1937–38 (with C. Stanley Brown)

The brief was for administrative, processing and
manufacturing buildings in Britain's second garden city.
The office block projects forward to the road, with a
covered entrance, and the clearly visible glazed stair tower,
originally of glass brick, but later reglazed in conventional
style. The factory lay behind but was not concealed, in
the convention of British factories such as Hoover in west
London. The whole building was carefully detailed and
included furniture designed by the architect.

NEW HOUSE

13 Arkwright Road, Hampstead, London NW3, 1937–38

Built for Cecil Walton, headmaster of the nearby University College School, this house has an infill site on a steeply sloping street, so that the dining-room is at garden level, below the living-room. The design was essentially by Harding. The garden front is a regular composition in brick on a concrete frame, similar to Ernö Goldfinger's Willow Road houses (see pp. 120–21) near by. The roadside plays games with a glass-brick wall in the recessed entrance area (with a piano behind it) and a cutaway shape in the end wall. A fireplace faced in flints adds a Paul Nash Surrealist touch to the living-room.

BELOW LEFT: The steep slope across the site can be seen from the road frontage – conditions similar to those facing Ernö Goldfinger at 1–3 Willow Road. This accounts for some of the strange features of the plan and elevation. The cutaway in the wall on the right recalls the similar device at Benjamin and Samuel's East Wall (see pp. 50–51).

OPPOSITE: The rear elevation is calm and classical, with the pleasant feature of the raised garden terrace overlooking a lower area of lawn. The lower-ground floor was occupied by the dining-room, kitchen and servants' quarters.

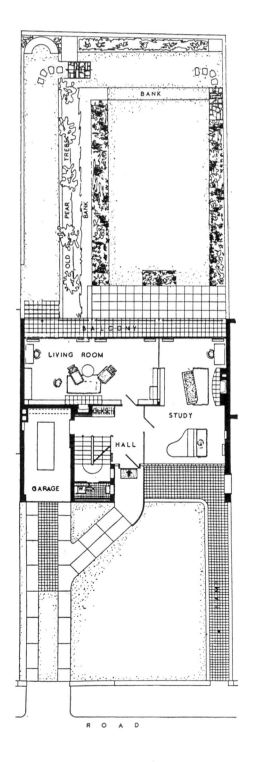

Samuel & Harding

GODFREY SAMUEL, 1904–1983;
VALENTINE HARDING, 1905–1940

Harding was educated at Rugby and Oxford, before going on to the Architectural Association, where he was one of the generation that joined with Berthold Lubetkin in the formation of the Tecton partnership in 1932. He remained with Tecton until 1936, when he formed a partnership with Godfrey Samuel. The house Six Pillars, Dulwich (see p. 173), which was one of his principal works within Tecton, showed an even more quirky approach to Modernism than was normal in the practice at that time. His own house at Egypt End, Farnham Common, Buckinghamshire, had a Continental self-assurance, with a wide first-floor terrace reached by a spiral stair, but this has sadly been much altered. Harding was killed in action in Flanders in the summer of 1940.

Godfrey Samuel was the son of the Liberal politician Herbert (later Lord) Samuel, a member of a distinguished Anglo-Jewish family, and was educated at Balliol College, Oxford, and the Architectural Association as a contemporary of Harding. In partnership with Harding, he was the less dominant figure as a designer but a good diplomat and organizer. Their work as a whole deserves further study.

REFERENCES

F.R.S. Yorke, *The Modern House in England*, London (Architectural Press), 2nd edn, 1944, pp. 90–91

Architectural Review, vol. 86, October 1939, pp. 149–51

Architects' Journal, vol. 91, 11 January 1940, pp. 44–46

BELOW: Several alterations
have been made to the garden
front, including the removal of
a roof pergola and the addition
of openings at ground level.

OPPOSITE: The individual
windows were part of Sisson's
resistance to Corbusian
Modernism, and the general
effect of banded ornament recalls
Dutch architecture of the 1920s.

31 MADINGLEY ROAD
Cambridge, 1931–32

Sisson's house for A.W. Lawrence, archaeologist and brother
of T.E. Lawrence (of Arabia), whom he met in Rome, was
built with multicoloured facing bricks with broad flush joints;
the grooved lintels were cast in artificial stone, and the
windows were timber-framed. The search for modern effects
by means of traditional materials was more typical of the
later 1930s, but the slightly De Stijl treatment of asymmetry
and of window bands wrapping round corners represents
the early 1930s.

The roof terrace, intended as a playing space for the
Lawrences' children, has been partly infilled and its distinctive
original pergola lost as a result.

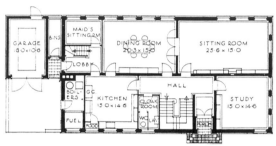

GROUND FLOOR PLAN

FIRST FLOOR PLAN

Marshall Sisson 1897–1978

Marshall Sisson was born in Gloucester, to a Quaker family with a mechanical
engineering business, and served in the First World War in a Quaker ambulance unit.
In 1920 he entered the Bartlett School of Architecture in London, before going on
to win the Henry Jarvis Studentship at the British School at Rome in 1924. He later
worked in New York. One of his tutors, James Burford, influenced him both politically
(towards Fascism) and architecturally (towards Modernism). Sheets of Sisson's
drawings show him experimenting with alternative treatments for the same scheme.

When Sisson had completed the evidently Modernist house in Madingley
Road, Cambridge, he wrote: "Essentially 'Traditional' in that it is not a 'stunt' but
represents a serious attempt to find a contemporary expression for the directional
character of Western culture … predominantly realistic and factual … expressed
in the emphatic horizontality, simplification and rigid systematization of buildings
such as this". He entered several competitions, including that for the De La Warr
Pavilion, Bexhill, with Burford, and built houses at Carlyon Bay, Cornwall, and
Frinton Park, Essex, in a modern manner, before reverting to Georgian classicism
with the Colchester Public Library, Essex (1935). After 1945 Sisson was mainly
concerned with repairs to old buildings.

REFERENCES
Architect
James Bettley, 'Marshall Sisson,
    1897–1978', *Royal Institute of
    British Architects: Transactions*,
    vol. 1, no. 2, 1982, pp. 93–100

31 Madingley Road
Architectural Review, vol. 71,
    December 1932, pp. 266–68
F.R.S. Yorke, *The Modern House*,
    London (Architectural Press)
    1934, pp. 154–55

Tayler & Green HERBERT TAYLER, 1913–2000; DAVID GREEN, 1913–1998

Tayler and Green, who met as students at the Architectural Association, were opposite characters: the former was the youngest of a large family raised in Indonesia, and a major creative talent, while the latter, an architect's son from Lowestoft, Suffolk, was happiest when dealing with practical building problems. The partnership was a professional and personal one and lasted for sixty years.

After launching their practice with The Studio in Highgate, north London, Tayler and Green moved to Lowestoft and laid the foundations for a locally based practice, based on council housing in villages across the Loddon district of south Norfolk. Tayler & Green's terraces, based on evolving standard house types and built to rigorous budgets, were sensitive to the landscape setting, the local vernacular style and the needs of farmworkers as tenants. They were widely recognized as outstandingly successful in an otherwise meagre field of architecture.

Tayler & Green's more metropolitan style had less scope for expression, although their house, factory and showroom for A. Imhof, a maker of electrical goods, made a group of exemplary buildings; the showroom was described by Tayler as "neo-Oxford Street baroque". He and Green retired to Spain in 1973, leaving a rich archive of their drawings in the Suffolk Record Office.

REFERENCES
Architect
Sherban Cantacuzino, 'The Work of Tayler and Green', *Architecture and Building*, vol. 25, no. 1, January 1960, pp. 2–23

Elain Harwood and Alan Powers, *Tayler and Green, Architects 1938–1973*, London (The Prince of Wales's Institute of Architecture) 1998

The Studio
Architects' Journal, vol. 92, 19 September 1940, pp. 235–41

Architectural Review, vol. 88, September 1940, pp. 71–80

Country Life, vol. 192, 25 March 1998, pp. 90–93

ABOVE: The Studio mixes several architectural languages, including a possible Scottish source for the turret stair. Its rendered surface recalls the 'harling' revived as a proto-Modernist material by Charles Rennie Mackintosh, whose buildings Tayler researched while a student.

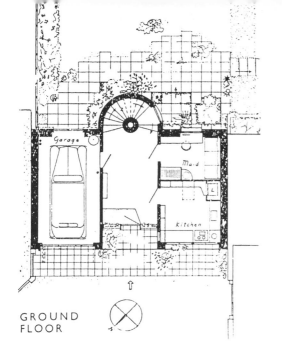

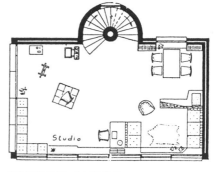

GROUND FLOOR

FIRST FLOOR

SECOND FLOOR

THE STUDIO

Duke's Head Yard, Highgate, London N6, 1938–39

The project for a studio for Roger Pettiward (the real name of the cartoonist Paul Crum) evolved into a house at the end of his garden. Vertical to catch the view and provide accommodation on the small site, the house is connected by a turret stair to the rear, with a food lift from the ground-floor kitchen to the dining space in the studio two floors up. Tayler & Green learned from earlier concrete houses how to avoid thermal and movement problems. They really wanted a black brick front wall but settled for a coloured render, a foretaste of their colourful rural housing.

ABOVE LEFT: The roof garden enjoys spectacular views, although a ground-level garden is also available. In the plans, the most interesting feature is the open-plan studio, with a dining-table and sitting area to one side, all planned by the architects in great detail with fitted furniture. The quality of constructional detail is exceptional, and came from David Green's obsession with elegant practicality.

BELOW LEFT: The entrance front has lost its band of continuous windows around the top of the circular stair tower, which at this level was a roof-top tank room. The windows have been replaced, but altogether the strong character of the design wins through these alterations. The architect's published justification for the circular shapes declared that "elevations were required to be carried out in a modern manner, and circular shapes were used on plan to soften the effect of hard horizontal lines".

BELOW CENTRE AND RIGHT: Internally, the stairs pass over the front door and arrive at a spacious landing, seen on the first-floor plan.

OPPOSITE: It is eccentric to have run the main chimney up the seaward elevation, but it succeeds in being convincing because it becomes such a dominant architectural feature. It would have enabled those seated before the fire to look out over the sea from windows on either side. Both corner rooms seen in this photograph feature a glazed 'turret', but it would appear from the plan that the two balconies did not originally wrap all around them. Perhaps the site boundary was too close, and this effect had to wait until the site was extended.

Harry Weedon 1887–1970

Trained in evening classes at the School of Architecture in his native Birmingham in 1904–08, Weedon opened his own office in the city in 1928. His reputation was based on his work for the Odeon chain of cinemas, for which his office designed around one third (over forty in total) of the buildings. The principal in-house designers were Cecil Clavering and Robert Bullivant, whose work included the Odeon cinemas at Kingstanding, Birmingham (1935), Scarborough (1936) and Sutton Coldfield (1936). Other designers employed by the company, such as George Coles and Andrew Mather, followed the pattern set out by the Weedon office for a streamlined look, with influences from Frank Lloyd Wright and W.M. Dudok. The early examples were clad in ceramic tiles, the later ones faced in brick similar to that of the Underground stations by Charles Holden. The architects needed to build cheaply and quickly, as well as providing audiences with sensational architecture.

After the death of Oscar Deutsch in 1941 and the saturation of the cinema market, Weedon turned to designing car factories and, in 1960, the Civic Centre at Solihull.

REFERENCES
Villa Marina
Building, vol. 12, February 1937,
p. 72

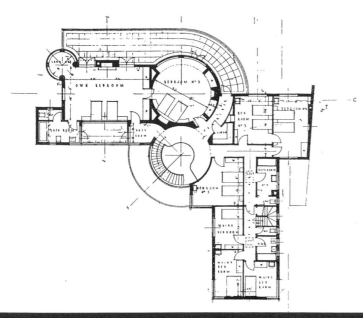

VILLA MARINA
The Promenade, Craigside, Llandudno, Gwynedd, 1936

Villa Marina was designed for Harry Scribbons, the joint
owner of a bakery business in Manchester. It occupies a site
beneath the large rock outcrop called the Great Orme,
looking north over the sea, and is planned on a generous
scale. As might be expected from a practice such as
Weedon's, there is a theatrical swagger to the seaward
elevation: its projecting concrete balcony and overhanging
roof, cut to the same profile, contrasted with the vertical of
the chimney. The stairs are the *tour de force*. The house has
been fortunate to survive with its principal features intact.

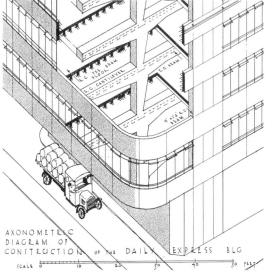

AXONOMETRIC DIAGRAM OF CONSTRUCTION of the DAILY EXPRESS BLG
SCALE 0   10   20   30   40   50 FEET

FAR LEFT: The staircase rises on the central axis from the lobby up the full height of the building. It was supplemented by twin lifts.

LEFT: A cutaway drawing shows how the building's concrete frame relates to the glass cladding. Reels of newsprint shelter beneath its overhang in Shoe Lane, waiting to be conveyed to the press room in the deep basement.

BELOW LEFT: The lobby, designed by Robert Atkinson (normally a rather sober classical architect), was London's most flamboyant piece of Art Deco. Most of the decoration is out of shot.

OPPOSITE: The exterior is of black glass embedded in mastic, with cover strips of Birmabright, one of the patent stainless steels of the time. The cradle rail for window cleaning emphasizes how this building could be kept in pristine condition in a London still heavily polluted by coal smoke.

Sir Owen Williams 1890–1966

Williams was born in north London and graduated in engineering from the University of London in 1911, after part-time study during apprenticeship. He soon became a specialist in reinforced concrete, handling the design of large contracts for dock works and factory buildings. During the First World War he designed slipways and a concrete tug. His major opportunity came in 1924 with the Empire Exhibition at Wembley, north London, where he designed the concrete structure behind the stripped classical façades by architects Simpson & Ayrton (including those of the former Wembley Stadium).

After the architect W. Curtis Green was called in to soften his original design for the Dorchester Hotel, London, Williams told an audience at the Architectural Association in 1934: "There are two types of racketeer: those who get out their guns and those who get out their elevations."

It has not been possible to include all Williams's worthwhile projects here; one notable omission is the Empire Pool, Wembley (1933–34), with its rows of solid concrete counterweights for the roof structure that hang along the sides.

DAILY EXPRESS BUILDING

120–129 Fleet Street, London EC1, 1929–32 (with Ellis & Clarke)

Williams was consulting engineer for this mould-breaking newspaper building, commissioned by the flamboyant Lord Beaverbrook for the leading popular daily of its time. Williams had worked on the *Daily Telegraph* building next door (by Burnet & Tait) and argued for a reinforced-concrete frame to reduce vibration from the presses in the basement. The commissioning period came at the 'moment of Modernism' in Britain, and Williams made the architects Ellis & Clarke rework their elevations, creating the first glass curtain wall building in Britain.

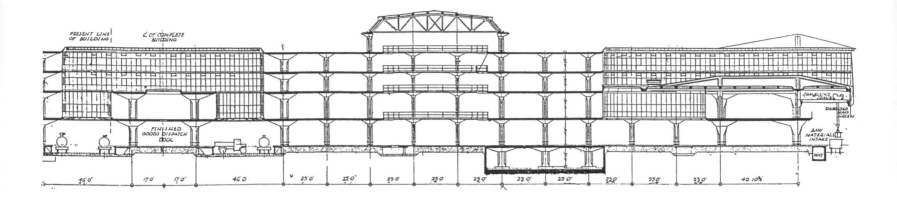

Owen Williams

BOOTS PACKED WET GOODS FACTORY (D10)
Beeston, Nottingham, 1930–32

The locally based chemist's company founded by Jesse Boot was taken over by an American company in 1926, leading to expansion on the Beeston site. Williams's first building, D10, was the most spectacular and radical, based on a downward flow for products through packing processes in the five-storey open atria, surrounded by broad galleries, with loading docks down the side. The elevations would originally have been sheer-glazed, but the floor slabs are expressed in the final version.

The original glazing was replaced c. 1993 after much discussion, in a slightly altered form, but the building remains heroically in its original use, to the credit of the company.

ABOVE LEFT AND TOP: The exterior photograph of D10 shows the narrow side of the rectangle, while the cross-section shows the profile of the atrium-like packing hall located along the central spine. The perimeter of the building was indented above ground-floor level to provide lighting to the transverse spaces.

ABOVE RIGHT: The entrance atrium, in line with the packing hall, stands immediately behind the glass façade.

OPPOSITE: Goods for packing were originally fed down chutes from the various higher levels. Apart from the loss of this technology, the feeling of the packing hall has not changed substantially during the building's lifetime.

BELOW AND RIGHT: The narrower frontage of the 'Drys' building compared with that of the 'Wets' encouraged Williams to dramatize it with a tower, which was originally surmounted by a flagstaff. The photograph below suggests the extent of the building, which is sixteen bays long.

Owen Williams

BOOTS 'DRYS' BUILDING (D6)

Beeston, Nottingham, 1935–38

On a site parallel to the 'Wets' building Williams was responding to different functional requirements, without the need for the large atrium spaces of his earlier masterpiece. His Z-beam concrete construction allowed for large column-free spaces and cantilevered overhangs of 30 feet (9 metres) for the loading dock. He chose to emphasize the entrance with a symmetrical tower feature and projecting ledges to shade the windows.

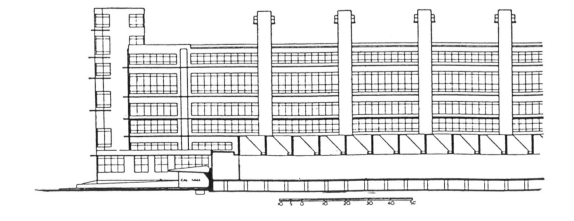

LEFT AND BELOW: The diagonal lattice of the fire station tower indicates that Williams had recourse to the vocabulary of concrete design used in France by Auguste Perret and his followers. The concrete surfaces were treated with a bush-hammered finish more common after the War.

BOOTS FIRE STATION

Beeston, Nottingham, 1935–38

Without a strong brief to respond to, Williams had more difficulty in rationalizing the form for this small building, involving a more typically architectural task of finding an appropriate expressive language.

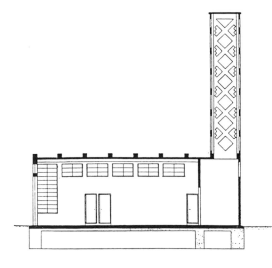

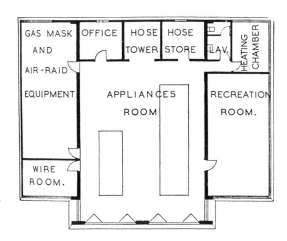

PIONEER HEALTH CENTRE
St Mary's Road, Peckham, London SE15, 1933–35

In 1926 the Peckham Health Centre was founded by two doctors as an experiment in community preventive medicine. Funds were raised for a new building (including a major donation from Jack Donaldson of The Wood House, Shipbourne, Kent), and Williams replaced the architect E.B. Musman. The brief required a variety of sports and medical facilities, all visible from one another so far as was possible. Williams produced a solution that was functionally and aesthetically satisfying, and provided good value for money.

The centre's role was to some extent superseded by the National Health Service, and after educational use it was sold in the late 1990s for conversion into dwellings.

BELOW: The swimming pool is in the centre of the rectangular plan of the health centre and was overlooked by many of the social spaces. These have now been subdivided, although Williams's elegant, bowed frontage remains unaltered. The pool has survived as a facility for the new residents.

Owen Williams

REFERENCES
Architect
David Cottam *et al.*, *Sir Owen Williams, 1890–1966*, London (Architectural Association) 1986

Daily Express building, London
Architects' Journal, vol. 76, 1932, pp. 2, 5–9
Architectural Review, vol. 72, 1932, pp. 3–12
Susie Barson and Andrew Saint, *A Farewell to Fleet Street*, London (English Heritage) 1988, pp. 44–49

Boots Packed Wet Goods factory (D10)
Architect and Building News, vol. 129, 8 January 1932, pp. 50–53, 93
Architects' Journal, vol. 76, 3 August 1932, pp. 125–39
Architectural Review, vol. 72, September 1932, pp. 86–88

Boots 'Drys' building (D6)
Architect and Building News, vol. 156, 25 November 1938, pp. 266–68
Architects' Journal, vol. 90, 29 December 1938, pp. 1053–60

Pioneer Health Centre
Architectural Review, vol. 77, May 1936, pp. 203–16
I.H. Pearse and L.H. Crocker, *The Peckham Experiment*, London (Allen & Unwin) 1943

Daily Express building, Manchester
Architect and Building News, vol. 158, 9 June 1939, pp. 312–15
Zodiac, vol. 18, 1968, pp. 11–13

Dollis Hill Synagogue
Architects' Journal, vol. 89, 24 March 1938, pp. 489–91
Building, vol. 14, April 1938, pp. 156–58

DAILY EXPRESS BUILDING
Great Ancoats Street, Manchester, 1935–39

This was the third of Williams's buildings for the newspaper (the second is in Glasgow), following the black glass of Fleet Street but dramatically raising the presses to street level in the three-storey open hall, designed to be seen working at night. The construction employs a flat slab of concrete for the floors, with careful provision for accessible services running in ceiling ducts and through the columns. The building was extended several times before newspaper production ceased there in the 1980s, after which it was eventually converted into offices.

BELOW: This was the only architecturally significant synagogue of the early Modern Movement in Britain, and is unique in other ways. It is the only one of Williams's buildings in which he involved himself in overt architectural symbolism and form-making, without which it would have been a quasi-industrial structure. Opinion has divided on the success of his venture.

C.H. Reilly commented: "Sir Owen in his design for a synagogue has let me down. Architects are bad at engineering but engineers are very good at architecture – provided always that they are not aware that it is architecture. Sir Owen has been consciously putting art on his synagogue and he seems to be aware that it is art."

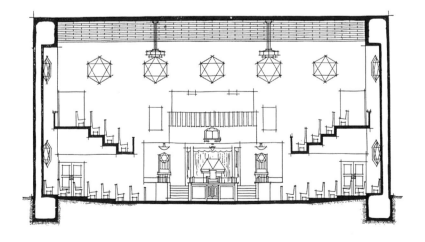

DOLLIS HILL SYNAGOGUE
Park Side, Cricklewood, London NW2, 1936–38

This is a building that seems out of its period: it is more suggestive of the formal inventiveness of Louis Kahn in the 1960s than of 1930s rationality, even in the unintended roughness of the finishes. These ensured it an adverse reception at the time of construction but add considerably to its interest today.

TORILLA

Wilkins Green Lane, Nast Hyde, Hatfield, Hertfordshire, 1934–35 (extended by Yorke and Breuer, 1936)

Torilla was designed for Barbara Macdonald and built by her mother, Christabel Burton, a valuable patron for Yorke on several occasions. It was built of 6-inch and 4-inch reinforced concrete and originally finished in pinky cream paint. The first project was raised on piloti, but, as built, the design seems to reflect a Czech interest in anchoring the modern house in the ground. The plan was simple, with its large double-height room containing the stairs. Yorke built a close copy at Lee on the Solent, Hampshire, in 1936.

Torilla was nearly demolished in 1993 but was saved by listing and restored by John Winter.

F.R.S. Yorke 1906–1962

The son of an architect with Arts and Crafts roots, Yorke trained at Birmingham. In London in 1932, with little work, he established himself as a technical expert, writing the 'Trade Notes' column for the *Architects' Journal*. Yorke was clubbable and unafraid of language barriers, so that his travels in Europe, especially in Czechoslovakia, brought new contacts for the Architectural Press's magazines and the commission for the book *The Modern House*. Its publication in 1934 was a landmark in raising awareness in Britain of a wide range of foreign examples. Similar books, primarily visual in content, followed.

Yorke's practice began in earnest with Torilla in 1934–35, and progressed mainly with houses. Partnership with Marcel Breuer brought polish. The War was spent building munitions factories in convivial company, researching the availability of materials, and making prototype prefabricated houses. In 1944 Yorke formed what was initially a loose partnership with the Czech émigré Eugene Rosenberg and the part-Finnish Cyril Mardall (born Sjöstrom); this went on to become one of the leading post-war architectural practices. Yorke appeared to lose interest in design at times but recruited highly able staff and was good at bringing in work. His interest in contemporary art was shared by his partners, to the benefit of users of his buildings.

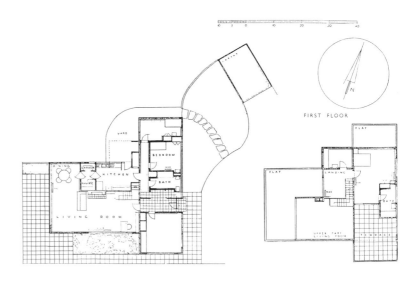

FIRST FLOOR

60–72 (EVEN NUMBERS) BIRMINGHAM ROAD
Stratford upon Avon, Warwickshire, 1938–39
(with F.W.B. Yorke)

Yorke wrote that he was "personally rather fond" of these cottages and that they gave an impression of the way his work would have developed, had it not been interrupted by the War (undated typescript by Yorke, quoted in Melvin, p. 38). The client was Flowers Brewery, building for its employees. Yorke's father, Francis Walter Bagnall Yorke, already undertook pub work for Flowers in the Midlands, and later published a book on pub design. The commission was therefore undertaken jointly.

The monopitch roof follows examples that include Mary Crowley's houses at Tewin, Hertfordshire, and works well with the form of the yellow stock brick terrace, set at right angles to the main road, with gardens for each house. The end wall is of rough local stone, laid in courses, and the horizontally sliding timber frames on the upper-floor windows are a vernacular style, known as a Yorkshire sash.

Yorke designed houses at Harlow New Town twenty years later that are almost identical, so he did not neglect this precedent after all.

SITE PLAN

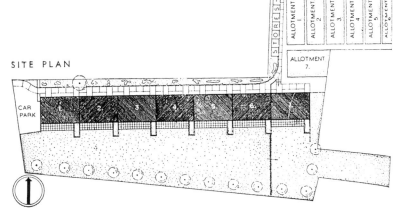

ABOVE: This early photograph shows the row of houses as seen from the road. The architecture remains largely unaltered, but the view has been lost behind garden fences and protection against late twentieth-century traffic levels.

REFERENCES
Architect
F.R.S. Yorke, *The Modern House*, London (Architectural Press) 1934; 2nd edn, 1935
F.R.S. Yorke, *The Modern House in England*, London (Architectural Press) 1937; 2nd edn, 1944
In the Line of Development: F.R.S. Yorke, E. Rosenberg and C.S. Mardall to YRM, 1930–1992, exhib. cat. by Alan Powers, London, Heinz Gallery, 1992
Jeremy Melvin, *F.R.S. Yorke and the Evolution of English Modernism*, Chichester (Wiley–Academy) 2003

Torilla
F.R.S. Yorke, *The Modern House*, London (Architectural Press) 1934, pp. 171–79
Architectural Review, vol. 77, March 1935, p. 105; vol. 78, September 1935, pp. 97–100
Architects' Journal, vol. 82, 5 September 1935, pp. 336–38
F.R.S. Yorke, *The Modern House in England*, London (Architectural Press) 1937, pp. 106–08
Jeremy Melvin, 'A Modern in the Making: F.R.S. Yorke and Torilla', *Architecture Today*, no. 148, May 2004, pp. 46–53

60–72 Birmingham Road
F.R.S. Yorke, *The Modern House in England*, London (Architectural Press), 2nd edn, 1944, pp. 60–61

The Royal Festival Hall dominates the South Bank in this image of the Festival of Britain. Its river frontage was extended in 1962, and all the other Festival structures were cleared away in October 1952 or soon after. These included the Skylon, the 'vertical feature' by Powell & Moya, and the Dome of Discovery by Ralph Tubbs, seen on the far side of Hungerford Bridge (right). The Shot Tower (left) was demolished in the early 1960s to make way for the Queen Elizabeth Hall and the Hayward Gallery.

The Post-War Legacy

Is it true to say that modern architecture in Britain after the Second World War was the fulfilment of the groundwork prepared during the 1930s? It would be a reasonable assumption, since many architects saw the earlier decade as a rehearsal for the real action that they hoped would follow. The welfare state of the Beveridge Report and the 1945 Labour government provided the state patronage and control that were essential to realizing the Modernist programme for building houses, factories, hospitals, schools and universities. Wartime work in camouflage and active service provided many architects with first-hand experience of teamwork as an effective way of solving problems. There were also new and talented men and women who had been students during the War.

Despite appalling shortages of materials and labour, there were beginning to be achievements in new building by 1951, the year of the Festival of Britain. From this event survives the Royal Festival Hall on London's South Bank, in which both Leslie Martin and Peter Moro played key design roles. This was seen as an important moment, when modern design as a whole was introduced to a more or less accepting public as a matter of daily routine. The Festival had a recognizable continuity from the 1930s, in the main architects involved and in its slightly earnest pursuit of frivolity, with scarcely a note of irony. Among buildings as a whole there was a different 'look' from the 1930s, however. As Ian McCallum wrote in 1951: "Gone is the black-and-white 'photographer's architecture', to be replaced for one reason or another … by brick facings and a generous display of bright colours."[1] He had apparently forgotten how much brick and how much colour were already around in 1939.

On the South Bank, as in the New Towns and schools, the sensitivity to landscape and the design quality of the spaces between buildings, which was emerging in the architectural community before the War, became as important as the design of the built structures themselves. McCallum saw that "the architect's scope is broadening to include all the paraphernalia of town and country, not just the buildings. The great battle is already under way against the ideas, or lack of them, which make towns by the method, or lack of it, of scrap heap assembly, bespattering the countryside, too, with visual muck."[2] His comments reflected the continuous concern after 1900 that in a country with an increasing population, with changing social patterns and land uses, a higher level of control should be exercised over

every aspect of the environment, something that was achieved in legislative terms through the 1947 Town and Country Planning Act, although the clearing up took the rest of the century, and even then could scarcely be called complete.

If one country dominated in its influence over Britain at this time, it was Sweden. The reasons were the same as they had been in 1930. In Sweden there was a strong culture of architecture, backed by sufficient investment and construction skills, and a model of a democratic society to stimulate production. Almost unscarred by war, Sweden had kept building during the 1940s in a romantic Modernist manner, sensitive to nature rather than formalistically rigorous, and this suited the tastes and limitations of most British architects in the immediate post-war years, broadening out to a re-engagement with Alvar Aalto, based on his later work, and with a number of Danish architects.

In no country except Britain were there so many architects still in practice after the War whose professional careers predated the beginnings of Modernism and who were unconvinced by its claims. H.S. Goodhart-Rendel, Vincent Harris and Albert Richardson arguably

produced better work after the War than before, although there was a
growing effort to deny them equal coverage in magazines and then to
persuade public and private patrons to choose Modernists instead.[3] The
new Modernist architectural establishment worked hard to keep a 'party
line' in favour of the movement, resulting in a regrettable loss of diversity
in the next generation and driving the non-Modernists into a position of
resentful reaction, believing that Modernism's claims to provide cheaper
or better solutions were unproven.

The persistence of the traditionalists was evidence that Modernism
was far from generally accepted. Was this simply conservatism, or could
the architectural language of Modernism be considered as inadequate?
The abolition of ornament left a gap that could partially be filled by
adding murals or sculpture to a building, something done occasionally
in the 1930s and much more often after the War, yet the effect was
quite different from the fully developed architectural languages of the
past. Textiles and paint colours helped, but these are mostly now lost,
except for what can be made out from black-and-white photographs.
Writing in 1935, John Summerson noted that most architecture in the

past depended on "the complete detachment of the architectural
'language' from its functional background" for its expression, and that,
although the classical language was now at the level of cliché, something
was needed to fill its place, as perhaps Le Corbusier demonstrated
most effectively by drawing expression from the functional elements
themselves.[4] In a letter to the painter Ben Nicholson in 1940, however,
Summerson feared that "modern architecture will have to beat a retreat,
simply because the public can't understand it, never will, and hates it like
poison".[5] Modern architecture had become a historical subject, to the
slight alarm of some of its practitioners, but when the hidden historical
roots or analogies contained in Le Corbusier's work were revealed by
Colin Rowe in 1949, Modernism could be seen, after all, as a style like
any other.[6]

In its most reductive form Modernism denied itself any vocabulary
of expressive power other than the provisions of a building programme
and a choice of materials. As with the design of engineering structures,
the results could be accidentally highly aesthetic, but, as Summerson
indicated, such self-denial was ineffective as an instrument of social

cohesion, and even the inner circle of CIAM itself began to discuss 'the new monumentality'.[7] The monumental tendencies in Berthold Lubetkin's work before the War had been a cause of criticism, but use of symmetry and patterned surfaces was not out of place in the post-war world. Without being monumental, Tayler & Green walked a narrow line between Modernism and tradition, and in 1962 Nikolaus Pevsner made an early use of the term 'post-modern' to describe their housing in Norfolk villages.[8]

At the *Architectural Review* H. de C. Hastings brought his campaigns for a resensitized and responsive form of modern urban design, based on the picturesque landscape tradition, to a culmination with 'Townscape', a major article of 1949, written in collaboration with Gordon Cullen, and later adapted in book form by Cullen alone.

All these trends would make it appear that Modernism was making a gradual accommodation with tradition and popular taste after the War, but a younger generation of architects refused to accept what they saw as this backsliding and were joined by members of the older generation. One of these was Denys Lasdun, who took over the Hallfield flats in Paddington from Lubetkin. Lasdun retained Lubetkin's general concept of patterned elevations, but designed the school there on his own in a much more sculptural and less decorative manner, and went on to specialize in large-boned concrete construction. New Brutalism, the loosely applied blanket term for the reaction against softness and the picturesque, was an attempt to take Modernism back to its European roots in the 1920s, but it could never be the same. The other aspect of the movement was in fact much closer to the picturesque in its fascination with dense vernacular settlement patterns, texture and architectural drama.

The shifts in post-war architecture could be considered simply as cycles of taste. By the end of the 1960s, however, signs of much more deep-rooted change began to appear. Almost everything that the Modern Movement had ever stood for was called into question as a result of a crisis of public confidence in architects. Arguably, it was the attempt to put Modernism back on the rails that had caused the crash, although numerous other causes were involved. The concept of Postmodernism was assembled among the ruins, involving practices such as rehabilitation of older buildings; the rediscovery of the importance of the street, as argued by Jane Jacobs; the empowerment of ordinary building users to the point of building their own homes, a contribution that came from the émigré Walter Segal; and the need for buildings to save energy.

Acceptance of modern architecture has unexpectedly increased in recent years, so that the buildings in this book have become symbols of both nostalgia and aspiration, something their original designers can scarcely have expected, although those who lived long enough to see it happen were generally pleased. As the buildings, many of which have suffered from lack of maintenance and insensitive alterations, are gradually restored, their attraction grows, and the same process has been taking place with post-war buildings.

The confused and inelegant design of the majority of new buildings should caution against any assumption that there is a widespread swing towards Modernism. The fact that the owner of a fine listed house, Greenside at Wentworth in Surrey, by Connell, Ward & Lucas, was able to win the support of local politicians for its demolition in 2003, and to carry out the deed, reinforces the reality of the division. Worse, perhaps, for those who write about architecture, it has revealed the absence of terminology through which the two sides can meaningfully discuss the issues.

Notes

1. Ian McCallum, *A Pocket Guide to Modern Buildings in London*, London (Architectural Press) 1951, pp. 8–9.

2. *ibid.*, p. 7.

3. There is still a dearth of literature on 'traditional' architecture of the twentieth century. Individual buildings are illustrated and described in Elain Harwood, *England: A Guide to Post-War Listed Buildings*, London (Batsford) 2002. Monographs include: Lucy Archer, *Raymond Erith: Architect*, Burford (Cygnet Press) 1985; Alan Powers, *H.S. Goodhart-Rendel, 1887–1959*, London (Architectural Association) 1987; and *Sir Albert Richardson, 1880–1964*, exhib. cat., London, Heinz Gallery, 1999.

4. John Summerson, 'Architecture', *The Arts Today*, ed. Geoffrey Grigson, London, 1935, p. 281.

5. John Summerson to Ben Nicholson, 31 December 1940, Tate Archive 8717.1.24621. After his marriage to Elizabeth Hepworth, the sister of the sculptor Barbara Hepworth, in 1938, Summerson became Nicholson's brother-in-law.

6. See Colin Rowe, *The Mathematics of the Ideal Villa and Other Essays*, Cambridge MA (MIT Press) 1976.

7. Sigfried Giedion's essay 'The Need for a New Monumentality' was published in 1944 in Paul Zucker's collection *New Architecture and City Planning*, and the 'monumentality debate' was the theme of the *Architectural Review* in September 1948.

8. Nikolaus Pevsner, *The Buildings of England: North-West and South Norfolk*, Harmondsworth (Penguin Books) 1962, p. 69: "Tayler and Green's rural housing … can almost be called post-modern, if by modern one still understands what is now familiar as the international style of the 1930s."

Burnet & Tait, Craig Angus, Silver End, Essex, 1927. This photograph shows the house's current condition. The peeling paint is unsightly, but – provided the structure is sound – not difficult to repair.

Wells Coates, Embassy Court, Hove, East Sussex, 1935. This famous block fell on hard times and maintenance was neglected. Owing to the efforts of residents, however, a full repair scheme is in progress (2005) under Paul Zara of Conran Architects.

Berthold Lubetkin, Holly Frindle, Whipsnade, Bedfordshire, 1936. This photograph was taken in 1991, before the house's repair following a long period of abandonment. The result might have been demolition had a campaign not been mounted to rescue the building.

OPPOSITE: Maxwell Fry, Sun House, Frognal Way, London NW3, 1935. The contrast between the original and current photos shows the subtle effect of thin-section windows in the aesthetic of the original design. These were changed over twenty years ago. The replacements are far from being the worst of their kind, but with the double-glazed metal windows currently available, a much closer resemblance to the original could be achieved.

Conservation of the Modern Movement in Britain

Buildings of the Modern Movement have been especially prone to alteration and demolition since they were first built. Sometimes this has been hard to avoid, owing to radical changes of land or building use, but on many occasions damage has been done by owners who do not appreciate the architectural importance of the buildings.

The things that make these buildings special are in themselves often a cause of difficulty. Technically, they were making experiments with materials that have not lasted well, or have been difficult to maintain. When replacement is sought, the original material may no longer be obtainable.

More subtly, their aesthetic is usually unforgiving even of small alterations to windows, the area where most owners wish to make changes. Despite the fact that many of the windows were more or less standard products in metal (although many more were one-off specials than is often realized), these contribute greatly to the 'reading' of the architecture because of their exceptionally thin bars and surrounds, the proportions of which were usually integrated into the design as a whole. Replacements in UPVC and other recent materials can scarcely ever match these thin lines, and the difference can be devastating to the overall effect. Yet metal-framed

windows have often created maintenance problems and were built without thermal breaks, which prevent condensation. Crittall is fortunately now able to supply double-glazed sealed windows with thermal breaks, and the profiles are only marginally thicker than the originals.

Concrete has created many difficulties, owing to inadequate knowledge at the time of construction, reinforcement bars close to the surface, water penetration and movement. In this field considerable expertise has been developed by specialist contractors and the architects they have worked for on many of the buildings illustrated here. Decay can be arrested, or even reversed, with careful and limited intervention in the original fabric of the building, so that repairs can be made that conform to the standards required for historic buildings of earlier periods. As in the case of older buildings, the application of additional coatings, whether of paint or other supposedly protective materials, is usually a wrong move, since the buildings need to be able to 'breathe'. Paints have been developed recently with this in mind. Steel frames can also suffer from water penetration, and the task of investigating them requires the removal of external wall surfaces, which can be hard to replace invisibly.

Private owners of houses may suffer from any of these problems, and it has often been said that owning a Modern Movement building is akin to owning a vintage car. It is a mark of considerable prestige and something from which great pleasure can be gained, but it is a heavier commitment than the ownership of most buildings of other periods. It is very encouraging that over the past twenty-five years many of the houses that have survived have been bought by enthusiasts and treated with care. There are still many more awaiting their turn, but, given that for reasons of planning policy it is currently very difficult to build a new house of modern character, the only alternative for those seeking surroundings of this type is to acquire an existing one.

This is not the occasion to give detailed technical advice, but owners of buildings seeking guidance are encouraged to contact the Twentieth Century Society, which is the national amenity society in Britain concerned with buildings after 1914. The Society can provide details of architects who have done relevant conservation work, and can offer other advice. Its members support the Society's conservation work and in return receive publications and the opportunity to attend visits and events.

English Heritage is also a source of advice and information. For buildings in other countries the equivalent would be the national chapter of DOCOMOMO International.

Many of the best Modern Movement buildings are now protected by listing. It is possible for anyone to recommend a building for listing by writing to English Heritage, and most effective when good factual and visual information is provided at the same time. The Twentieth Century Society may be able to assist in preparing an application. There are undoubtedly many important Modern Movement buildings still undiscovered in Britain and worthy of listing, while others may be due for upgrading.

Further Reading

Books and articles on individual architects and projects already cited are not repeated here.

PRIMARY SOURCES (PUBLISHED UP TO 1940)

Patrick Abercrombie (ed.), *The Book of the Modern House*, London (Waverley Book Company) 1939
A well-illustrated pluralist survey. Essays include 'The Contemporary House' by Oliver Hill.

Anthony Bertram, *Design*, Harmondsworth (Penguin Books) 1938
Based on broadcasts made in 1937, with substantial architectural content.

Reginald Blomfield, *Modernismus: A Study*, London (Macmillan) 1934
Described in The Listener as "the hasty outpouring of impotent rage against the younger generation", but Blomfield often hits his target.

John Burnet, with Thomas Tait and Francis Lorne, *The Information Book of Burnet, Tait and Lorne*, London (Architectural Press) 1933
Standard details to speed production in the machine age.

Noel Carrington, *Design in the Home*, London (Country Life) 1933
One of the best picture sources for early Modernist interiors and objects in Britain.

Hugh Casson, *New Sights of London*, London (London Transport) 1938
Lists of buildings worth visiting, including some in semi-traditional styles.

Elizabeth Denby, *Europe Re-Housed*, London (George Allen & Unwin) 1938
Based on first-hand research in six countries. The conclusion, applying the findings to British conditions, is full of wisdom, largely unheeded in the post-war world.

R.A. Duncan, *The Architecture of a New Era: Revolution in the World of Appearance*, London (Denis Archer) 1933
An English architect coming to terms with the European revolution in design.

John Gloag (ed.), *Design in Modern Life*, London (George Allen & Unwin) 1934
Based on a BBC broadcast series of 1933 representing DIA (Design and Industries Association) values.

Henry-Russell Hitchcock, *Modern Architecture in England*, New York (Museum of Modern Art) 1937
A valuable outsider's view of English Modernism, with selected exemplars and essays by Hitchcock and the housing expert Catherine Bauer.

John Leslie Martin, Ben Nicholson and Naum Gabo (eds.), *Circle: International Survey of Constructive Art*, London (Faber & Faber) 1937
The classic English contribution to the international abstract movement.

Raymond McGrath, *Twentieth Century Houses*, London (Faber & Faber) 1934
An attempt to write (in 'basic English') the history of the modern house internationally, concluding with English examples.

Raymond McGrath and A.C. Frost, *Glass in Architecture and Decoration*, London (Architectural Press) 1936
A massive technical survey, including much interesting history and high-quality illustrations of buildings of all kinds.

Steen Eiler Rasmussen, *London, The Unique City*, London (Jonathan Cape) 1937
A Danish architect's admiring history of London, including many comments on the architectural present and future.

Herbert Read (ed.), *Unit One: The Modern Movement in English Architecture, Painting and Sculpture*, London (Cassell) 1934
Wells Coates and Colin Lucas are the two architects among such artists as Moore, Hepworth and Wadsworth.

J.M. Richards, *Introduction to Modern Architecture*, Harmondsworth (Penguin Books) 1940
A history and survey, with a final section on British examples responsive to the regionalist turn of the late 1930s.

Howard Robertson, *Modern Architectural Design*, London (Architectural Press) 1932
Robertson's attempt to embrace Modernism within the compositional conventions of the previous generation.

International Architecture, 1924–1934, exhib. cat., London, Royal Institute of British Architects, 1934
The exhibition staged for the opening of the RIBA's new building in Portland Place, boldly upholding worldwide Modernism for admiration.

Thomas Sharp, *Town Planning*, Harmondsworth (Penguin Books) 1940
The most popular of several books by a campaigning planner.

Bruno Taut, *Modern Architecture*, London (The Studio) 1929
Introducing a range of European Modernism to English-language readers, with a special section about English traditions.

F.E. Towndrow, *Architecture in the Balance: An Approach to the Art of Scientific Humanism*, London (Chatto & Windus) 1933
One of the more thoughtful assessments at a critical date.

Christopher Tunnard, *Gardens in the Modern Landscape*, London (Architectural Press) 1938
An eclectic scrapbook of past and present examples rather than a coherent theory.

Bryan Westwood, *Smaller Retail Shops*, London (Architectural Press) 1937
Exemplars of modern design in an important experimental field.

Clough Williams-Ellis and John Summerson, *Architecture Here and Now*, London (Thomas Nelson) 1934
A large-format book, combining survey and polemic, largely written and researched by Summerson.

Myles Wright, *Design of Nursery and Elementary Schools*, London (Architectural Press) 1938
Includes illustrations of the News Chronicle competition winners and international examples.

F.R.S. Yorke, *The Modern House*, London (Architectural Press) 1934
A collection of photographs and plans, with a technical bias. For many years after its publication, this book was the key that opened the door to the world of Modernism for many aspiring architects.

F.R.S. Yorke, *The Modern House in England*, London (Architectural Press) 1937 (2nd rev. edn 1944)
A brief survey, connecting back to the Arts and Crafts movement, followed by copious examples of modern houses. The second edition omits some entries and replaces them with more recent examples.

F.R.S. Yorke and Frederick Gibberd, *The Modern Flat*, London (Architectural Press) 1938
An international survey with high-quality illustrations.

F.R.S. Yorke and Colin Penn, *A Key to Modern Architecture*, London (Blackie) 1939
A popular account of the subject with the standard justifications for Modernism.

SECONDARY SOURCES

Architectural Review, '30s: Special number on The Thirties, London, November 1979
A mixture of new research, reprinted texts and retrospects by those who were there, including Ove Arup, Serge Chermayeff and H. de C. Hastings.

Architecture Club, *Recent English Architecture 1920–1940*, London (Country Life) 1947
A useful collection of pictures published by a dining club set up in the 1920s to broaden interest in architecture.

Martin Battersby, *The Decorative Twenties*, London (Studio Vista) 1969
A pioneering survey of France, Britain and the United States by a collector and artist. Well illustrated.

Martin Battersby, *The Decorative Thirties*, London (Studio Vista) 1969
Sequel to the above. Both books fuelled the nostalgic cult of the 1930s.

Lionel Brett, *The Things We See: Houses*, Harmondsworth (Penguin Books) 1947
Includes many famous 1930s examples in an attempt to define an English Modernist doctrine of pragmatism and civility for post-war reconstruction.

Donatella Calabi (ed.), *Architettura Domestica in Gran Bretagna 1890–1939*, Milan (Electa) 1982
Never translated, but excellent as a visual source for public housing in the period, with well-researched texts.

David Dean, *The Thirties: Recalling the English Architectural Scene*, London (Trefoil Books) 1983
An entertaining and well-illustrated survey based on the resources of the RIBA Library and Drawings Collection.

John Gold, *The Experience of Modernism: Modern Architects and the Future City, 1928–1953*, London (Spon) 1997
A fresh reappraisal, with a focus on planning.

H.S. Goodhart-Rendel, *English Architecture Since the Regency: An Interpretation*, London (Constable) 1953 (new edition with introduction by Alan Powers, London [Century Hutchinson] 1989)
Based on lectures given in 1934. Places Modernism at the end of a hundred years of architectural confusion, in which Goodhart-Rendel thought the wrong paths had been followed.

Jeremy Gould, *Modern Houses in Britain 1919–1939*, London (Society of Architectural Historians of Great Britain) 1977
Valuable for its clear mapping of the subject, first-hand anecdotes and gazetteer (the last updated in the Twentieth Century Society's The Modern House Revisited).

Richard Gray, *Cinemas in Britain: One Hundred Years of Cinema Architecture*, London (Lund Humphries) 1996
An excellent source of pictures and information.

Anthony Jackson, *The Politics of Architecture: A History of Modern Architecture in Britain*, London (Architectural Press) 1970
A pioneer work in the field.

Modern Britain, exhib. cat., ed. Donna Loveday and James Peto, London, Design Museum, 1999
Exhibition catalogue with essays by Alan Powers, John Gold and others covering architectural themes.

Open University Arts, *British Design*, Milton Keynes (Open University Press) 1975
Covers design in Britain between 1915 and 1939 (Geoffrey Newman) and 'The Electric Home' (Adrian Forty). Still a valuable source of information and critical thinking.

Nikolaus Pevsner, *Studies in Art, Architecture and Design, Volume Two: Victorian and After*, London (Thames & Hudson) 1968
Collects Pevsner's essays on 'Pioneers' and DIA heroes such as Frank Pick and Gordon Russell.

Alan Powers, *Look Stranger at this Island Now: English Architectural Drawings of the 1930s*, London (Architectural Association) 1983
A revisionist and pluralist survey, with entries on selected architects.

Alan Powers, *The Twentieth Century House in Britain*, London (Aurum Press) 2004
Drawn from the archives of the Country Life picture library, it places inter-war Modernism in house architecture in a wider perspective.

Sam Smiles (ed.), *Going Modern and Being British: Art, Architecture and Design in Devon, c. 1910–1960*, Exeter (Intellect) 1998
Includes 'Architecture in Devon 1910–1958' by Jeremy Gould and 'Dartington – A Modern Adventure' by David Jeremiah.

Gavin Stamp (ed.), *Britain in the Thirties*, Architectural Design, Special Issue, November 1979
A response to the Arts Council exhibition The Thirties in 1979, pressing the claims of architects outside the MARS Group's inner circle, such as Goodhart-Rendel and Oliver Hill.

John Summerson, 'Introduction' in Trevor Dannatt, *Modern Architecture in Britain*, London (Batsford) 1959
A sceptical retrospect emphasizing the progress made by architecture in the 1950s.

Thirties, exhib. cat., London, Arts Council of Great Britain, 1979
A fat catalogue describing the exhibits and commenting on the whole range of art and design in the decade.

SELECTED PERIODICALS AND SERIAL PUBICATIONS

Architectural Association Journal
Monthly record of lectures, student activity and buildings by members.

Architectural Review
Premier monthly, central to the understanding of the 1930s in Britain.

Architect and Building News
Weekly that pioneered the publication of Modernist buildings in the 1920s. After 1933 John Summerson was a member of the editorial staff.

Architects' Journal
Companion weekly to *Architectural Review*. The 'Astragal' gossip column, mostly written during the later 1930s by Hugh Casson, is a valuable source of otherwise unrecorded information.

The Builder
Weekly with a comprehensive record in reporting and publishing designs, with no strong leaning towards Modernism.

Building (later retitled *Architecture and Building*)
Monthly begun in 1928 and containing more editorial commentary on buildings and issues than the other magazines.

Country Life
Between 1930 and 1935 an important source for illustration and commentary on modern design.

Design and Construction (later retitled *Architectural Design*)
Started as a monthly in 1930, edited by F.E. Towndrow. Good for commentary and illustrations not published elsewhere.

Design for Today
Monthly magazine published by the DIA (Design and Industries Association) in the middle years of the 1930s.

Master Builder
Trade monthly, hard to find. Notable for a period in the early 1930s during which it was owned by the architectural enthusiast Roger Fleetwood-Hesketh, who used it to promote German Modernism.

RIBA Journal
An official monthly record of the Institute, containing valuable full transcripts of lectures and discussions. The librarian – E.J. Carter, an ally of the young moderns – was the editor in the 1930s and influenced the content.

Studio
A monthly art magazine originating from the 1890s. Around the turn of the 1930s, it published some of the most avant-garde architecture in Europe with intelligent commentaries at a time when it was still neglected by the professional journals. The annual Year Book of Decorative Art is also a useful source of pictures.

Thirties Society Journal
Seven issues between 1981 and 1992. Contains articles on architects of all styles.

Twentieth Century Architecture
Journal of the Twentieth Century Society. Seven issues since 1994, which cover 1930s themes in *Industrial Architecture* (no. 1, 1994), *The Modern House Revisited* (no. 2, 1996) and *The Twentieth Century Church* (no. 3, 1996).

Index

Picture Credits

The illustrations in this book have been reproduced courtesy of the following:

Architectural Association Picture Library
    © E.R. Jarrett/Architectural Association: 152 (left and right)
Architectural Review: 76–77, 82, 124, 136–37, 160, 182, 228, 229
Lady Bliss: 134 (centre right), 135 (Bridgeman Art Library/© Estate of Edward Wadsworth 2005. All Rights Reserved, DACS/photo by Mark Fiennes)
H.T. Cadbury Brown: 70–71
Peter Chermayeff: 77 (colour image)
Michael Cooke-Yarborough: 230
The Dartington Hall Trust: 164–67
Herbert Felton (courtesy of Lynne Walker): 44–45
© FLC/ADAGP, Paris and DACS, London 2005: 28
David Green: 232 (left)
Millar & Harris 138–39, 141, 142–43, 144 (right)
Julian Honer: 187 (top)
National Monuments Record/English Heritage: 74, 134 (top), 188–89, 208–09, 231 (right)
Alan Powers: 13, 18, 20, 231 (left), 232 (right), 324 (centre and right)
RIBA Library Photographs Collection: 83, 104–05, 122–23, 140 (top), 153, 202–03
John Somerset Murray (courtesy of Lynne Walker): 50
John Stubbington: 118–19 (drawings)

The publisher has made every effort to trace and contact copyright holders of the illustrations reproduced in this book; they will be happy to correct in subsequent editions any errors or omissions that are brought to their attention.